Contributions to Political Science

More information about this series at
http://www.springer.com/series/11829

Andreas Jungherr

Analyzing Political Communication with Digital Trace Data

The Role of Twitter Messages in Social Science Research

Andreas Jungherr
University of Mannheim
Mannheim, Germany

The present work is based on the author's PhD thesis, accepted in 2014 at the University of Bamberg, Faculty for Social Sciences, Economics, and Business Administration under the title "The Use of Twitter in the Analysis of Political Phenomena: A Framework Based on Twitter Messages Commenting on the German Federal Election 2009"

ISSN 2198-7289　　　　　　　　ISSN 2198-7297　(electronic)
Contributions to Political Science
ISBN 978-3-319-20318-8　　　　ISBN 978-3-319-20319-5　(eBook)
DOI 10.1007/978-3-319-20319-5

Library of Congress Control Number: 2015943374

Springer Cham Heidelberg New York Dordrecht London
© Springer International Publishing Switzerland 2015
This work is subject to copyright. All rights are reserved by the Publisher, whether the whole or part of the material is concerned, specifically the rights of translation, reprinting, reuse of illustrations, recitation, broadcasting, reproduction on microfilms or in any other physical way, and transmission or information storage and retrieval, electronic adaptation, computer software, or by similar or dissimilar methodology now known or hereafter developed.
The use of general descriptive names, registered names, trademarks, service marks, etc. in this publication does not imply, even in the absence of a specific statement, that such names are exempt from the relevant protective laws and regulations and therefore free for general use.
The publisher, the authors and the editors are safe to assume that the advice and information in this book are believed to be true and accurate at the date of publication. Neither the publisher nor the authors or the editors give a warranty, express or implied, with respect to the material contained herein or for any errors or omissions that may have been made.

Printed on acid-free paper

Springer International Publishing AG Switzerland is part of Springer Science+Business Media (www.springer.com)

Meinen Eltern

Preface

The causes of scientific paradigm shifts can usually be found in the cultivation of new data sources, opening up new perspectives on well-examined phenomena. Technological advances—such as the telescope—or methodological innovations—such as the experimental method—have disrupted scientific practices in the past and provided researchers with scores of new data, illuminating hitherto invisible aspects of reality. The digitalization and relentless chronicling of digitally mediated interactions provide such a technological advance, challenging researchers to make sense of digital data traces and incorporate them into their research.

For this to happen successfully, though, researchers have to examine these new data sources critically: Which practices in data collection, preparation, analysis, and storage have to be observed to guarantee the privacy of those users whose interactions were documented in the data and the accuracy of scientific findings? Which new analytical methods have to be developed and taught in order to handle the deluge of data now readily available for anyone with a computer and an Internet connection? Most fundamentally, which phenomena are documented by this new technology and which are neglected? These are undoubtedly only some of the challenging questions to be addressed by the current generation of researchers, attempting to integrate digitalization's promises into their respective fields.

As a political scientist, I am naturally fascinated by the question of what digital data traces can reveal about political phenomena and behavior. Given these interests, the microblogging service Twitter has proved to be a valuable research environment. In 2009, when I first started on the course that would later lead to this book, Twitter was a new phenomenon in political communication. At that time, the service also offered more than generous access to its data through an open Application Programming Interface (API), providing access to the postings and interactions of politically vocal Twitter users on the cheap. As luck would have it, Twitter is still around, the service's API is still open to researchers, and it is still a popular platform for political campaigns as well as political talk; moreover, a slew of research uses Twitter data as a basis for the analysis of political phenomena, attitudes, and public opinion.

This research has provided many fascinating results, regarding Twitter's political uses and opened the eyes of many a scholar to the potential of Twitter as a data source in research. Even researchers not necessarily interested in the particularities of political talk in 140 characters or less but instead in political science's more fundamental questions, such as the identification and categorization of citizens' political leanings or the assessment of trends in societies' political polarization, start turning to Twitter as a data source. Most of this research—expecting Twitter data to hold information on larger political phenomena—has treated Twitter somewhat as a mirror to political reality with its data offering a true reflection of political phenomena.

In this book, I take issue with this view. In contrast, I present a framework for the use of Twitter in the analysis of politics, that interprets data traces collected on Twitter as a mediated reflection of political reality, skewed by the attention, interests, and intentions of politically vocal Twitter users. This is not to say that Twitter data hold no information on political reality at large. Instead, the framework emphasizes the need to account for this mediation process of political reality through Twitter in the analysis and interpretation of data collected on the service. Some political phenomena, such as the dynamics of attention to politics or even aspects of political discourse by the section of a population likely to be found on Twitter, might be very likely to leave identifiable data traces. Other research objects, such as political attitudes, voting intentions, or inferences on the public in general, might prove much harder to be realized. As such, the framework presented here is an invitation to examine critically which type of political phenomena one can reasonably expect to be accurately examined through digital trace data collected on Twitter, given the service's data generating process.

The argument presented in this book follows similar lines to the long ongoing discussion involving the mediation of reality through coverage in traditional media. As in the case of digital trace data, traditional media were first supposed—and normatively expected—to mirror reality. Gradually scholars have come to see all media forms as mediators of reality, filtering by systematically emphasizing or neglecting specific aspects in accordance with various mediating factors, be they connected with the nature of a news item, professional codes and practices, or individual characteristics of journalists and editors—such as their political leanings or personal connections. This debate, continuing since the 1970s, has done much to enrich our understanding of news as well as the use of media coverage in the analysis of political phenomena. I see the argument presented in this book as an invitation to think about digital trace data as products of a similar mediation process. To be sure, the mediating factors will very likely be different from those identified by communication scholars analyzing the mediation of reality through traditional media, but by the end of the book, I hope I will have convinced you that at its heart the process is very much the same.

My largest debt in the process of writing this book is to Pascal Jürgens with whom I developed the first ideas for this project in 2009. Without his tireless help and efforts in the collection and preparation of the data used in this study, this book could not have been written. Also, his continuous feedback on earlier versions of the ideas presented in the following pages was instrumental in helping me to develop the argument presented here.

I want to thank Harald Schoen for providing me with a challenging academic environment and giving the book room to grow from its early stages to its current form and for encouraging me to start with what would later become this book back in 2009 when it was far from obvious that this would become a promising research field. His comments during various stages of the project provided me with crucial input and the necessary critique to allow the book to develop into its current form.

Also, I want to thank Damien Schlarb and Roland Parr for reading the manuscript and providing me with a wealth of comments and copyedits, allowing me to advance my argument and present the reader with a book doing a passable impression of being written in English.

During the writing of this book, I was lucky enough to participate in a series of workshops and conferences that brought me into contact with various scholars working on related topics. I benefited immensely from these encounters and discussions. I want to, therefore, thank Lance Bennett, Grant Blank, Andrew Chadwick, Rachel Gibson, David Karpf, Daniel Kreiss, Mona Krewel, Darren Lilleker, Axel Maireder, Helen Margetts, Takis Metaxas, Eni Mustafaraj, Rasmus Kleis Nielsen, Zizi Papacharissi, Travis Ridout, Jan-Hinrik Schmidt, Alexandra Segerberg, Markus Strohmaier, Jennifer Stromer-Galley, and Cristian Vaccari.

In 2010, I had the chance to participate in the Summer Doctoral Programme organized by the *Oxford Internet Institute*. The programme was a great place to present an early version of the arguments presented here and get multifaceted feedback by tutors and participants alike. The highly interdisciplinary and supportive environment of the Summer Doctoral Programme provided the basis of various ongoing friendships and proved vital for the development of this book. I owe the participants, tutors, and organizers, therefore, a great deal.

Any research project is based in the academic communities an author started in. For me these were the environments provided by the Universities of Mainz and Bamberg, Germany. I also want to include, therefore, my thanks to my friends and colleagues at these institutions: Kai Fischbach, Robert Greszki, Matthias Mader, Johannes Marx, Marco Meyer, Daniel Odinius, Ersin Özsahin, Oliver Posegga, Thomas Rixen, Thomas Saalfeld, Carolin Stange, Philipp Wackerbeck, and Christian Zettl.

I want to thank my immediate family—Ursula, Hans-Gerd, Joachim, and Ingeborg—for providing me with constant support, trust, and love, enabling me to venture forward on this and other projects.

Finally, I want to thank Valeska for making it all worthwhile.

Some of the material presented in Chap. 6 appeared previously in Andreas Jungherr (2014) "The Logic of Political Coverage on Twitter," *Journal of Communication* and has been reproduced here courtesy of *John Wiley and Sons*.

Mannheim, Germany   Andreas Jungherr

Contents

1 **Introduction: How to Use Twitter in the Social Sciences** 1
   1.1 Digital Trace Data as Information Source for Political Phenomena 1
   1.2 A Map of the Territory 4
   1.3 Research Goals 6
   1.4 Structure of the Book 7
   References 9

2 **Twitter, Usage and Research** 11
   2.1 Why Twitter? 11
   2.2 What is Twitter and How is it Used? 12
      2.2.1 What is Twitter? 12
      2.2.2 Usage Patterns 15
   2.3 Political Uses of Twitter: Politicians, Activists, Citizens, and the Media 16
   2.4 Rise to Prominence 18
   References 21

3 **Twitter in the Analysis of Social Phenomena: An Interpretative Framework** 25
   3.1 Analyzing Social Phenomena with Digital Trace Data............... 25
   3.2 What Are Digital Trace Data? 27
   3.3 Computational Social Science, Digital Methods, and Big Data: What Is Missing? 29
      3.3.1 Computational Social Science 29
      3.3.2 Digital Methods 31
      3.3.3 Big Data 32
      3.3.4 Why We Need Theory 34
   3.4 Twitter: Macro-Phenomena, Micro-Behavior, and Macro-Patterns 35
      3.4.1 Approaches to the Analysis of Digital Trace Data 35
      3.4.2 Macro-Phenomena, Micro-Behavior, and Macro-Patterns.... 37

	3.4.3	Metrics for the Analysis of Social Phenomena Based on Twitter Data	40
	3.4.4	Different Services, Different Uses, Different Data-Generating Processes	42
	3.4.5	Politics Through the Lens of Digital Trace Data	45
3.5	A Mechanism Explaining the Publication of Tweets		48
	3.5.1	Social Context	50
	3.5.2	State of the Twittersphere	54
	3.5.3	External Stimuli	56
	3.5.4	A Person's Propensity to Tweet	61
	3.5.5	What Does This Mechanism Enable Us to Do?	62
3.6	A Framework for the Analysis of Social Phenomena with Twitter Data		62
References			63

4 Twitter as Political Communication Space: Publics, Prominent Users, and Politicians ... 69

4.1	The Political Communication Space		69
4.2	Data Collection and Preparation		70
4.3	Publics		73
	4.3.1	Publics: Message-Centric Analysis	73
	4.3.2	Publics: Dynamics Over Time	75
	4.3.3	Publics: User-Centric Analysis	78
	4.3.4	Publics: Political Support and Opposition	79
	4.3.5	Publics: Patterns in the Use of Twitter	82
4.4	Prominent Users		83
	4.4.1	Prominent Users: General Observations	85
	4.4.2	Prominent Users: Message-Centric Analysis	86
	4.4.3	Prominent Users: User-Centric Analysis	89
	4.4.4	Prominent Users: Political Support	91
	4.4.5	Prominent Users: Patterns in the Use of Twitter	92
4.5	Politicians		93
	4.5.1	Politicians: General Observations	93
	4.5.2	Politicians: Message-Centric Analysis	94
	4.5.3	Politicians: User-Centric Analysis	95
	4.5.4	Politicians: Content	97
	4.5.5	Politicians: Patterns in the Use of Twitter	101
4.6	Publics, Prominent Users, and Politicians in Their Use of Twitter		102
References			104

5 Sensor of Attention to Politics ... 107

5.1	Connecting Politically Relevant Events to Spikes in the Volume of Twitter Messages	107
5.2	How to Detect Spikes in Data Streams?	109
5.3	Identifying Politically Relevant Events	112

5.4	Political Events and Their Shadows on Twitter	117
	5.4.1 Event Detection by Differencing	120
	5.4.2 Event Detection by Regression Models	123
	5.4.3 Index of Political Relevance	128
	5.4.4 Parties	132
	5.4.5 Candidates	136
	5.4.6 Controversies	139
5.5	Twitter as a Sensor of Political Attention	150
References		151

6 The Media Connection ... 155
- 6.1 The Connection Between Political Media Coverage and Twitter Activity ... 155
- 6.2 Data Set and Method ... 156
- 6.3 Temporal Patterns in the Coverage of Politics on Twitter and Traditional Media ... 159
  - 6.3.1 Temporal Dynamics ... 159
  - 6.3.2 Common Patterns in the Mentions of Political Actors Across Media Types ... 161
- 6.4 What Do Users Tweet About in Reaction to Mediated Events? ... 168
  - 6.4.1 Ratification of the Access Impediment Act: Temporal Dynamics and Content ... 170
  - 6.4.2 State Elections: Temporal Dynamics and Content ... 174
  - 6.4.3 Televised Leaders' Debate: Temporal Dynamics and Content ... 178
  - 6.4.4 Election Day: Temporal Dynamics and Content ... 182
- 6.5 Twitter and Political Coverage by Traditional Media ... 185
- References ... 186

7 Predictor of Electoral Success and Public Opinion at Large ... 189
- 7.1 The Connection Between Attention on Twitter and Electoral Fortunes ... 189
- 7.2 Predicting Election Results Using Twitter Data: The Evidence ... 190
- 7.3 Mechanisms Linking Twitter Messages with Opinion Polls and Election Results ... 194
- 7.4 Method ... 197
- 7.5 Twitter Metrics and Their Relationship to the Electoral Fortunes of Parties ... 198
  - 7.5.1 Aggregates, Twitter Metrics: Users, Mentions and Sentiment ... 198
  - 7.5.2 Dynamics of Hashtag Mentions Compared to Shifts in Opinion Polls ... 203
- 7.6 No Indicator of Political Support or Public Opinion at Large ... 207
- References ... 208

8 Conclusion: Twitter and the Analysis of Social Phenomena 211
   8.1 Early Days 211
   8.2 Characteristics of Twitter as a Political Communication Space 212
   8.3 A Framework for the Use of Twitter in the Analysis
       of Social Phenomena 215
   8.4 Twitter: Political Communication Space and Mediator of Politics ... 217
   References 219

List of Figures

Fig. 3.1	Macro-phenomena, micro-behavior, macro-patterns................	38
Fig. 3.2	Example for the data-generating process of internet search engines...	43
Fig. 3.3	Example for the data-generating process of Twitter	44
Fig. 3.4	Random volume of messages per hour over time	51
Fig. 3.5	Number of all messages per hour over time	52
Fig. 3.6	Distribution of the message volume for each day of the week	53
Fig. 3.7	Distribution of the message volume for each hour of the day	53
Fig. 3.8	Autocorrelation for time series of twitter messages per hour, for lags 0 to 35 and lags 0 to 336	55
Fig. 3.9	Autocorrelation for time series of all twitter messages per day, for lags 0 to 20...	55
Fig. 3.10	Time series of hashtags referring to phenomena of media-, offline-, and online-culture	58
Fig. 3.11	Users ranked by total number of messages posted	61
Fig. 4.1	Data acquisition process...	71
Fig. 4.2	Number of active users per day	75
Fig. 4.3	Average number of messages per user	76
Fig. 4.4	Share of messages containing neither @messages, retweets, or URLs (in percent)	77
Fig. 5.1	Mechanism linking political events to shifts in the behavior of Twitter users	108
Fig. 5.2	All messages between June 18, and October 1, 2009	117
Fig. 5.3	Messages contributing to the political communication space between June 18, and October 1, 2009.......................	119
Fig. 5.4	Cumulative number of users who had contributed to the political communication space at any given hour	119
Fig. 5.5	First and seventh differences of the political communication space...	121

Fig. 5.6	Boxplots of two volatility regimes in differenced time series of political communication space	122
Fig. 5.7	All messages of the political communication space over time with outliers based on differencing	122
Fig. 5.8	Fitted values of regression model compared with actual message volume political communication space	125
Fig. 5.9	Outliers in the residuals of the regression model political communication space	125
Fig. 5.10	Political communication space over time with outliers based on regression models	126
Fig. 5.11	Index of political relevance per day (traditional political actors)	129
Fig. 5.12	Index of political relevance per day (traditional political actors and activists)	131
Fig. 5.13	Number of messages mentioning parties by hashtags	135
Fig. 5.14	Number of messages mentioning Angela Merkel and Frank-Walter Steinmeier by hashtags	137
Fig. 5.15	Number of messages mentioning the controversy over the Access Impediment Act in hashtags	141
Fig. 5.16	Number of messages mentioning Ulla Schmidt in hashtags	142
Fig. 5.17	Number of messages mentioning Karl-Theodor zu Guttenberg in hashtags	144
Fig. 5.18	Number of messages mentioning Josef Ackermann in hashtags	146
Fig. 5.19	Number of messages mentioning Kunduz in hashtags	147
Fig. 6.1	Candidate and party mentions in newspapers, on TV, and on Twitter, aggregated for each media type	160
Fig. 6.2	Scree plot of PCA	164
Fig. 6.3	Candidate and party mentions in newspapers, on TV, and on Twitter, aggregated for each component	167
Fig. 6.4	Daily aggregates of messages using at least one of the 2629 politically relevant hashtags between June 18 and October 1, 2009	169
Fig. 6.5	Messages contributing to the political communication space posted between June 18, and June 19	172
Fig. 6.6	Messages contributing to the political communication space posted between August 29, and August 31	176
Fig. 6.7	Messages contributing to the political communication space posted between September 12, and September 14	180
Fig. 6.8	Messages contributing to the political communication space posted between September 26 and September 28	184
Fig. 7.1	Potential mechanism allowing the detection of public opinion and/or electoral chances of political actors through Twitter data	197
Fig. 7.2	Votes and tweets per party (all parties)	201

Fig. 7.3	Votes and tweets per party (only parties with less than 250,000 votes)	202
Fig. 7.4	Party support polls with trend	204
Fig. 7.5	Mention share hashtags per party with trend	205
Fig. 8.1	Relationship between social phenomena and data patterns in aggregates of Twitter messages	216

List of Tables

Table 2.1	Usage conventions on Twitter	13
Table 2.2	Key moments in the evolution of Twitter as a popular and political medium	19
Table 3.1	Elements of the relationship between macro-phenomena, micro-behavior, and data aggregates	39
Table 3.2	Examples for various types of events leading to spikes in Twitter messages	60
Table 4.1	Hashtags used to identify politically vocal users	70
Table 4.2	Conventions used in all messages and the political communication space between June 18, and October 1, 2009	74
Table 4.3	Message to convention ratio	74
Table 4.4	Message to convention ratio reported in other studies	74
Table 4.5	User statistics aggregated between June 18, and October 1, 2009	78
Table 4.6	User counts explicitly supporting and opposing parties using hashtags	81
Table 4.7	Interpretations and operationalizations for influence on Twitter	84
Table 4.8	New and traditional political actors among the most prominent Twitter users	87
Table 4.9	Conventions used in all messages and the political communication space posted by the most prominent users between June 18, and October 1, 2009	88
Table 4.10	Message to convention ratio for the most prominent users	88
Table 4.11	Usage statistics for most prominent users, aggregated between June 18, and October 1, 2009	89
Table 4.12	Political support by prominent users	91
Table 4.13	Count of politicians who were using Twitter	93

Table 4.14	Conventions used in all messages and the political communication space posted by politicians between June 18, and October 1, 2009	94
Table 4.15	Message to convention ratio for politicians using Twitter	94
Table 4.16	Usage statistics of politicians aggregated between June 18, and October 1, 2009	95
Table 4.17	Functions in tweets posted by politicians	99
Table 4.18	Primary topic of tweets posted by politicians	100
Table 5.1	Key events during the campaign for the federal election of 2009 in Germany	115
Table 5.2	Days identified by differencing and corresponding events in the political communication space	123
Table 5.3	Regression model of time series political communication space	124
Table 5.4	Days identified by regression models and corresponding events political communication space	127
Table 5.5	Days identified by index of political relevance (traditional political actors)	130
Table 5.6	Days identified by index of political relevance (traditional political actors and activists)	132
Table 5.7	Descriptive metrics of messages referring to political parties	133
Table 5.8	Days identified by local maxima in party mentions by hashtag	136
Table 5.9	Descriptive metrics of messages referring to leading candidates	137
Table 5.10	Days identified by local maxima in candidate mentions by hashtag	138
Table 5.11	Descriptive metrics of messages referring to various controversies during the campaign	139
Table 5.12	Days identified by local maxima in the hashtag mentions of the Access Impediment Act	141
Table 5.13	Days identified by local maxima in the hashtag mentions of Ulla Schmidt	143
Table 5.14	Days identified by local maxima in the hashtag mentions of Karl-Theodor zu Guttenberg	145
Table 5.15	Days identified by local maxima in the hashtag mentions of Josef Ackermann	146
Table 5.16	Days identified by local maxima in the hashtag mentions of Kunduz	147
Table 6.1	Total mentions of political actors across different media types (June 28 to September 26)	158

Table 6.2	Summary of principle component analysis results for mentions of political actors in newspapers, on TV, and on Twitter ($n = 78$)	165
Table 6.3	User behavior in all messages posted compared to political communication space on the day of the ratification of the Access Impediment Act, June 18, 2009	171
Table 6.4	Usage patterns in the 137 top RTs on the day of the Access Impediment Act's ratification, June 18, 2009	173
Table 6.5	User behavior in all messages posted compared to political communication space on the day of the state elections, August 30, 2009	175
Table 6.6	Usage patterns in the 121 top RTs on the day of the state elections, August 30, 2009	177
Table 6.7	User behavior in all messages posted compared to political communication space on the day of the televised debate, September 13, 2009	179
Table 6.8	Usage patterns in the 116 top RTs on the day of the televised debate, September 13, 2009	181
Table 6.9	User behavior in all messages posted compared to political communication space on election day, September 27, 2009	182
Table 6.10	Usage patterns in the 137 top RTs on election day, September 27, 2009	184
Table 7.1	Predicting elections results with Twitter data	191
Table 7.2	Predictive metrics of election or poll results	192
Table 7.3	Twitter metrics shares between June 18, and October 1, 2009 compared to vote share	199
Table 7.4	Intercepts and slopes in models of poll and hashtag mention dynamics per party through the course of the campaign	206

Chapter 1
Introduction: How to Use Twitter in the Social Sciences

1.1 Digital Trace Data as Information Source for Political Phenomena

In 2010, a team of enterprising scholars from the Technical University of Munich, Germany, published a paper with a surprising finding. In an analysis of Twitter messages mentioning political parties during the run-up to the 2009 federal election in Germany, they found that the mention shares of parties were pretty similar to their vote shares on election night. Digital trace data thus seemed to mirror political phenomena accurately. The authors concluded:

> [...] the mere number of tweets mentioning a political party can be considered a plausible reflection of the vote share and its predictive power even comes close to traditional election polls. (Tumasjan et al. 2010)

Thus was born the idea of "predicting elections with Twitter". This has proven to be a very attractive endeavor for researchers. Its popularity is illustrated by there having been over 700 references made to the original paper, at the time of this writing.[1] Since then, many studies have followed the trail blazed by the team from Munich in finding correlations between Twitter-based metrics and metrics of political success in various cases. This literature is driven by the hope of supplementing, improving or even replacing survey-based polling by metrics based on digital trace data. If there was indeed a systematic relationship between Twitter mentions of political actors and their subsequent success at the polls, this would lead to a significant decrease in polling costs and offer polling-opportunities for races too small to warrant traditional survey-based polls. But here, as in other walks of life, what seems too good to be true, often simply is not true.

---

[1]Number of references based on count of *Google Scholar* on December 28, 2014.

Intrigued by the claims by Tumasjan and colleagues, Pascal Jürgens, Harald Schoen, and I decided to replicate their study. Our replication came to radically different findings from those presented in the original study. One of these differences goes far in illustrating the challenges of using digital trace data in social science research. We found that the accuracy in predicting the results of German parties running for the 2009 federal election depended on the choice of parties included in the analysis. While Tumasjan and colleagues had included only parties in their analysis that were already in Parliament by 2009, we added the German Pirate Party to our analysis. We did so based on the assumption that any Internet based metric of political success should also include the party most concerned with Internet related issues, even if its entering Parliament appeared to be a long shot. Lo and behold, predicting the results of the Pirate Party based on their share of Twitter mentions would have led us to expect the Pirates to be the strongest party in Parliament. Obviously, this had little correspondence with political reality. Apart from invoking this charming counterfactual alternative reality of election outcomes in Germany, this result spelt trouble for the general applicability of predicting election results by counting Twitter messages. If the relationship between shares of parties' Twitter mentions and their subsequent vote shares proved to be critically dependent on the choice of parties included in the analysis, Twitter data were obviously of only limited use in replacing survey based polls (Jungherr et al. 2012).

Tumasjan and colleagues answered this challenge by questioning the merit of including the Pirate Party in the analysis:

[...] given that they were neither represented in the German parliament nor specifically reported by name in the major election forecasts at the time of our study. (Tumasjan et al. 2012)

Thus, the authors explicitly stated the dependence of their Twitter prediction on decisions by polling institutes about which parties' polling results to report and which parties' results to lump into the "other parties" category. Let us leave aside for a moment that the Pirate Party's treatment by polling companies was startlingly different from the one chosen by Tumasjan and colleagues. After all, the polling companies did ask respondents if they intended to vote for the Pirate Party but decided not to report these results explicitly based on the small number of Pirates' supporters. In contrast, Tumasjan and colleagues did not query Twitter for mentioning the Pirate Party, thereby ignoring their substantial mention share online. More fundamentally, this response shows how much implicit dependence on traditional metrics of public opinion "forecasts" based on digital trace data have built into them.

With all its problems, the study by Tumasjan and colleagues and various studies like it show that Twitter data seem to hold information on political phenomena—albeit probably not the kind of information the authors hope to find. Twitter has become an important element in political communication by political elites and the public at large. Twitter users react to media appearances by political candidates, political news coverage or share their own political experiences and opinions with others. Thus, Twitter has become a crucial element in what Andrew Chadwick calls the "hybrid media system", a media system where many types of actors use many interconnected channels following various media logics to communicate and interact (Chadwick 2013). It is only natural to expect that the analysis of Twitter mentions of political actors will reveal information on political phenomena, such as campaigns. Still, without a clear understanding of Twitter uses for political communication by political elites and the public as well as its motivations, it is very hard to assess which kind of information on politics social scientists can expect in Twitter data. For this, we need a framework allowing the assessment of which part of political reality is documented by Twitter data, thereby offering context on how to use these data in the social sciences.

Studies, like the one by Tumasjan and colleagues, implicitly assume that mentioning a political actor on Twitter signals support for that actor—be it support by the user posting the message or the actor's relative importance indicated by users mentioning her. In contrast, I will show that empirical evidence speaks in favor of a different reading. Twitter data can be used to identify shifts in the attention of Twitter users towards political information. I will illustrate this point by examining data patterns in messages commenting on the 2009 federal election in Germany. To this empirical part of the argument, I will add the proposal of a mechanism leading Twitter users to post messages, providing an interpretative framework on how to use Twitter data in the analysis of political and social phenomena. This mechanism will include factors accounting for social, platform related, individual and external factors leading users to post messages, again supporting the argument that Twitter data hold information on the attention to political information paid by Twitter users but not on their political opinions or voting intentions.

The debate about potential uses of digital trace data in the social sciences has to mature. In its current state, we have many isolated single-shot case studies and proofs of concept that illustrate the relationship between some Twitter based metrics and some metrics of political phenomena in specific situations, like the one proposed by Tumasjan and colleagues. Without the proposal and systematic testing of potential mechanisms connecting the act of posting a Twitter message mentioning a given political actor with larger political phenomena, the authors of these case studies will always have to contend with the challenge that instead of reporting stable relationships between two variables, they are over-narrating spurious correlations. Researchers interested in the use of digital trace data in the social sciences, therefore, have to propose, discuss and test these potential mechanisms explicitly. The field thus has to develop and test a framework for the use of digital trace data in the analysis of political phenomena. With this book, I add to this discussion using data documenting political uses of Twitter during the campaign for the German federal election in 2009.

1.2 A Map of the Territory

All over the world, many digital tools have emerged and are routinely used in political campaigns. Some of these tools have become common place—such as email, websites, or Google—others still have that "new car smell"—such as Facebook, Twitter, or YouTube. While their period of influence has been relatively short, they have changed the way political campaigns are performed, organized, covered by the media and talked about by the public. Digital tools have created interconnected spaces contributing to communication spheres of traditional media and social interaction, thereby becoming influential channels through which politics and campaigns are mediated. These developments and their consequences have been subject to far reaching and ongoing scholarly debate (Chadwick 2006; Chadwick and Howard 2009; Dutton 2014; Jungherr and Schoen 2013; Stromer-Galley 2014).

But this extension of the political communication space is only part of the story. The growing use of digital tools in political communication also leads to the emergence of new data sources available to scientists. Each user interaction with a digital service creates data traces, documenting this interaction. While online services vary widely with regard to the accessibility of these data traces to researchers, in principle they hold significant research potential for social scientists since they document actual human behavior. Tapping into this data reservoir allows researchers to side-step problems associated with traditional approaches, such as potential biases introduced to answers on self-reported behavior in surveys or potentially artificial behavior measured in laboratory experiments. The research potential of data sources documenting all interactions of large numbers of users with specific online services is obvious.

However, despite these advantages there remain challenges to the use of digital trace data by researchers. First, while many digital services collect and retain data on user behavior, these services vary widely in the degree of access they grant researchers. For example, Google grants public access to aggregated standardized data on the use of search[2]; Facebook grants access to a selection of their data through a public application programming interface (API)[3]; while Twitter offers developers and researchers access to publicly posted messages through its public API.[4] These variations in data access make it hard to compare the behavior of users across platforms. Thus, instead of offering a comprehensive view on user behavior online, most studies using digital trace data can offer only glimpses of user behavior on specific platforms.

Also, as the data collected by digital services document user behavior in great detail, there are non-trivial privacy concerns to be addressed by services in their decisions to grant researchers data access and by researchers in analyzing these data

---

[2] http://trends.google.com/trends/.

[3] https://developers.facebook.com.

[4] https://dev.twitter.com.

1.2 A Map of the Territory

sets or making them publicly accessible for replication (Boyd and Crawford 2012; Puschmann and Burgess 2013).

To date, it remains unclear which part of political behavior is documented by online trace data. Does the fact that a user types the name of a political candidate into the search field of Google speak to her intention of voting for that candidate? Or, does the fact that a user posts a message mentioning a political party in context of otherwise positively connotated words indicate that she is a supporter of said party? Just because we have access to this type of data does not mean we understand how to interpret patterns in the data meaningfully; especially once we try integrating these data with existing concepts, theories, and research approaches to political behavior (Howison et al. 2011; Jungherr and Jürgens 2013).

While online activity might indicate users' awareness of political parties, candidates, or platforms and thus provide relevant information for scholars, much methodological and theoretical work has yet to be done to integrate these data sources fully into the social sciences. Most of the available research focuses on the presentation of single-shot case studies, which claim to show the relationship between some metrics of attention online with some metrics of political behavior. Any meaningful theoretical discussion of potential mechanisms between specific patterns in online trace data and political phenomena is missing from the literature. Thus, it is very difficult to assess whether or not case studies offer more than accounts of spurious correlations between otherwise unconnected variables. This unsatisfactory state of the field is due to the fact that most of the research analyzing political behavior through online trace data has been presented by computer scientists who work in a publication culture that favors short peer-reviewed conference papers. Most of these papers present case studies that are best understood as proofs of concept and not necessarily as systematic analyses of political behavior through online data. In addition, some of the case studies which were seemingly successful in connecting political phenomena with patterns in online trace data have led some authors to overemphasize the potential of these data sources. Much of this discussion centers around the term *big data* (Mayer-Schönberger and Cukier 2013). As with any hype, the exaggeration of potentials and simplistic interpretations of novelty findings warrants criticism. Still, both, overly optimistic hype and overzealous critique, undermine any serious discussion of how online trace data can be used for the analysis of social and political phenomena.

This books aims to address the significant research gap by offering an exemplary analysis of a data set comprising 10,085,982 Twitter messages posted by 32,731 users who commented on politics during the campaign for the federal election of 2009 in Germany. I will be proposing a framework for the analysis of social phenomena through digital trace data and presenting analyses illustrating the dynamics of Twitter as a communication space.

1.3 Research Goals

For this project, my research goals are twofold: first, I aim to examine the specific usage patterns of Twitter during a political campaign. Second, I will examine how some metrics of attention to political actors on Twitter can be used to examine larger political phenomena to which Twitter users were reacting by posting messages. These goals are closely interconnected as any meaningful discussion of links between Twitter data and political phenomena presupposes an understanding of the specific patterns and dynamics of political communication on Twitter. Without such an understanding, any discussion of links between online trace data and political phenomena is bound to be bogged down in attention to spurious correlations and overly optimistic generalizations based on single-shot case studies.

The analyses presented in this book are based on a unique dataset collected by Pascal Jürgens and myself during three and a half months preceding the 2009 federal election in Germany. We collected all messages posted by users who used one of 19 politically relevant hashtags between June 18, and October 2, 2009. This resulted in a data set of 10,085,982 messages—not all of them referring to politics—posted by 32,731 users. These messages were collected during the course of the campaign through regular queries of Twitter's API. The data set thus offers a very broad account of Twitter's use by politically vocal users.

The election of 2009 offers a promising basis for the analysis of these questions. First, in 2009, Twitter was still at a very early stage of adoption in Germany, being used by only a very small percentage of the German population. While this might possibly date the results presented here, an analysis at this early stage might offer an early snapshot of patterns and dynamics characterizing political communication on this online service which can be used later to examine larger data sets as Twitter's user base continues to grow and the volume of messages keeps on rising. Second, messages referring to the 2009 campaign in Germany are part of a very specific language area, thus probably following a limited set of common stimuli for users to post messages referring to the campaign. In contrast, US campaigns elicit much stronger reactions by international users than campaigns in Germany, since candidates for the US Presidency are political symbols of interest to an international audience. Thus, introducing a myriad of potential stimuli for international users to comment on candidates or the campaign, thereby potentially introducing "noise" in the data. In contrast, an analysis of messages referring to a campaign in Germany should allow for a pretty clear view of the relationship between the campaign, political media coverage and dynamics in Twitter messages referring to politics.

For social scientists who want to include Twitter data in their research, the findings presented in this book have clear implications. Twitter data appear to have high potential in the analysis of the flow of political information and the role of various actors—media, political elites, social networks—in its dissemination. On the other hand, it appears to be much harder—if at all possible—to use digital trace data to draw valid inferences on the political opinions and voting intentions of Twitter users or the public at large. As such, these findings offer a challenge to much of the current research which is trying to use digital trace data collected on Twitter to draw wide reaching inferences on public opinion or election results. For this ongoing discussion, the study aims to provide a rudimentary framework for Twitter data's use in the analysis of political phenomena.

1.4 Structure of the Book

In Chap. 2, Twitter Usage and Research, I will give an overview of how Twitter is used and which events led to its increasing prominence in political campaigns. I will start with a general discussion of Twitter and various usage practices. Subsequently, I will discuss several studies that document current use of the Internet and Twitter in the USA and Germany. Beyond that, I will survey studies that focus on socio-demographic attributes differentiating Twitter users from the general public. Building on these findings, I will discuss various examples of Twitter's political uses that will serve to document the relevance of the microblogging service for public discourse, political campaigns, political activism, and the public performance of politics. In this chapter, I will also discuss the events that led to Twitter's growing prominence in political campaigns.

In Chap. 3, Twitter in the Analysis of Social Phenomena, I will offer an interpretative framework for the use of Twitter in the analysis of political phenomena. I will start by offering a definition of digital trace data and discussing various approaches in the social sciences that analyze data traces of human interaction with online services and integrate the results in the body of established research—such as *computational social science*, *digital methods*, and *big data*. I will show that the inference of social phenomena based on digital trace data is, in fact, a special case from a larger debate in sociology about how to explain macro-phenomena based on micro-behavior. Connecting the relatively new debate on how to analyze social phenomena based on online trace data with the much explored discussion about macro-micro-macro linkages (Coleman 1990) goes a long way to anchor the current debate in the larger context of the social sciences. I will propose a mechanism leading users to post Twitter messages. This mechanism includes elements based on individual behavior, social influence, opportunities offered by social context, and external events.

In Chap. 4, Twitter as Political Communication Space: Publics, Prominent Users, and Politicians, I will offer a detailed analysis of messages posted by politicians and the public during the course of the federal election campaign of 2009 in Germany. For this analysis, I differentiate between patterns in the messages posted by the public, prominent users—identified by the number of @messages and retweets received by them—and politicians. The analysis will show that new political actors achieved prominence on Twitter, and most of the time, the attention paid to them surpassed by far the attention paid to traditional political actors. Politicians tended predominantly to post messages containing information on the campaign while interacting with other Twitter users only sporadically. This one-sided behavior shows that Twitter was used predominantly as a broadcasting medium not as a platform for public dialogue. There was only little evidence of messages in which politicians actively tried to mobilize their followers to vote or to volunteer in their campaign.

In Chap. 5, Sensor of Attention to Politics, I examine whether or not shifts in the dynamics of time series documenting the daily volume of Twitter messages referring to politics, political actors, and political controversies were indicative of politically relevant events during the campaign. I will show that Twitter users reacted to media events—such as election night coverage or the televised debate—with a significant increase in running commentary on these events. I will also show that political events which were associated with topics of interest for Internet users and which allowed for humor, personalized scandalization, and the linking to content on the Web tended to be accompanied by local peaks in the volume of messages referring to politics. The evidence presented in this chapter points to the fact that Twitter offers a promising data source in analyzing objects of attention for politically vocal Twitter users during a campaign. Still, Twitter data appear to be a much less reliable source for the identification and analysis of all politically relevant events during a campaign.

Political activities on social media are clearly interconnected with the coverage of politics by traditional media. In Chap. 6, The Media Connection, I analyze temporal dynamics of Twitter messages commenting on politics during the campaign for the 2009 federal election in Germany. I will show that the temporal dynamics and content of Twitter messages follow a hybrid logic of political coverage; this follows on occasions the same logic as the coverage of political actors in traditional news media, while in other cases a logic specific to political expression on Twitter. A detailed analysis of message contents posted during four prominent mediated events shows that these events led to a significant increase in messages referring to politics. Prominent content on Twitter during mediated events tended to provide commentary, links to further information on the Web with sometimes competing context to the event coverage, thereby opening the political discourse around prominent political events to the views of new political actors.

As the microblogging service Twitter becomes an increasingly popular tool enabling the public and politicians to comment on and discuss politics, researchers increasingly turn to the relationship between tweets mentioning parties or candidates and their respective electoral fortunes. In Chap. 7, Predictor of Electoral Success and Public Opinion at Large, I offer a detailed analysis of Twitter messages posted during the run-up to the 2009 federal election in Germany and their relationship to the electoral fortunes of German parties and candidates. The findings indicate that during the campaign of 2009 Twitter messages commenting on parties and candidates showed little—if any—systematic relationship with subsequent votes on election day. To determine the political opinions or voting intentions of Twitter users or the public at large based on digital trace data thus seems to be a highly dubious prospect.

Finally, in Chap. 8, Conclusion: Twitter and the Analysis of Politics, I will discuss the meaning of results from previous chapters for the interpretation of political communication on Twitter and the analysis of larger political phenomena with digital trace data.

Overall, unless otherwise stated, the analyses in this book were performed using the statistics software R (R Core Team 2014). For the creation of the plots, I used the R packages ggplot2 (Wickham 2009), grid, scales (Wickham 2012), and plyr (Wickham 2011). For the analysis of time series, I used the packages zoo (Zeileis and Grothendieck 2005) and xts (Ryan and Ulrich 2013).

References

Boyd D, Crawford K (2012) Critical questions for big data: provocations for a cultural, technological, and scholarly phenomenon. Inf Commun Soc 15(5):662–679. doi:10.1080/1369118X.2012.678878

Chadwick A (2006) Internet politics: states, citizens, and new communication technologies. Oxford University Press, Oxford

Chadwick A (2013) The hybrid media system: politics and power. Oxford University Press, Oxford

Chadwick A, Howard PN (eds) (2009) Routledge handbook of internet politics. Routledge, Oxon

Coleman JS (1990) Foundations of social theory. Harvard University Press, Cambridge

Dutton WH (ed) (2014) Politics and the internet. Routledge, Oxon

Howison J, Wiggins A, Crowston K (2011) Validity issues in the use of social network analysis with digital trace data. J Assoc Inf Syst 12(12):767–797

Jungherr A, Jürgens P (2013) Forecasting the pulse: how deviations from regular patterns in online data can identify offline phenomena. Internet Res 23(5):589–607. doi:10.1108/IntR-06-2012-0115

Jungherr A, Schoen H (2013) Das Internet in Wahlkämpfen: Konzepte, Wirkungen und Kampagnenfunktionen. Springer, Wiesbaden

Jungherr A, Jürgens P, Schoen H (2012) Why the pirate party won the German election of 2009 or the trouble with predictions: a response to Tumasjan, A., Sprenger, T.O., Sander, P.G. & Welpe, I.M. Predicting elections with Twitter: what 140 characters reveal about political sentiment. Soc Sci Comput Rev 30(2):229–234. doi:10.1177/0894439311404119

Mayer-Schönberger V, Cukier K (2013) Big data: a revolution that will transform how we live, work, and think. Houghton Mifflin, New York

Puschmann C, Burgess J (2013) The politics of Twitter data. In: Weller K, Bruns A, Burgess J, Mahrt M, Puschmann C (eds) Twitter and society. Peter Lang Publishing, New York

R Core Team (2014) R: A language and environment for statistical computing. R Foundation for statistical computing, Vienna, Austria. http://www.R-project.org

Ryan JA, Ulrich JM (2013) xts: eXtensible time series. http://CRAN.R-project.org/package=xts

Stromer-Galley J (2014) Presidential campaigning in the internet age. Oxford University Press, Oxford

Tumasjan A, Sprenger TO, Sandner PG, Welpe IM (2010) Predicting elections with Twitter: what 140 characters reveal about political sentiment. In: Hearst M, Cohen W, Gosling S (eds) ICWSM 2010: Proceedings of the 4th international AAAI conference on weblogs and social media, Association for the Advancement of Artificial Intelligence (AAAI), Menlo Park, pp 178–185

Tumasjan A, Sprenger TO, Sandner PG, Welpe IM (2012) Where there is a sea there are pirates: response to Jungherr, Jürgens, and Schoen. Soc Sci Comput Rev 30(2):235–239. doi:10.1177/0894439311404112

Wickham H (2009) ggplot2: elegant graphics for data analysis. Springer, New York
Wickham H (2011) The split-apply-combine strategy for data analysis. J Stat Softw 40(1):1–29. http://www.jstatsoft.org/v40/i01/
Wickham H (2012) scales: scale functions for graphics. http://CRAN.R-project.org/package=scales
Zeileis A, Grothendieck G (2005) zoo: S3 infrastructure for regular and irregular time series. J Stat Softw 14(6):1–27. http://www.jstatsoft.org/v14/i06/

Chapter 2
Twitter, Usage and Research

2.1 Why Twitter?

We witness a continually increasing public adoption of the Internet and various online services, such as Facebook or Twitter. These services enable their users to publish information, document seemingly mundane aspects of their lives, interact online with friends, family, and strangers, and perform daily tasks with greater ease. These tools not only complement the daily lives of their users, they also change political participation, campaigning, and activism. Fascinating narratives on the role of the Internet and various online services abound: examples include Barack Obama's presidential campaigns of 2008 and 2012, the enabling role the Internet played during the revolutions in the Arab world in 2010 and 2011 or in various single issue campaigns (e.g. #zensursula, #acta, #aufschrei). These episodes show that digital tools have become integrated in campaigning, political discourse, and activism. To understand today's politics, one has to understand the interplay of politics online and offline. While many online services are used by campaigners, activists, and the general public to inform, organize, or discuss politics, the microblogging service Twitter is one of the most popular tools and one of those most open to researchers.

As the use of online services becomes more popular with the general public, so the interest of researchers shifts. Recent years have seen increasing research activities into usage patterns on online communication platforms, the ethnography of various online services, and how these services are integrated in the communication repertoires of *normal* users and elites. With time, researchers have grown increasingly interested in data that document users' interactions on online platforms. Each action a user takes on an online service leaves digital data traces. These data are highly interesting as they go well beyond the breadth and detail to which social scientists are accustomed. At present, there is a vital debate going on as to how these data can be used in understanding computer mediated human behavior but also how insights gained from these new data sources can be integrated in the traditional social science corpus. My book aims to add to this debate.

In this chapter, I will give an overview of how Twitter is used and which events led to its increasing prominence in political campaigns. I will start with a general discussion of Twitter and various usage practices. Next I will look at several studies that document the current use of the Internet and Twitter in the USA and Germany, followed by studies examining how Twitter users are different from the general public, following which, I will discuss various examples of Twitter's political uses that will serve to document the relevance of the microblogging service to public discourse, political campaigns, political activism, and the public performance of politics. I will also present a timeline of Twitter's rise to prominence in general and specifically with regards to politics.

2.2 What is Twitter and How is it Used?

2.2.1 What is Twitter?

Twitter[1] is a microblogging service that allows its users to post short text messages of up to 140 characters in length on personalized profiles. These messages are called *tweets*. In the early days of the service users who wanted to update their profiles with messages were greeted by the question "What are you doing?" With this short question Twitter prompted users to post new messages. Later in its development Twitter changed the question to "What's happening?" This was an attempt to accommodate the steadily growing variety of the service's uses (Stone 2009). In 2011 the question was completely dropped in favor of the much more neutral prompt "Compose new Tweet..." . The evolution of this seemingly simple phrase shows the service's ongoing evolution together with the corporate and public narrative about its purpose.

The service allows its users to *follow* other twitterers. This means a user is able to subscribe to the message feeds of other users. This relationship can be asynchronous: followers do not necessarily have to be followed by their counterparts to receive their messages. On each profile page Twitter documents who the author of this account is *following* (i.e. subscribed to) and who her *followers* are (i.e. who her subscribers are). The messages of all accounts to which a user subscribes appear on her personalized *news feed* in chronological order.

Users can access their accounts (e.g. read their news feed, post messages, or perform a search) through various interfaces (e.g. through Twitter's website, through various applications for desktop computers, tablet computers, and mobile phones). In the early days of the service, Twitter encouraged third-party developers to program and market applications that allowed users to interact with their accounts

---

[1] https://twitter.com.

2.2 What is Twitter and How is it Used?

on various devices by providing them with relatively comprehensive access to Twitter's own databases through an application programming interface (API). This led to the rapid development of many competing applications for users to choose from and contributed to the fast adoption of Twitter as the microblogging service of choice. Since then, in an effort to monetize the service, Twitter has become much more restrictive in its API policies and the interaction with third-party developers which has led to some backlash among developers.

With its limit of 140 characters, Twitter offered its users a highly restrictive communication environment. Unsurprisingly, users started to experiment by using emerging cultural conventions to extend uses of the service by sidestepping this limitation. Some of these cultural usage conventions became so successful that Twitter implemented them in its own software. This is an interesting example of the interdependent relationship between software that enables but restricts users and usage practices that feed back into the design of the software, thus leading to an extension of possibilities for users. Some of the most commonly used conventions merit closer discussion because they fundamentally determine the user experience on Twitter (see Table 2.1 for a short overview).

The most common usage convention on Twitter is probably the *@reply*: if a user wants to contact another user directly on Twitter or reply directly to a tweet, she has the option to start her Twitter message by an @-sign followed by the username of the user she wants to contact (e.g. if she wanted to write a tweet addressed to Steffen Seibert, spokesman for the German government, she would start her message with *@RegSprecher*[2]). @Replies appear only in the news feeds of those

Table 2.1 Usage conventions on Twitter

Usage convention	Description
@reply to another user	To address publicly other Twitter users, one precedes the text of a message with the username of the addressee and an @ (i.e. @username)
@mention of another user	One can also use the @username convention in the text of a message instead of the beginning, this is called an @mention
RT verbatim	A retweet (RT) is an exact copy quote of another tweet; to do this one copies the tweet and precedes it with the character string *RT @username*
RT modified	One can also comment or modify a quote message; this is called a modified retweet
#keywords	To establish an explicit context for a tweet, one can use keywords preceded by the # sign, so called hashtags
Links to other Web content (e.g. websites, pictures, videos et al.)	One can also post links in messages to content on the Web, these links are often shortened to accommodate Twitter's 140 character limit

---

[2]https://twitter.com/RegSprecher.

users following the account of the user who posted the tweet as well as the user she addressed in the message. Notably, @replies are public and thus appear openly in the list of published messages on the profile of the user who sent them and can be found by using the Twitter search function. It is also possible to use the @*username* combination not at the start but in the body of a message. This is called an @*mention*. Different from @replies, messages containing @mentions appear in the news feeds of every user who follows the author of the tweet. Users are notified if they have received @replies or @mentions by Twitter and thus are prompted to react to them. Messaging a user privately is also possible by prefacing a tweet with *d* @*username* (e.g. *d* @*RegSprecher*). Naturally these direct messages are not accessible through Twitter's API and, therefore, cannot be used as the basis for research that uses Twitter's API as data source.

Another popular convention among Twitter users is the *retweet*. If a user likes a message she sees in her news feed and wants to share the message with her followers, she can re-post the message on her profile. To do this, she copies the message in question, precedes it with *RT* @*username (of the original author)*, and posts this new message on her account. It is also possible for the person retweeting a message to alter or add to the message she wants to re-post. This is known as a *modified retweet*. Since Twitter implemented this convention in its software, most applications offer a simple retweet button under each tweet so the posting of retweets has become much easier. The retweet convention is one reason why information and news travel very fast on Twitter since the re-posting of interesting messages has becoming an important aspect of its usage culture.

The conventions mentioned above focused on the interaction between users, as opposed to the hashtag (#) convention which focuses on the interaction of users around topics. In the early days of Twitter, users already identified a tweet's topical keywords by prefacing with a # (i.e. hashtag) sign. Doing so enabled users to anchor their short messages in topical contexts. Beyond that, this practice made it possible to find all messages referring to a given topic by searching on Twitter for relevant hashtags. This usage convention has also been implemented as a standard feature by Twitter, thereby simplifying the search for relevant hashtags. Twitter also added the feature *trends*, which shows each user the most popular topics and hashtags based on her location together with the people she follows. Recently Twitter introduced trends relevant to specific countries and even some selected cities. Hashtags are an important feature for Twitter users to interact and browse on the basis of topics.

Since Twitter restricts its users to post messages of up to 140 characters in length, users began using so called *link shorteners*. Link shorteners are third-party services that allow users to shorten URLs to webpages or other content on the web significantly. This allowed users to post links and their own accompanying comments on Twitter without violating the 140 character limit. Early on, a wide variety of link shorteners were in use. Currently, only a few services remain. One reason for this is that Twitter implemented a link shortener of its own which automatically abbreviates links of URLs that users post on the service.

These and other usage conventions help in enriching the user experience of Twitter. They help twitterers to interact with each other and around topics. These conventions as highly formalized modes of interaction and topical discussion hold potential for researchers who can use automated tools to analyze Twitter data and discover patterns in the interaction of its users without having to resort to coding each message by hand. The restriction of human interaction by the code of the services people use to interact, therefore, makes it easier to analyze these interactions automatically with tools created through the code.

2.2.2 Usage Patterns

By 2013, 18 % of US online users claimed to use Twitter while 8 % claimed to use it on a daily basis (Duggan and Smith 2013). In 2014, 9 % of German online users identified themselves as Twitter users, while 5 % claimed to use it at least once a week (van Eimeren and Frees 2014). This difference already shows that the importance of Twitter in both countries should be evaluated differently. Interestingly the usage gap, which clearly exists between the USA and Germany with regard to Twitter, is not grounded in a fundamentally different usage intensity of the Internet itself. By 2013, 85 % of American adults (18 years and older) used the Internet while 70 % did so using a broadband connection at home (Zickuhr and Smith 2013). In 2014, 79.1 % of the German population (14 years and older) used the Internet (van Eimeren and Frees 2014) while roughly 58.4 % did so using a broadband connection (Initiative D21 2014). Although these numbers are not directly comparable since they address the Internet use of different demographic groups, they can serve as rough indicators suggesting that while the Internet is more broadly used in the USA than in Germany, this usage gap is far smaller than the gap seen with regard to Twitter use.

Without further research and the collection of data sets that allow country-to-country comparisons on who uses Twitter and why, one can only speculate on the reason for the divergent adoption rates in the USA and Germany. One reason could be that in the US celebrities, established media and corporations flocked to Twitter quite early and thus, while promoting their presence on Twitter, also contributed to the service's growing adoption among the public. Meanwhile in Germany these groups kept their distance from Twitter for much longer; hence the platform was less visible in public discourse and received less media coverage. However, it is certainly true that the differences in Twitter use have led to differences in the evaluation of Twitter's relative importance within the political process by political elites.

There are only a handful of studies examining the demographic makeup of Twitter users, all of them pointing to their being far from a representative sample of underlying populations. Twitter users seem to skew towards the age bracket of 18–29 year olds, being better educated, and slightly more politically interested than the general population (Gainous and Wagner 2014; Rainie et al. 2012; Smith and Brenner 2012; Vaccari et al. 2013). Motives for political Twitter use seem to include quick information gathering, feeling connected with politicians, social utility, entertainment, and self-expression (Gainous and Wagner 2014; Parmelee and

Bichard 2012). Given these observations, it is not surprising to find that politically vocal Twitter users also tend to be partisan supporters of political parties (Barberá and Rivero 2014; Gainous and Wagner 2014). Given this nature of Twitter use, it seems highly unlikely—or at the very least surprising—for metrics calculated on the basis of Twitter users' messages to correspond with population-wide political phenomena or trends.

2.3 Political Uses of Twitter: Politicians, Activists, Citizens, and the Media

Twitter clearly was not created as a tool for political expression, activism, or campaigning. Still, the service, which was founded to allow users to share details of their lives, content on the Web, or pithy remarks, has been taken up by politicians, government officials, activists, and political supporters. Twitter has, therefore, become a medium for talking and fighting about politics, organizing collective action, and showing support for, or critique of politicians and political issues. While a majority of registered users use the service for social or entertainment purposes (e.g. Hargittai and Litt 2012; Java et al. 2007), a relevant number of users employ Twitter to engage with politics.

In the aftermath of Barack Obama's successful presidential bid in 2008 and the highly promoted use of the Internet and Twitter by his campaign, Twitter suddenly became a prominent campaigning tool. Since the autumn of 2008 many campaigns, politicians, and government officials have started using Twitter (e.g. Golbeck et al. 2010; Jackson and Lilleker 2011; Kreiss 2014; Vergeer and Hermans 2013). These actors display a variety of usage patterns. For some, Twitter serves as a new communication channel to publish information or updates; some use Twitter as an opportunity for other Twitter users to make contact with them; some use Twitter as a marketing stunt, to generate positive press; while others use Twitter just like *normal* users to interact and socialize with other Twitter users (for an overview of the relevant literature see Jungherr 2014b).

Twitter has also become a popular tool for political activists. Some well documented examples for the use of Twitter by activists include protests in reaction to the results of the Iranian presidential election 2009 (e.g. Web Ecology Project 2009), the Arab Spring 2010/2011 (e.g. Howard and Hussain 2013; Lotan et al. 2011), and the Spanish *Indignados* 2011/2012 (e.g. González-Bailón et al. 2013). In Germany political activists are also increasingly using Twitter. Some examples include the campaign in support of the e-petition against the *Zugangserschwerungsgesetz* (Access Impediment Act) in 2009 (e.g. Jungherr and Jürgens 2010), the *Yeaahh Flasmobs* during the campaign for the federal election of 2009 in Germany (Jungherr 2012a), protests against working conditions for students at universities in Germany and Austria (Maireder and Schwarzenegger 2012), and protests against an infrastructure project in Stuttgart, S21 (Jungherr and Jürgens

2014). In these cases, Twitter served as a tool not only for the organization and coordination of collective action but also for the distribution of information about the events.

Twitter has also been used successfully to coordinate relief efforts after natural disasters or civil unrest. Some examples include the relief efforts after the Haiti earthquakes in 2010 (e.g. Pew Research: Journalism Project 2010), the clean-up after the London riots of 2011 (Ball and Lewis 2011), and the coordination of the relief efforts in the aftermath of hurricane Sandy on the east coast of the USA in 2012 (Stricker 2012). In these cases, Twitter users serve as sensors who document their rapidly changing environment. Their messages might offer information on the changing conditions, relevant to rescue workers or to the relief efforts. The messages could thus be used to document the current state of a situation and might serve as a basis for the coordination of relief efforts. This shows that Twitter has become a tool not only for marketing by political elites but also for the documentation and coordination of political activists as well as relief workers. Thus, Twitter has the potential to empower the coordination and promotion of collective action (e.g. Bennett and Segerberg 2013).

In addition to professional political actors—such as politicians, campaigners, government officials, and political activists—*normal* Twitter users also use the microblogging service to comment on political topics, events, voice their support or critique political initiatives and politicians. Of course, these users view politics as one topic among many issues fit for discussion on Twitter. Accordingly, these discussions tend to arise in reaction to political events—such as televised debates or inaugurals (e.g. Jungherr 2014a; Lin et al. 2014; Shamma et al. 2011), protests (e.g. Jungherr and Jürgens 2014) or during campaigns (e.g. Bruns and Burgess 2011; Hanna et al. 2011; Jürgens and Jungherr 2015; Mustafaraj et al. 2011). Thus, Twitter messages contribute to the political discourse online, albeit restricted to 140 characters or less.

Twitter messages commenting on politics are not only of interest for researchers analyzing political discourse online. Journalists also use Twitter in their coverage of political events, scandals, and campaigns as a source for ad hoc opinion surveys (e.g. Anstead and O'Loughlin 2014). Even classic horse-race reporting has found a new outlet in the shape of Twitter (Jungherr and Schoen 2013, p. 94). In general, Twitter has become a medium for political discourse and a source for journalists and researchers—rightly or wrongly—to assess the level of political support for political actors.

Additionally, journalists use Twitter increasingly as a research tool (e.g. Broersma and Graham 2012; vom Hofe and Nuernbergk 2012). Thus, Twitter messages can become inspiration or sources for news stories. Twitter contributes to a transformation of the traditional *news cycle*. The result of this transformation is something Andrew Chadwick calls *political information cycle*:

> They are assemblages in which the personnel, practices, genres, and temporalities of supposedly 'new' online media are increasingly integrated with those of supposedly 'old' broadcast and press media. They are set to become the systemic norm for the mediation of high-profile political events in Britain. (Chadwick 2011a, p. 25)

The political information cycle is different from its older sibling the news cycle. It is faster, recognizes more actors, and shows more complicated reciprocal effects on the participating actors. Nevertheless, these new dynamics do not necessarily subvert traditional political elites (Chadwick 2011b). Twitter is not the only contributor to the political information cycle. That being said, by its mix of users belonging to political elites, the media, and *normal* users Twitter offers a data set with unique potential to examine the dynamics of the new environment for political communication.

2.4 Rise to Prominence

On 21 March 2006, Twitter co-founder Jack Dorsey posted the first tweet: "just setting up my twttr" (Dorsey 2006). This seemingly innocuous message was the beginning of one of the big Web 2.0 success stories and the start of a communication phenomenon whose reach is still growing and whose consequences are far from understood. The microblogging service Twitter is used by celebrities, athletes, brands, politicians, political activists, and normal users to post opinions, to communicate or to inform themselves. Topics range from the mundane details of day to day life (e.g. what did I have for lunch?), shocking events (e.g. natural or man made disasters, terrorist attacks), TV shows, sports events, product launches, political campaigns, and collective action. It seems that any topic fitting into 140 characters or less is suitable for Twitter. Table 2.2 shows a timeline of major steps in the evolution of Twitter as a popular and political medium both in Germany and internationally.

International events illustrate Twitter's growing popularity over the years and its various uses. We see events that illustrate Twitter's growing general popularity (e.g. the first tweet by Oprah Winfrey; the first live tweet from the International Space Station; the first tweet by the pope), its potential as a fast information distribution platform (e.g. the emergency landing of US Airways Flight 1549 on the Hudson river; news about Jakarta bombings break on Twitter), its use as a tool for the coordination of collective action or disaster relief (e.g. students used Twitter to coordinate protests in Moldova and Twitter was also used as a tool in support of disaster relief in the aftermath of the Haiti earthquakes) and Twitter's growing adoption in the communication repertoire of campaigns and politicians (e.g. Barack Obama's campaign team reacts to the results of the 2008 presidential election: "We just made history"; British PM David Cameron announces major cabinet reshuffle on Twitter; Obama's campaign team reacts to the results of the 2012 presidential election: "Four more years").

The table also illustrates Twitter's growing popularity with politicians and campaigns in Germany. In late 2008 and early 2009, we find some early adopters among Germany's politicians at federal and state level, no doubt motivated by the upcoming election campaigns in 2009 (e.g. Hubertus Heil, SPD; Volker Beck, Bündnis 90/Die Grünen; Thorsten Schäfer-Gümbel, SPD; Kristina Schröder, CDU). We also see that

2.4 Rise to Prominence

Table 2.2 Key moments in the evolution of Twitter as a popular and political medium

Date	Description	Country
2006-03-21	First tweet is published	USA
2008-04-10	Journalist James Buck uses Twitter to inform his followers about his arrest in Egypt—soon after he is released	Egypt
2008-08-25	Hubertus Heil (General Secretary SPD) posts his first tweet while visiting the nomination convention of the US Democrats	Germany
2008-09-17	First tweet by Volker Beck (Bündnis 90/Die Grünen)	Germany
2008-11-05	Barack Obama's campaign team reacts to the results of the 2008 presidential election: "We just made history"	USA
2008-11-26	Eye witnesses use Twitter to post their observations of the Mumbai terrorist attacks	India
2009-01-01	First tweet by Thorsten Schäfer-Gümbel (SPD)	Germany
2009-01-08	First tweet by Kristina Schröder (CDU)	Germany
2009-01-19	Emergency landing of US Airways Flight 1549 on the Hudson river	USA
2009-01-23	First tweet by Oprah Winfrey	USA
2009-04-07	Students use Twitter to coordinate protests in Moldova	Moldova
2009-05-07	Online petition against the Access Impediment Act reaches 50,000 signatures	Germany
2009-05-24	MPs Klöckner (CDU) and Kelber (SPD) tweet the result of the election of Germany's Bundespräsident before the official announcement	Germany
2009-06-12	Twitter is heavily used by activists during protest against the contested 2009 presidential election in Iran	Iran
2009-06-16	The US State Department asks Twitter to delay scheduled downtime so protesters in Iran can keep using the service	USA
2009-07-16	News about Jakarta bombings breaks on Twitter	Indonesia
2009-10-20	Start of the #unibrennt protests in Vienna	Austria
2009-11-15	Barack Obama states in an interview: "I Have Never Used Twitter"	USA
2010-01-13	Twitter is used as a tool in support of disaster relief in the aftermath of the Haiti earthquakes	Haiti
2010-01-22	First live tweet from the International Space Station	Space
2010-09-30	Protesters against Stuttgart 21 use Twitter heavily	Germany
2010-12-17	Twitter and other social media channels are heavily used during the protests of the Arab Spring	Egypt
2011-02-28	First tweet by Regierungssprecher Steffen Seibert	Germany
2011-05-01	Tweet refers to helicopters hovering above Abbottabad thus documenting the raid against the compound of bin Laden	Pakistan
2011-09-18	The Pirate Party gains enough votes to enter the state parliament of Berlin	Germany
2011-09-25	First tweet by Peter Altmaier (CDU)	Germany
2012-03-20	First tweet by Hannelore Kraft (SPD)	Germany
2012-08-31	Obama's campaign team reacts to Republican nomination convention: "This seat's taken"	USA

(continued)

Table 2.2 (continued)

Date	Description	Country
2012-09-04	British PM David Cameron announces major cabinet reshuffle on Twitter	UK
2012-11-06	Obama's campaign team reacts to the results of the 2012 presidential election: "Four more years"	USA
2012-12-12	First tweet by the pope	Italy
2013-01-24	Activists use the hashtag #aufschrei to raise awareness about everyday sexism	Germany

Twitter has been increasingly adopted in protests by political activists in Germany (e.g. online petition against the Access Impediment Act reaches 50,000 signatures; start of the #unibrennt protests in Vienna; protesters against Stuttgart 21 use Twitter heavily). It seems also worthwhile pointing out that after the surprising success of the Pirate Party in the Berlin state elections (September 2011) a greater number of established German politicians started including Twitter in their communication repertoires (e.g. Peter Altmaier, CDU; Hannelore Kraft, SPD).

Examining the role of Twitter during the federal election campaign of 2009 in Germany, we have to understand that this campaign was heavily influenced by the 2008 presidential bid by Barack Obama. Or to be more precise, the campaign was heavily influenced by the public perception of Barack Obama's presidential bid. In Germany, nearly everybody—journalists, consultants, campaign professionals, and politicians—spoke of the transformative and mobilizing powers of the Internet for campaigns. Since 2009, the discussion about the role of the Internet in Barack Obama's campaign and its contribution to his successful bid for the presidency has evolved, resulting in a much more nuanced picture. Researchers point to the fact that Obama's team used the Internet in support of traditional campaign functions—such as fundraising or get-out-the-vote mobilization (Kreiss 2012; Nielsen 2012), functions which Matthew Hindman has called the "infrastructure of politics" (Hindman 2009).

In 2009, these elements of Obama's campaign were largely absent from discussion about the Internet's political potential in Germany. Back then, the discussion instead focused on the vague hope that the Internet could mobilize politically disinterested people, would lead to the sudden emergence of grassroots movements or perhaps even facilitate more meaningful dialogue between politicians and the electorate. Political campaigns in Germany focused on another political function of the Internet. Political parties used the Internet and digital services predominantly to visualize political support by heavily investing in the *digital horse-race*—the race between parties and candidates to generate high counts of supporters on various online channels and countable interactions. All cyber- and Web 2.0-rhetoric by politicians, campaigners, and consultants aside, the Internet was used in the campaign for the German federal election of 2009 largely as a publicity tool with which parties could stage events online that in turn led to coverage by traditional media and thus fed back into the larger campaign narrative (Jungherr 2012b).

2009 was a special election year in Germany. Not only was there a federal election in September but also six state elections, the election of Germany's *Bundespräsident* as well as the election for the European Parliament. Parties and politicians in Germany could thus test various online campaigning tools before committing to their use during the federal election campaign. This led to some experimentation with Twitter by politicians prior to the Hessen state election early in 2009. These promising experiments came to a sudden halt when two Members of Parliament, Julia Klöckner (CDU) and Ulrich Kelber (SPD), tweeted the results of the election of Germany's *Bundespräsident* before their official announcement (Heeg 2009). Media reactions were so critical of the two politicians' behavior that others reduced their experiments with the microblogging service during the federal election campaign a few months later. While politicians and campaigns thus approached Twitter cautiously leading up to the campaign, political activists used Twitter successfully to mobilize supporters of an e-petition to the German Parliament to stop a controversial piece of Internet legislation (Jungherr and Jürgens 2010) and to coordinate flashmobs at Merkel campaign events during the last week of the campaign (Jungherr 2012a). Supporters of the *Piratenpartei* also used Twitter extensively to post information about the campaign, comment on the political opponent, and to coordinate campaign activities. In summary, traditional political actors approached Twitter somewhat cautiously and hesitantly during the campaign of 2009 while political activists and supporters of the Pirates used Twitter extensively. This led to vibrant political discussions on Twitter during the election campaign of 2009.

As this chapter has shown Twitter is well on its way to becoming a significant online service that people use not only in their personal lives but also to participate in political discourse. The process has been facilitated by the readiness of political elites, activists, and the media to incorporate Twitter into their communication repertoires. This has undoubtedly contributed to the public perception of Twitter as a legitimate communication channel for political talk and interaction.

References

Anstead N, O'Loughlin B (2014) Social media analysis and public opinion: the 2010 UK general election. J Comput-Mediat Commun. doi:10.1111/jcc4.12102

Ball J, Lewis P (2011) Twitter and the riots: how the news spread. The Guardian. http://www.guardian.co.uk/uk/2011/dec/07/twitter-riots-how-news-spread

Barberá P, Rivero G (2014) Understanding the political representativeness of Twitter users. Soc Sci Comput Rev. doi:10.1177/0894439314558836

Bennett WL, Segerberg A (2013) The logic of connective action: digital media and the personalization of contentious politics. Cambridge University Press, Cambridge

Broersma M, Graham T (2012) Social media as beat: tweets as a news source during the 2010 British and Dutch elections. Journal Pract 6(3):403–419. doi:10.1080/17512786.2012.663626

Bruns A, Burgess J (2011) #ausvotes: how Twitter covered the 2010 Australian federal election. Commun Polit Cult 44(2):37–56

Chadwick A (2011a) Britain's first live televised party leaders' debate: from the news cycle to the political information cycle. Parliam Aff 64(1):24–44. doi:10.1093/pa/gsq045

Chadwick A (2011b) The political information cycle in a hybrid news system: the British Prime Minister and the "Bullygate" affair. Int J Press/Polit 16(1):3–29. doi:10.1177/1940161210384730

Dorsey J (2006) Just setting up my twttr. Twitter. https://twitter.com/jack/status/20

Duggan M, Smith A (2013) Social media update. Pew Internet & American Life Project. http://pewinternet.org/Reports/2013/Social-Media-Update.aspx

Gainous J, Wagner KW (2014) Tweeting to power: the social media revolution in American politics. Oxford University Press, Oxford

Golbeck J, Grimes JM, Rogers A (2010) Twitter use by the U.S. Congress. J Am Soc Inform Sci Technol 61(8):1612–1621. doi:10.1002/asi.21344

González-Bailón S, Borge-Holthoefer J, Moreno Y (2013) Broadcasters and hidden influentials in online protest diffusion. Am Behav Sci 57(7):943–965. doi:10.1177/0002764213479371

Hanna A, Sayre B, Bode L, Yang JH, Shah D (2011) Mapping the political Twitterverse: candidates and their followers in the midterms. In: Nicolov N, Shanahan JG, Adamic L, Baeza-Yates R, Counts S (eds) ICWSM 2011: proceedings of the 5th international AAAI conference on weblogs and social media, Association for the Advancement of Artificial Intelligence (AAAI), Menlo Park, pp 510–513

Hargittai E, Litt E (2012) Becoming a tweep: how prior online experiences influence Twitter use. Inform Commun Soc 15(5):680–702. doi:10.1080/1369118X.2012.666256

Heeg T (2009) Die Weinkönigin und der Bundes-Hotte. FAZNET. http://www.faz.net/-gpf-12k3v

Hindman M (2009) The myth of digital democracy. Princeton University Press, Princeton

Howard PN, Hussain MM (2013) Democracy's fourth wave? Digital media and the Arab Spring. Oxford University Press, New York

Initiative D21 (2014) D21-Digital-Index: Die Entwicklung der digitalen Gesellschaft in Deutschland. Initiative D21, Berlin, DE. http://www.initiatived21.de/portfolio/d21-digital-index-2014/

Jackson NA, Lilleker DG (2011) Microblogging, constituency service and impression management: UK MPs and the use of Twitter. J Legis Stud 17(1):86–105. doi:10.1080/13572334.2011.545181

Java A, Song X, Finin T, Tseng B (2007) Why we Twitter: understanding microblogging usage and communities. In: Zhang H, Mobasher B, Giles L, McCallum A, Nasraoui O, Spiliopoulou M, Srivastava J, Yen J (eds) WebKDD/SNA-KDD '07: proceedings of the 9th WebKDD and 1st SNA-KDD 2007 workshop on web mining and social network analysis. ACM, New York, pp 56–65. doi:10.1145/1348549.1348556

Jungherr A (2012a) The German federal election of 2009: the challenge of participatory cultures in political campaigns. Transform Works Cult 10. doi:10.3983/twc.2012.0310

Jungherr A (2012b) Online campaigning in Germany: the CDU online campaign for the general election 2009 in Germany. Ger Polit 21(3):317–340. doi:10.1080/09644008.2012.716043

Jungherr A (2014a) The logic of political coverage on Twitter: temporal dynamics and content. J Commun 64(2):239–259. doi:10.1111/jcom.12087

Jungherr A (2014b) Twitter in politics: a comprehensive literature review. Soc Sci Res Netw. http://papers.ssrn.com/sol3/papers.cfm?abstract_id=2402443

Jungherr A, Jürgens P (2010) The political click: political participation through e-petitions in Germany. Policy Internet 2(4):131–165. doi:10.2202/1944-2866.1084

Jungherr A, Jürgens P (2014) Through a glass, darkly: tactical support and symbolic association in Twitter messages commenting on Stuttgart 21. Soc Sci Comput Rev 32(1):74–89. doi:10.1177/0894439313500022

Jungherr A, Schoen H (2013) Das Internet in Wahlkämpfen: Konzepte, Wirkungen und Kampagnenfunktionen. Springer, Wiesbaden

Jürgens P, Jungherr A (2015) The use of Twitter during the 2009 German national election. Ger Polit Forthcoming.

Kreiss D (2012) Taking our country back: the crafting of networked politics from Howard Dean to Barack Obama. Oxford University Press, Oxford

References

Kreiss D (2014) Seizing the moment: the presidential campaigns' use of Twitter during the 2012 electoral cycle. New Media Soc. doi:10.1177/1461444814562445

Lin YR, Keegan B, Margolin D, Lazer D (2014) Rising tides or rising stars? Dynamics of shared attention on Twitter during media events. PLoS One 9(5):e94093. doi:10.1371/journal.pone.0094093

Lotan G, Graeff E, Ananny M, Gaffney D, Pearce I, Boyd D (2011) The revolutions were tweeted: information flows during the 2011 Tunesian and Egyptian revolutions. Int J Commun 5. http://ijoc.org/ojs/index.php/ijoc/article/view/1246

Maireder A, Schwarzenegger C (2012) A movement of connected individuals. Inform Commun Soc 15(2):171–195. doi:10.1080/1369118X.2011.589908

Mustafaraj E, Finn S, Whitlock C, Metaxas PT (2011) Vocal minority versus silent majority: discovering the opinions of the long tail. In: SocialCom 2011: the 3rd IEEE international conference on social computing. IEEE, Washington, DC

Nielsen RK (2012) Ground wars: personalized communication in political campaigns. Princeton University Press, Princeton

Parmelee JH, Bichard SL (2012) Politics and the Twitter revolution: how tweets influence the relationship between political leaders and the public. Lexington Books, Lanham

Pew Research: Journalism Project (2010) Social media aid the Haiti relief effort. PEJ New Media Index January 11–15, 2010. http://www.journalism.org/index_report/social_media_aid_haiti_relief_effort

Rainie L, Smith A, Schlozman KL, Brady H, Verba S (2012) Social media and political engagement. Pew Internet Am Life Proj. http://pewinternet.org/Reports/2012/Political-engagement.aspx

Shamma DA, Kennedy L, Churchill EF (2011) Peaks and persistence: modeling the shape of microblog conversations. In: Hinds P, Tang JC, Wang J, Bardram J, Ducheneaut N (eds) CSCW 2011: proceedings of the ACM 2011 conference on computer supported cooperative work. ACM, New York, pp 355–358. doi:10.1145/1958824.1958878 10.1145/1958824.1958878

Smith A, Brenner J (2012) Twitter use 2012. Pew Research Center's Internet & American Life Project. http://pewinternet.org/Reports/2012/Twitter-Use-2012.aspx

Stone B (2009) What's happening? Twitter Blog. http://blog.twitter.com/2009/11/whats-happening.html

Stricker G (2012) Hurricane Sandy: resources on Twitter. Twitter Blog. http://blog.twitter.com/2012/10/hurricane-sandy-resources-on-twitter.html

Vaccari C, Valeriani A, Barberá P, Bonneau R, Jost JT, Nagler J, Tucker J (2013) Social media and political communication: a survey of Twitter users during the 2013 Italian general election. Rivista Italiana di Scienza 43(3):325–355. doi:10.1426/75245

van Eimeren B, Frees B (2014) 79 Prozent der Deutschen online—Zuwachs bei mobiler Internet-468 nutzung und Bewegtbild. Media Perspektiven (7–8):378–396

Vergeer M, Hermans L (2013) Campaigning on Twitter: micro-blogging and online social networking as campaign tools in the general elections 2010 in the Netherlands. J Comput-Mediat Commun 18(4):399–419. doi:10.1111/jcc4.12023

vom Hofe HJ, Nuernbergk C (2012) Twitter im professionellen journalismus: Ergebnisse einer Redaktionsbefragung. Journalistik Journal 15(1):30–31

Web Ecology Project (2009) The Iranian election on Twitter: the first eighteen days. Web Ecology Project. http://www.webecologyproject.org/2009/06/iran-election-on-twitter/

Zickuhr K, Smith A (2013) Home broadband 2013. Pew Internet & American Life Project. http://pewinternet.org/Reports/2013/Broadband.aspx

Chapter 3
Twitter in the Analysis of Social Phenomena: An Interpretative Framework

3.1 Analyzing Social Phenomena with Digital Trace Data

As the use of online services grows and capabilities in data storage as well as analytics keep on rising, researchers become increasingly interested in what digital trace data might tell them about patterns of human behavior. These new data sources document human behavior in unprecedented detail and scale (Freelon 2014; Howison et al. 2011; Lazer et al. 2009). Thus, they potentially hold new information for researchers on the mechanisms of human interaction and social phenomena. But before we can proceed in unlocking the potential of these data, we have to establish how such data traces connect to social phenomena of interest.

The underlying thesis of this book is that Twitter data may provide researchers with insights about objects and shifts in politically vocal Twitter users' attention to political information but are much less reliable in drawing inferences on public opinion or voting intentions of the general public. In the following chapter, I will provide a framework for this argument by introducing a micro-foundation to the analysis of social phenomena on a macro-level through patterns in aggregate data, documenting human interactions online.

Although there is an increasing number of studies trying to connect patterns in human data traces online with social phenomena—such as political polarization (e.g. Conover et al. 2011), protest recruitment (e.g. González-Bailón et al. 2011), or election results (e.g. Gayo-Avello 2013)—little attention has been paid to the mechanisms driving users' reactions to an offline phenomenon or event by interacting with an online service. Without a better understanding of a user's motivation for posting a tweet or googling a search term, it is difficult to interpret the resulting patterns within digital trace data collected on the respective services. Beyond that, a systematic discussion of how the various data-generating processes of different online services impact the interpretation of digital trace data is conspicuously absent from the literature. Data collected on services that document non-public behavior of users—for instance, searching a term in a search engine or the automatic logging of geographical coordinates by cell phones—should be interpreted differently than data collected on a service through which users consciously and publicly document their behavior, such as micro-publishing platforms like Twitter or location services like Foursquare. Analyses of politically relevant keywords' frequency on Google (e.g. Weber et al. 2012) and on Twitter (e.g. Jungherr 2013)—to pick just two examples—should not be interpreted as documenting the same aspect of social reality but instead as documenting different shadows of the same social phenomenon, mediated through different mechanisms that led users to interact with Google and Twitter. For the field to advance beyond the establishment of a relationship between some metrics of online trace data and some social phenomena, we have to address systematically the mechanisms leading individuals to interact with different online services. In this chapter, I will address these questions with special attention to the analysis of Twitter messages commenting on politics.

As a first step, I will offer a definition of digital trace data. Then, I will discuss various approaches in the social sciences attempting to analyze data traces of human interaction with online services and incorporate the results in the body of established research. The most popular strands are grouped under the terms *computational social science*, *digital methods*, and *big data*. I will show where these approaches originated and how they emphasize different aspects of conducting research with digital trace data. While there is an increasing body of research that links offline phenomena to patterns in digital trace data, there is surprisingly little research focusing on the social mechanisms that lead users to interact with online services in the first place. This is a serious deficit in the literature, as digital data traces do not offer us a direct view on social phenomena or events; instead, they offer us a view of these phenomena mediated through the interests and behavior of users moving in the constricted, semi-public communication spaces provided by various digital services. I will show that the inference of social phenomena based on digital trace data is, in fact, a special case within the larger sociological debate, on how to explain macro-phenomena based on micro-behavior. Connecting the relatively new debate on how to analyze social phenomena based on online trace data with the much older debate on how to explain macro-phenomena based on micro-behavior goes a long way in anchoring the current debate within the larger context of the social sciences. Following this, I will show that digital trace data collected on different online services have to be interpreted on the basis of each online service's respective data-generating process. In the analysis of political phenomena, it is also necessary to approach digital trace data differently than for the analysis of other social phenomena—such as the commercial success of products or brands. Based on this discussion, I will propose a mechanism that might lead users to post Twitter messages. This mechanism includes elements based on individual behavior, social influence, opportunities offered by social context, and external events.

3.2 What Are Digital Trace Data?

James Howison, Andrea Wiggins, and Kevin Crowston define digital trace data as:

> (...) records of activity (trace data) undertaken through an online information system (thus, digital). A trace is a mark left as a sign of passage; it is recorded evidence that something has occurred in the past. (...) The second part of the definition of digital trace data is that the data are both produced through and stored by an information system. Not all trace data are digital in this sense, including patent citations. Moreover, trace data could be produced through direct observation. (Howison et al. 2011, p. 769f.)

Each user interaction with an online service leaves these data traces, documenting activity on the service. Each Google search term, each tweet, each login on Facebook or Foursquare leaves a digital trace. The aggregates of these interactions especially are of interest to researchers and engineers and may have a variety of applications in research: patterns and dynamics of user interactions in these data sets can be used to understand user behavior better, improve the technological design of services, or offer new features.

It is important to differentiate further between different types of digital trace data. On the one hand, we have data directly produced by the user in interaction with the service in question. This could be the keyword typed by a user into Google or the text of a tweet, all of which might be called primary data. On the other hand, we have data that the service uses to contextualize interaction by its users. This may refer to a time-stamp marking the moment a keyword was searched on Google, the GPS coordinates of where a user posted a tweet, or the name of the application someone used to post a message. These data might be called meta-data. The analysis of meta-data allows researchers to establish potentially meaningful contexts for the interpretation of patterns found in primary data.

In their article, Howison and colleagues identify a number of digital trace data characteristics that are important for interpretation:

> 1) it is found data (rather than produced for research), 2) it is event-based data (rather than summary data), and 3) as events occur over a period of time, it is longitudinal data. (Howison et al. 2011, p. 769)

With their first characteristic, found data, the authors address the fact that digital trace data are a by-product of interactions with an online service and are not collected by a dedicated research instrument. Hence, these data do not lend themselves as readily to scientific research as data collected explicitly with a research question in mind. Instead, researchers have to address consciously how these found data can be used in the context of their research. This raises the importance of understanding the data generating processes of digital services and burdens researchers with the task of providing a link between these data generating processes, identified patterns in data aggregates, and the social phenomena they wish to address.

The second characteristic of digital data traces has similar implications. Howison et al. (2011) describe this type of data as "event-based", by which they mean that digital trace data document events during which users interacted through an online service, thus allowing for the establishment of a link between them in a social network. Howison, Wiggins, and Crowston contrast this with summary-based data which might be the answer to a survey question asking for social contacts of an individual. In essence, Howison et al. (2011) raise the valid point that these different modes of data collection might document different types of social relationships. Does a link between two actors established by an @mention, posted by one of them in a tweet, allow the same inferences as a link between the same actors established by the survey question asking a respondent to list her friends? The authors discuss digital trace data from the perspective of social network analysis; but their point remains valid for other research contexts. Researchers have to remain conscious of how they interpret patterns in data documenting individual interactions of users with a service, whilst using theoretical concepts established in other research contexts.

The third characteristic discussed by Howison et al. (2011) is that they are longitudinal data. Thus, they document a user's interactions with the service at different times. The question for the researcher then becomes how to deal with the data. Does one aggregate the number of @mentions between two users during a given time interval; and if so, what time interval? In constructing a time series based on these interactions, what are the time bins in which one decides to aggregate the interactions; is the correct bin size 1 min, 10 min, an hour, or a day? These choices influence the patterns that emerge from the data. These choices have to be addressed by researchers, therefore, when interpreting the results, especially when trying to use these data in the context of well established theories in the social sciences, which were developed using different data types.

Still, the characteristics discussed above also contribute to the potential of these data sources in advancing social science research. Digital trace data are available as individual and process-produced data, documenting the actual behavior of people over time. Thus, a series of issues with data reliability documenting self-reported behavior can be avoided. Another benefit of these data is that they allow the analysis of all actors' behavior in a system (i.e. all users that interacted with an online service over a given time span), not just within a sample.

The second part of the definition by Howison et al. (2011) is also important to keep in mind: digital trace data are produced and stored in the context of the technological design of an information system. The design of each service and the format in which its programmers decided to store information has crucial impacts on how the data can be used by researchers.

The potential of digital trace data for social science is considerable. Still, their special characteristics will have to be addressed before researchers can productively integrate results of research based on digital trace data in the body of established research.

3.3 Computational Social Science, Digital Methods, and Big Data: What Is Missing?

The increasing use of digital devices, online services, and the accompanying growth in data-sets documenting human behavior have led to the emergence of research efforts in various branches of the social sciences. The three terms most often connected with the analysis of digital data traces of human behavior are *computational social science*, *digital methods*, and *big data*. As each of these terms stems from a different research tradition and is connected with different approaches with regard to research practice and research interest, it pays to look at them a bit more closely.

3.3.1 Computational Social Science

The concept *computational social science* has its roots very firmly in computer science, physics, and various quantitative research traditions in the social sciences. Its main focus is on unlocking new research potential in digital data sources by using advanced quantitative methods and computational models (Cioffi-Revilla 2010, 2014; Conte et al. 2012; Gilbert 2010; Lazer et al. 2009).

The intellectual and professional roots of many proponents of this approach can be found in complex systems research and generative social science. Both these fields understand social phenomena on the macro level—examples include segregation, economic processes, information diffusion—as based on individual level decision, that can be modeled by computer programs. These models are then used to create data sets—for example through agent based modeling—that document how a social system would look if the assumptions researchers had formulated in their models were true. Recent studies combine this approach based on quantitative models of human behavior with data sets documenting actual human interaction with digital devices or online services (Epstein 2006; Miller and Page 2007; Mitchell 2009).

Another group of researchers, not entirely distinct from the first, starts from the quantitative analysis and statistical modeling of networks. Since the 1990s, an increasing number of mathematicians, physicists, and computer scientists have used the growing computational power to analyze large-scale data sets of networks—be they technical, biological, or social—and build statistical models of their dynamics (Easley and Kleinberg 2010; Jackson 2008; Kolaczyk 2009; Newman 2010). With this approach, they have also increasingly contributed to the field of social network analysis, which up until then had almost exclusively been dominated by sociologists and had mainly focused on the analysis of networks of small social groups (Scott 2013; Wasserman and Faust 1994). Today, the quantitative analysis of social networks—constructed from interactions of users with digital devices and online services—is one of the dominating fields in computational social science.

Another group of researchers contributing to computational social science is interested in using digital devices as sensors for human behavior offline. Here examples include all forms of communicational interactions and non-verbal communication. They either use data collected by digital devices during their everyday use, customize standard devices such as smart-phones with special apps for data collection, or even equip people with custom-made sensors (Eagle and Pentland 2006; Lane et al. 2010; Pentland 2008).

Researchers from both traditions are connected by their interest in the ever growing data traces of human behavior, captured by digital devices and online services. Leading practitioners in the field described the research potential of these conjoined fields in manifesto form:

> Each of these transactions leaves digital breadcrumbs which, when pulled together, offer increasingly comprehensive pictures of both individuals and groups, with the potential of transforming our understanding of our lives, organizations, and societies in a fashion that was barely conceivable just a few years ago. [...] To date the vast majority of existing research on human interactions has relied on one-shot self-reported data on relationships. New technologies, such as video surveillance, e-mail, and 'smart' name badges offer a remarkable, second-by-second picture of interactions over extended periods of time, providing information about both the structure and content of relationships. [...] In short, a computational social science is emerging that leverages the capacity to collect and analyze data with an unprecedented breadth and depth and scale. (Lazer et al. 2009, p. 721ff.)

This begs the question of which social phenomena are computational social scientists studying? Claudio Cioffi-Revilla lists the main research areas of the approach:

> The main computational social science areas are automated information extraction systems, social network analysis, social geographic information systems (GIS), complexity modelling, and social simulation models (Cioffi-Revilla 2010, p. 259).

Examples of this approach include studies that used data from the photo website Flickr to detect and classify popular international landmarks successfully (e.g. Crandall et al. 2009), data collected by a global instant messaging network to determine whether social contagion processes were based on prior similarity of its users or genuine influence (e.g. Aral et al. 2009), and location data collected by telephone companies to detect regular movement patterns of commuters (e.g. González et al. 2008). Because of its relatively open data access policy, Twitter is a very popular data source for studies in this tradition. Twitter data has successfully been used to detect stages in televised political events (e.g. Shamma et al. 2011) and protests (e.g. Jungherr and Jürgens 2014a). There is also a steadily increasing number of studies focusing on the network structure of interactions between Twitter users (e.g. Cha et al. 2010; Kwak et al. 2010). The geography of Twitter interaction has also become the focus of an increasing number of studies (e.g. Frank et al. 2013). Already this brief selection shows that Twitter is at the centre of the rapidly developing field of computational social science.

3.3.2 Digital Methods

The term *digital methods* stems from a tradition of qualitative research. Its origins lie mainly in culture studies and the ethnography of human interaction online. Its focus is on using digital artifacts—such as websites, links, search results—not only to research online phenomena but also to draw inferences on offline phenomena—such as power relationships between organizations or state censorship of specific Internet aspects (Rogers 2004, 2013b).

The roots of this approach lie with Richard Rogers and the *Digital Methods Initiative* at the University of Amsterdam. Through an annual summer school and a series of easy-to-use software packages, such as the *Issuecrawler*,[1] the digital methods approach has become popular among researchers coming to Internet studies from the humanities or more qualitative fields of the social sciences. The popularity of the term has led many researchers to use it synonymously with Internet research.

However, in its original conception digital methods aimed to use digital objects and medium specific methods to learn more about the Internet and reality. Richard Rogers formulates as the basic goal of digital methods, that:

> [...] web research be put to new uses, given an emphasis on the study of natively digital objects and the methods that routinely make use of them. That is, I will strive to shift the attention from the opportunities afforded by transforming ink into bits, and instead inquire into how Internet research may move beyond the study of online culture only. How to capture and analyze hyperlinks, tags, search engine results, archived websites, social networking sites' profiles, Wikipedia edits, and other digital objects? How may one learn from how online devices (e.g., engines and recommendation systems) make use of the digital objects, and, crucially, how may such uses be repurposed for social and cultural research? Ultimately, I propose a research practice that learns from the methods of online devices, repurposes them, and seeks to ground claims about cultural change and societal conditions in web data, introducing the term 'online groundedness.' The overall aim is to rework methods for Internet-related research, developing a novel strand of study, digital methods. (Rogers 2013b, p. 19)

At first, this quote sounds like something a proponent of computational social science could have written. Indeed, the differences between the two lie not so much in their general approach of how to do research in, on, and with an online environment; instead, they stem from researchers' backgrounds and the methodological tool set they bring with them. This becomes clearer once we look at some studies from this field. In his 2013 book *Digital Methods*, Richard Rogers showcases a number of studies that used the digital methods approach: the study of link networks from nationally accessible or blocked websites in Iran, the comparison of Wikipedia pages on politically controversial historical events in different languages or the presence of political actors in the search results from politically relevant search terms in Google (Rogers 2013b). While these studies share an interest in online artifacts with computational social science, their research interest and methods

---

[1] https://www.issuecrawler.net.

are much more clearly anchored in qualitative social science. One indicator for these different sensibilities is the scale of the data collection. While studies in computational social science often use data sets with data points numbering in the hundred thousands or millions, studies in digital methods use much smaller data sets. What they might give away in scale, they make up for in a deeper interpretation of the phenomena in question. Still, the differences of the two approaches are mostly grounded in different backgrounds of researchers interested in online data, not in the general idea—using online data and artifacts to study not only online but also offline phenomena. Some studies already show that researchers explicitly anchor their work in both traditions (e.g. Weber et al. 2012). Thus, the borders between the approaches become increasingly blurred.

As with computational social science, Twitter is increasingly becoming a popular research topic in digital methods (Rogers 2013a). Nevertheless, the prominence of Twitter in digital methods is less than in computational social science. One reason for this divergence in interest might be that the comparative wealth of data with which the Twitter API provides researchers is less relevant to the questions that digital methods are concentrating on than for the analysis of quantitative patterns on which computational science is focused.

3.3.3 Big Data

Another term associated with the potential to gain insights from digital data sources documenting human behavior is *big data*. Originally, the term stems from computer science and was first used to describe database technology and software that allowed for the distributed storage and analysis of data, such as Google's *MapReduce* or *Apache Hadoop*[2] (O'Reilly Media 2012). However, the term is now increasingly adopted not only to describe data management techniques, but for instance is also used to describe business practices that rely on the analysis of user data pioneered by firms like Amazon or Google (McAfee and Brynjolfsson 2012). Beyond that, it is also often used as shorthand to describe the analytical potential of data-mining, machine learning, or predictive modeling (Miller 2014; Siegel 2013).

In their general-interest introduction to big data, Viktor Mayer-Schönberger and Kenneth Cukier outline the concept in more general terms:

> At its core, big data is about predictions. Though it is described as part of the branch of computer science called artificial intelligence, and more specifically, an area called machine learning, this characterization is misleading. Big data is not about trying to 'teach' a computer to 'think' like humans. Instead, it's about applying math to huge quantities of data in order to infer probabilities: the likelihood that an email message is spam; that the typed letters 'teh' are supposed to be 'the'; that the trajectory and velocity of a person jaywalking mean he'll make it across the street in time—the self-driving car need only slow slightly. The key is that these systems perform well because they are fed with lots of data on

---

[2]http://hadoop.apache.org.

which to base their predictions. Moreover, the systems are built to improve themselves over time, by keeping a tab on what are the best signals and patterns to look for as more data is fed in. (Mayer-Schönberger and Cukier 2013, p. 11)

This statement illustrates the difference between big data and computational social science. Big data, in its current conception, is strongly rooted in business analytics not in science. A business like Amazon does not need to know why people who bought book A are more likely to buy book B than those who bought book C; for the company it is important to know only that they are and thus make for more valuable addressees in advertising book B. In business, correlations between two relevant phenomena—for instance between sales of various articles, specific motor vibrations and the failure of motor parts, or sales of specific items and pregnancies—are valuable points of information in how to focus resources. In the words of Mayer-Schönberger and Cukier this is:

> [...] a move away from the age-old search for causality. As humans we have been conditioned to look for causes, even though searching for causality is often difficult and may lead us down the wrong paths. In a big-data world, by contrast, we won't have to be fixated on causality; instead we can discover patterns and correlations in the data that offer us novel and invaluable insights. The correlations may not tell us precisely why something is happening, but they alert us that it is happening. (Mayer-Schönberger and Cukier 2013, p. 14)

This reads like a typical example for an approach to social science known as *statistical explanations*:

> The defining characteristic of what here is referred to as a statistical explanation is that an appropriate explanation is at hand when we have identified factors that seem to make a difference to the probability of the event one seeks to explain. The identification of such factors is typically accomplished by decomposing the relevant population into different categories. (Hedström 2005, p. 20)

This approach stands in stark contrast to the goals of computational social science—and, for that matter, the goals of most scientific endeavors. In fact, if taken seriously, the claims of big data proponents can be read as a direct challenge of the role of interpretation in science and with this the foundations of the humanities and social sciences (Couldry 2014). Addressing this challenge, Jon Kleinberg states, in describing the potential of online data for scientists:

> The challenge is to do more than just notice the patterns; it is to begin inferring some of the high-level structures that generate the principles we humans are familiar with but also those that have eluded our limited powers of observation and analysis. (Kleinberg 2011, p. 75)

Using broad strokes, we can thus characterize computational social science as being interested in the psychological and social mechanisms producing patterns in aggregate data and big data as being interested in the predictive power of large data sets when analyzed by machine learning techniques. In this, the difference between the two approaches resembles the difference between an instrumentalist and a realistic approach to science. The instrumentalists see the value of a scientific theory not in the realism of its observations but in the precision of predictions based on as few assumptions as possible (Friedman 1953; Jasso 1988). This position has been subsequently criticized by social scientists that have been characterized as realists. The latter are interested in explaining social phenomena based on realistic assumptions about the processes contributing to an outcome of interest. The focus on their work does not lie in producing predictions about social phenomena but in their explanation (Hedström 2005). In line with these scientists, the analyses presented in the following chapters address potential mechanisms producing patterns in data documenting online interactions and accordingly what these patterns tell about social reality.

Computational social science thus stands in a clear line of social science, using new data sources, but still attempting to determine causal mechanisms in human behavior or social processes (Hedström and Ylikoski 2010). In contrast, big data is probably best understood as a label for specific analytical and business practices that build on new data sources to invent new or improve existing business models. This difference is crucial and should be kept in mind in light of recent attempts to adopt the term big data and the corresponding practices in scientific contexts.

3.3.4 Why We Need Theory

For all their differences, computational social science, digital methods, and big data share an underlying conviction: new data sources and new techniques for the storage and analysis of data might lead to the next paradigm shift in the social sciences. They are all very clear about the fact that digital data traces document human behavior in, up to now, unknown detail and scale. Instead of relying on carefully selected samples of a given service's users, there is no reason not to analyze the behavior of all users. Instead of surveying users at given intervals on their usage behavior of a given service, researchers can now analyze their behavior in real time. This new scale and depth of data potentially opens up a way to deeper understanding of those aspects of social life that are, at least in part, accompanied by the use of digital tools or services.

At present, most studies following these approaches focus on providing examples of offline phenomena that can be analyzed or even predicted using digital trace data. As with any new method, successful case studies generate the necessary interest among researchers and funding agencies to pursue these new research approaches further. We are currently at a point in time when the potential for conducting research based on digital data traces has been firmly established. This gives researchers the chance to approach the new data sources and new methods more systematically.

Two larger questions have to be addressed by social scientists in using digital trace data. First, practical questions in doing research with these data have to be addressed. These new data sources offer access to all aspects of human behavior that are accompanied by the use of digital tools and online services. Naturally, this raises questions regarding user privacy, methods of data access, data retention, and new analytical methods, which have to be answered before these new data sources will become common among social scientists (King 2011).

Second, researchers have to determine what part of reality, social interaction, and communication is documented by data collected through these devices and online services. Only then can we answer if and how these data supplement, or maybe even substitute, other data sources. In answering this question, it is crucial to determine what data-generating mechanisms are connected with various digital devices and online services, as well as how these mechanisms influence what we can deduce about reality when analyzing the resulting data. This indirect link between reality and data aggregates is mediated by users' decisions to react to social phenomena or events by interacting with an online service. The underlying mechanisms of this relationship have to be addressed for social scientists to be able to explain data patterns based on individual behavior.

3.4 Twitter: Macro-Phenomena, Micro-Behavior, and Macro-Patterns

3.4.1 Approaches to the Analysis of Digital Trace Data

Many studies interested in data documenting human interactions online identify patterns in the aggregates of users' interactions with the online service that provides the data under analysis. Such studies provide us with an increasingly detailed view of how the aggregates of digital trace data look while allowing us to examine differences in the patterns when we examine the online reactions of users to different social phenomena and online reactions of users to the same phenomena but on different online services. In the case of Twitter, we know typical interaction patterns between users across multiple thematic topics (e.g. Cha et al. 2010), differences in the structure of interaction networks between users commenting on US-politics depending on the form of interaction (i.e. @mention or retweet) (e.g. Conover et al. 2011), communication patterns between different types of users (e.g. Wu et al. 2011), and the role of individuals in the distribution of information on Twitter (e.g. Bakshy et al. 2011).

There is also an increasing number of studies developing statistical models of patterns of human online interaction. For example, there have been successful demonstrations on how to determine characteristic shapes in temporal activity for specific topics on various online channels (e.g. Kleinberg 2003; Yang and Leskovec 2011) or how to model the spread of information through various online channels based on algorithms inferring hidden dynamic networks (e.g. Gomez-Rodriguez et al. 2013). These two approaches, quantitative descriptions and statistical models, are both valuable for our understanding the shapes and dynamics of human interactions online; but they allow analyses only of this phenomenon's macro aspects. And even if we are able to model the flow of information through various online channels, this does not explain the behavior of users giving rise to these patterns.

Another group of studies tries to address the mechanisms giving rise to patterns in data aggregates. They do so by analyzing the effects of micro-level characteristics within a communication environment on macro-patterns or by performing experiments in online environments to determine data pattern changes given specific incentives (e.g. Anderson et al. 2013; Bond et al. 2012), variation in network structure (e.g. Ugander et al. 2012), the amount of information users have about the behavior of other actors (e.g. Muchnik et al. 2013; Salganik and Watts 2008, 2009; Salganik et al. 2006), the spread of various types of topics (e.g. Romero et al. 2011), and the difference between homophily and influence based mechanisms in information contagion (e.g. Aral 2011; Aral et al. 2009). These studies go a long way to providing a micro-foundation for studies providing descriptives of aggregate data patterns and statistical models of system level dynamics.

The empirical analyses in this book contribute to a fourth type of study based on digital trace data. Studies in this group use digital trace data to draw inferences on social phenomena or events inspiring users to interact with online services. There are two types of studies in this group, one focusing on inferring the occurrence of social events, the other trying to predict offline phenomena.

Some researchers use patterns in online trace data to detect events that users were commenting on—these events range from the spread of infectious diseases (e.g. Ginsberg et al. 2009), earthquakes (e.g. Sakaki et al. 2010), political protests (e.g. Jungherr and Jürgens 2014b), to rocket attacks in Israel (e.g. Zeitzoff 2011). In cases of events inspiring a high level of commentary, such as sport events, media broadcasts, or political protests, researchers have also shown that digital trace data allow for the identification of an event's specific stages (e.g. Chakrabarti and Punera 2011; Jungherr and Jürgens 2014a; Shamma et al. 2011).

Studies of the second type in this group are not only interested in detecting events in digital trace data streams; they also aim to establish a statistical relationship with specific patterns in digital trace data and the development of offline phenomena—such as the development of movies' box office results (e.g. Asur and Huberman 2010), stock-market movements (e.g. Bollen et al. 2011), and even election results (e.g. Gayo-Avello 2013) (for recent reviews on the use of digital trace data for predictions see Kalampokis et al. 2013; Schoen et al. 2013). Thus, these studies are interested in what the aggregates of users' interactions with online services can tell researchers about social phenomena or events that might have inspired the use of said online service. Following this approach, aggregates of digital trace data offer a mirror image of social phenomena and events.

3.4.2 Macro-Phenomena, Micro-Behavior, and Macro-Patterns

The analysis of Twitter data—or, for that matter, any source of digital trace data—can be understood as a special case in the attempt to explain macro-phenomena based on micro-behavior in sociology (Coleman 1990; Hedström 2005). In a nutshell, the basic reasoning behind this approach can be summed up thus: an event is witnessed by a user, be it an event of social importance—such as the television coverage of a campaign event of a politician—of entertainment value—such as the performance of a leading artist—or of personal relevance—such as an especially delicious meal. A user's incentive for reacting to the event in question can range from mere acknowledgment in a tweet to in-depth research and information gathering on Google and even public engagement with the event to further a personal agenda. These different motivations might lead users to interact with an online service. For example, if an event spiked a user's interest, she might tweet spontaneously her immediate emotional reaction. If an event garnered general interest that leads a user to engage with a topic, she might use a search engine to look for topically relevant keywords. Alternatively, if a user perceived an event as fit to further her own agenda, she could use Twitter as a means of spreading the message out to her followers, in order to rally support for her agenda that may, incidentally, be independent from the original event that spawned her reaction. All these uses leave digital data traces, albeit without information about the motives of the users producing them.

While the data on these individual reactions might not hold much value in themselves, in aggregate the data traces of reactions by many users during the same time span might show clear patterns. If, for example, users had used an online service in reaction to incidents only of relevance to them personally, the data would appear scattered. If, in contrast, users interacted with an online service in reaction to an incident of collective relevance, their data traces would show either temporal or semantic clusters. These patterns may in turn be used to identify the social phenomena or events that led users to use digital services in reaction to them.

Thus, macro-level phenomena or events, mediated through individual-level behavior, might indirectly lead to the emergence of recognizable data patterns, which in turn might be used to infer the social phenomena or events that gave rise to them. Figure 3.1 shows this process based on Coleman's schematic of the relationship between macro-level phenomena versus micro-level behavior and processes (Coleman 1990). Arrow 1 shows the relationship between social phenomena or events on the macro-level and reactions by individuals on the micro-level. Arrow 2 represents the relationship between the initial reaction of individuals and their resulting use of online services. Arrow 3 shows the relationship between those digital traces and the emergence of recognizable data patterns in data aggregates. Arrow 4, from element A to D, is dashed in order to illustrate that the relationship

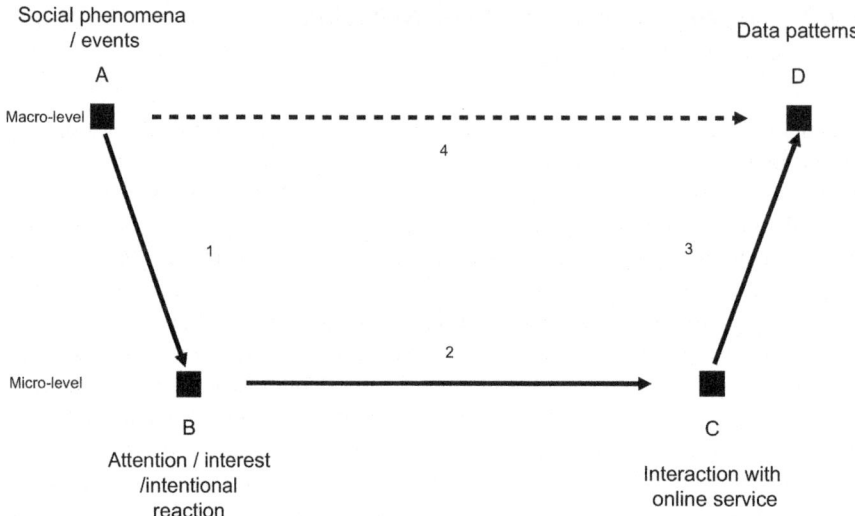

Fig. 3.1 Macro-phenomena, micro-behavior, macro-patterns

between macro-level phenomena or events and patterns in data aggregates is indirect because the relationship between these two macro-elements is mediated by behavior on the individual level. Patterns in data aggregates can be used to infer the presence of social phenomena or events giving rise to them. Still, as the dashed line in Fig. 3.1 indicates, we should be careful not to mistake patterns in data aggregates as direct results of social phenomena or events. Instead, information on their occurrence are filtered through the behavior of online services' users. This means that the data document social phenomena or events mediated through the desires, beliefs, and opportunities of online users.

Figure 3.1 also helps us to group schematically the various approaches to the analysis of digital data traces, described above. Table 3.1 shows such an attempt. The column *level of analysis* shows the element from the graph of interest to a specific research approach. The column *relationship of interest* documents the focus of interest from approaches trying to determine the processes leading to the emergence of patterns, rather than merely describing specific patterns found in digital trace data. The column *approach* shows the research approaches identified in the section before, while the column *example* lists a number of studies for each grouping. The empirical analyses presented in the remaining chapters are clearly interested in the nature of the relationship between social phenomena or events and patterns in aggregate data of individual behavior by users of the online service Twitter.

3.4 Twitter: Macro-Phenomena, Micro-Behavior, and Macro-Patterns

Table 3.1 Elements of the relationship between macro-phenomena, micro-behavior, and data aggregates

Level of analysis	Relationship of interest	Approach	Examples
Analysis of usage patterns in user groups (D)		Quantitative and qualitative descriptions	Chap. 4
Identification of characteristic patterns in data aggregates of individual behavior (D)		Quantitative descriptions	Cha et al. (2010), Conover et al. (2011), Wu et al. (2011), and Bakshy et al. (2011)
Development of statistical models of dynamics in data aggregates (D)		Statistical models	Kleinberg (2003), Yang and Leskovec (2011), and Gomez-Rodriguez et al. (2013)
	Identification of statistical relationships between attributes and behaviors on the individual level and the emergence of patterns on the aggregate level (3)	Statistical relationships between variables and outcomes & experiments	Anderson et al. (2013), Bond et al. (2012), Ugander et al. (2012), Salganik et al. (2006), Romero et al. (2011), and Aral et al. (2009)
	Relationship of media coverage and Twitter activity (1–2–3–4)	Statistical relationships and qualitative similarities	Chap. 6
	Inference of social phenomena or events based on patterns in data aggregates (4)	Event detection	Ginsberg et al. (2009), Sakaki et al. (2010), Zeitzoff (2011), Shamma et al. (2011), Jungherr and Jürgens (2014a), and Chakrabarti and Punera (2011); Chap. 5
	Prognosis of social phenomena based on patterns in data aggregates (4)	Prediction	Asur and Huberman (2010), Bollen et al. (2011), and Gayo-Avello (2013); Chap. 7

3.4.3 Metrics for the Analysis of Social Phenomena Based on Twitter Data

The usage conventions of Twitter, described in the previous chapter, allow for the detection of stimuli that led Twitter users to post messages. The simplest approach to the identification of events relevant to Twitter users is the analysis of sudden spikes in the volume of messages. This approach is based on the assumption that an external stimulus—such as a political event—observed by a large number of Twitter users—including events witnessed directly or through coverage in traditional media or online—might lead to an increase in the publication of Twitter messages. This is a very coarse approach and easily disrupted by spam or the posting of automated messages—for example, by accounts automatically tweeting links to content in online media. Alternatively, one could focus on spikes in the volume of messages using specific words, phrases, or hashtags. This approach is based on the assumption that if users experience the same stimulus, they might react to it by using similar keywords or semantic constructs (Kleinberg 2003). Human interactions on the micro-level thus can be identified in aggregates of their digital data traces.

It is also sensible to differentiate between messages containing hashtags and those without. Messages without hashtags can be read as indicators that users' postings are primarily addressed to their direct followers. These messages might also contain comments on recent events, which can be identified by the analysis of words and phrases used. By choosing to avoid the use of hashtags, users may explicitly try to reach only their immediate circle of followers. In contrast, with the use of a relevant hashtag, a user might intentionally be trying to reach beyond her immediate circle of followers and contribute to a larger "issue public" concerned with the topic to which the hashtag is referring.

Fluctuations in the use of usage conventions might also lead to the emergence of messages, content, or people that Twitter users deemed relevant during a given time span. Messages, pertaining to a specific event or of relevance during a specific time span, can rise to prominence by their retweet count. Users see these messages and, by retweeting them, alert followers to their content. This can either be because they think the content of the message holds relevant information—a funny quip, for instance, or a declarative statement to which they wish to see themselves connected. Either way, by analyzing the top retweets of all messages, or the messages publicly contributing to a given issue, or the messages posted by a predetermined subpopulation of Twitter users during a given time span, we are able to detect messages that many users then thought to be relevant.

A similar logic holds true for websites linked to from Twitter messages. Heavily linked content from messages posted during a given time span is obviously of interest to Twitter users commenting on an issue occurring at that time and, therefore, might hold information on the phenomena to which Twitter users were reacting.

It is also possible to analyze who Twitter users were explicitly referencing in their messages. If, for example, the @messages or retweet count of a Twitter user rises during a given time span (i.e. if this person is mentioned more often than usual in the messages of other users), we can deduce that this person was seen by other Twitter users as a relevant actor during a given time span or related to unfolding events. Thus, analyzing the users most prominently referred to by other Twitter users during a specific time span might also hold information on the events users were referring to.

These practices can be understood as a collective *curating* process, to which all Twitter users contribute, be it intentionally or unintentionally by emphasizing specific actors, objects, or topics in their messages, thereby filtering the stream of all messages posted (Jungherr and Jürgens 2014b). Various other terms for this collective filtering process can be found in the relevant literature. It has been called *gatekeeping* or *gatewatching* (Bastos et al. 2013; Bruns 2005; Papacharissi and de Fatima Oliveira 2012; Segerberg and Bennett 2011). Regardless of the term used for this practice, collective filtering is a highly relevant practice on social media services, as it determines which messages, links, and users come to dominate the discourse on a given channel with regard to specific topics. Thus, collective filtering is important for how participants and outsiders perceive online discourses. Apart from this, through collective filtering users' individual decisions lead to the emergence of recognizable patterns in aggregated data that allow researchers to identify those elements of a phenomenon that Twitter users collectively deemed to be of importance.

As an alternative to the analysis of total or relative spikes in the volume of tweets, hashtags, retweets, links, or mentions, one could also focus on shifts in user behavior. Various studies have shown that different types of offline events tend to preface discernible pattern shifts in the behavior of Twitter users. For example, researchers successfully showed that shifts in semantic patterns, identified in Twitter comments about televised events and collective action, could be used to identify distinct stages in the events (e.g. Jungherr and Jürgens 2014a; Shamma et al. 2011). Other papers demonstrated that there were differences in the ratio of messages containing @mentions, retweets, and links between tweets commenting, for example, on disaster relief or television coverage (e.g. Bruns and Stieglitz 2013). Researchers were also able to show that various events during the campaign for the US Presidential election in 2012 were detectable by shifts in user behavior (e.g. Lin et al. 2014). These studies show that various offline phenomena lead to shifts in the micro-behavior of users that can be detected in aggregate data. Specific types of events may even create specific patterns in aggregates of digital trace data, so that the detection of these patterns could make automated classification feasible.

In drawing inferences on the phenomena prompting users to post messages, another possibility could be sentiment analysis. Various studies have shown that large-scale Twitter data can be used to draw inferences on Twitter users' mood shifts (e.g. Dodds et al. 2011), connect sentiment patterns in messages to demographic factors of the city in which the messages were posted (e.g. Mitchell et al. 2013), and also connect expressions of happiness with movement patterns of individuals (e.g. Frank et al. 2013). These results show the possibility of consistently detecting Twitter users' mood shifts based on the content of messages they post. If sentiment shifts could also be consistently connected with reactions to offline phenomena—such as natural or man-made disasters, election outcomes, or TV shows—shifts in the sentiment voiced in messages could also serve as an interesting metric for the analysis of events prompting Twitter users to post messages.

This discussion shows that patterns and pattern-shifts in aggregates of digital trace data can be used to detect and analyze social phenomena together with events that led users to post messages in reaction to them. Still, for the analysis of social phenomena or events on the macro-level based on micro-level data, we need a clear understanding about the data-generating process leading individuals to use various digital services. The differences in these data-generating processes clearly have implications for what kind of information can be gained from the analysis of aggregate data collected on different services.

3.4.4 Different Services, Different Uses, Different Data-Generating Processes

The interpretation of analyses based on data patterns in aggregates of digital trace data depends on the specific data-generating process of the service from which the data was collected. Different services offer different uses, thus their data-generating processes also differ. Clearly, this has implications on which type of social phenomena can be identified and which element of a phenomenon can be validly analyzed using data collected by online services (Jungherr and Jürgens 2013).

We have to differentiate between digital trace data collected during the interactions of users with devices or online services which the users did and did not intend to be public. Analyses based on data intentionally and unintentionally produced by users have to account for these different data-generating processes in the interpretation of their results.

Many devices and online services document user behavior that those users did not necessarily intend to be public; in fact, many users may not even be aware that they left behind data traces of their interactions. Examples of these data include geo-logs of mobile-phone users' locations or logs of search engines collecting user queries. These data traces are usually put in context by metadata—such as the device in use, a location where the interaction took place etc. Thus, in principle, unintentionally produced data might allow researchers to infer users' interests or habits at specific locations during specific time intervals. What these data hold as potential, is offset with privacy concerns. Since users did not actively publish the information collected in data sets of their digital traces, these data are very sensitive and, if at all, usually accessible only to researchers in high-level aggregates, thus somewhat limiting their research potential.

Data on behavior that users did not intend to be public are of obvious interest. Using these data, we might, in fact, approximate the *real* interests of users,

3.4 Twitter: Macro-Phenomena, Micro-Behavior, and Macro-Patterns

unmediated by the impression they are trying to make on their social environment. This is especially of interest for researchers interested in political phenomena. A politician's mediated public appearances, interviews, and articles, for instances, may lead users to search for said politician on the Internet. If many users read the same interview and search for the same politician we can identify this collective interest by a sudden rise in the use of the politician's name in search engine logs. The use of topically relevant search terms by people interested in a politician is completely independent from their political convictions. If, in contrast, we were to analyze a data source that documented users' public messages, we would not receive such a direct documentation of the interest the interview spiked in online users. Search engine logs thus offer a relatively direct view of a user's interest in a political candidate, irrespective of her attitude towards the candidate. The data-generating process for unintentionally produced data is schematically shown in Fig. 3.2. Comparable data have been used to analyze mobility in metropolitan areas (e.g. González et al. 2008), track diseases (e.g. Ginsberg et al. 2009), predict prices (e.g. Choi and Varian 2012), and follow political discourse (e.g. Weber et al. 2012).

Data collected on other services show intentionally published information, including status messages posted on services like Facebook or Twitter. Digital trace data of this kind show the content of status messages posted by users, hashtags users wanted to contribute to by posting their message, links to websites linked to from the message, and mentions of other users. As before, these data are contextualized by metadata, about which users can be conscious or not. This could, for example, be the name of the device with which a message was posted, the application used

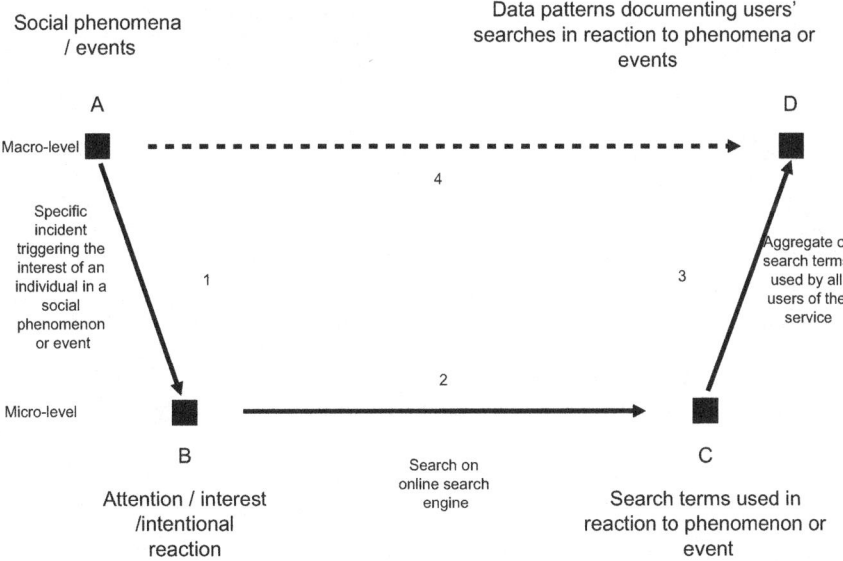

Fig. 3.2 Example for the data-generating process of internet search engines

or the location and time of publication. These data allow researchers to identify the interest and interactions that users intended to be public at a specific time and place.

These observations illustrate the crucial difference between intentionally published data and unintentional data traces. With politically motivated use of online services the difference becomes even more obvious. Users commenting online on an interview by a politician may voice support or criticism. The body of the messages posted to that effect may yield the name of the politician, the name of a party, and perhaps also a link to the interview that led our exemplary online user to post a tweet. In this sense, the data might initially resemble the information we might collect through search engine logs; however, these data traces emerged from two very different data generating processes. For users to tweet about a stimulus—be it a politician, an event, or a link to content on the Web—they must act upon the intention of making their opinion and commentary available to a broader public. Accordingly, digital data traces of interactions with online services do not allow inferences on users' *real* interests but only on the slice of their interests they wanted to be publicly seen. This data-generating process is schematically shown in Fig. 3.3. Data of this type have been used to track earthquakes (e.g. Sakaki et al. 2010), coordinate disaster relief (e.g. Verma et al. 2011), and identify specific phases in mediated events, and political protests (e.g. Jungherr and Jürgens 2014a; Shamma et al. 2011).

Following these observations, we find that people use different online services with different intentions and the data generated by their interactions with those online services have, therefore, to be interpreted in light of the data-generating

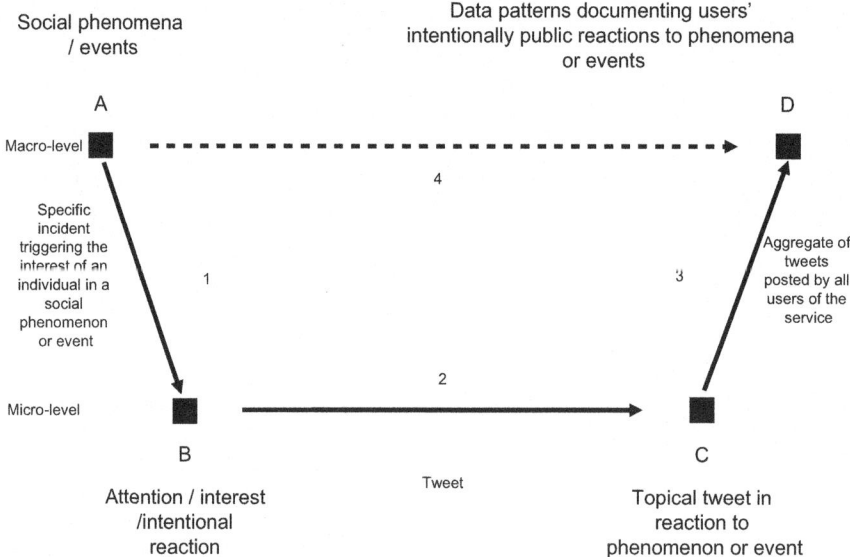

Fig. 3.3 Example for the data-generating process of Twitter

processes of the respective service. As shown above, using a search engine like Google and a microblogging service like Twitter are markedly different acts of communication, indicating their users' distinct intentions and considerations prior to interacting with the service. The data collected by these services thereby document different parts of social reality. Consequently, analyses of politically relevant keywords' frequency on Google (e.g. Weber et al. 2012) and on Twitter (e.g. Jungherr 2013) should not be interpreted as documenting the same aspect of reality but instead as documenting different shadows of the same social phenomenon mediated through different mechanisms, leading users to interact with Google and Twitter.

Data generated on the microblogging platform Twitter correspond with intentionally produced data. When analyzing Twitter data we thus have to keep in mind that we are dealing with the reactions of people to a social phenomenon or event, that they wanted to be public. This is especially relevant to the analysis of political phenomena.

3.4.5 Politics Through the Lens of Digital Trace Data

The attempt to analyze political phenomena and events based on the data of online services—such as Twitter—has its roots within early successes in the detection of large-scale social phenomena, such as influenza outbreaks (e.g. Ginsberg et al. 2009), the commercial success of consumer products (e.g. Jansen et al. 2009)—for example, books (e.g. Gruhl et al. 2005) or movies (e.g. Asur and Huberman 2010)—and the analysis of broadcast events' structure—such as sports fixtures (e.g. Chakrabarti and Punera 2011). In this, the analysis of political events with digital data traces follows a similar path to early work on public opinion based on techniques prevalent in consumer research (Chaffee and Hochheimer 1985; Lazarsfeld et al. 1944). Similar to these early studies, this new approach has to face challenges specifically connected with political research.

Early studies successfully showed that, at least in some cases, it was possible to find statistical relationships between mentions of brands or specific consumer products with metrics of their offline success—such as sales numbers for books or box-office results for movies. In this, they established a connection between the attention a product received online with its offline success. These relationships seem to hold, irrespective of the fact that Twitter's user base is not representative of the general population of the USA—or any other state for that matter. Still, what seems to work for brands and popular consumer goods does not necessarily have to be true for politics. There is no automatism for a link between references to political actors online and their respective electoral success. Nevertheless, more and more studies attempt to link metrics for the popularity of political actors on various online services with their electoral success (Gayo-Avello 2013). This approach has been shown to yield far from robust results (Gayo-Avello 2012; Jungherr 2013; Metaxas and Mustafaraj 2012). Still, as digital trace data documenting politically motivated activities on online services rise, scholarly interest rises as to how these data might be used in the analysis of political phenomena.

In a recent article, Harald Schoen and colleagues discuss the relationship between digital data traces and more traditional measures of public opinion research—such as surveys, statistical models, and prediction markets. They show that although social media data seem to share some surface characteristics with more traditional approaches to data collection, there are significant deeper differences that influence the validity of the inferences (Schoen et al. 2013).

These observations have special significance for the question of how digital data traces can be used by researchers interested in political phenomena and events. Performing surveys or prediction markets on social media channels is certainly possible. However, researchers have to find ways to account for the biases inherent in the demographic composition of users of the service in question. Recent studies suggest that, by the careful design of surveys and the collection of detailed demographic information on the respondents, valid inferences of election results are possible, even if the survey is based on a very biased selection of respondents (Wang et al. 2014). Still, for the discussion of inferences based on digital trace data, the survey, and the prediction-market approach both require researchers to post explicit questions to users, not just to analyze data traces of their regular online behavior. Connecting existing data traces of human behavior online to offline phenomena corresponds with the discussion of statistical models by Schoen et al. (2013).

To establish a stable statistical relationship between Twitter messages mentioning political actors and political phenomena—such as a politician's chances of electoral success—researchers have to show that two preconditions are met. First, there must be a systematic connection between references to a political actor in a message as well as the variable of interest. This seems to be a reasonable assumption for the mention of political actors based on their connection to a political event or broadcast. If a politician's name appears in clusters uncharacteristic to her mentions in the past, therefore, these data patterns allow for the inference that a recent event happened which Twitter users connected with the politician—be it a statement, or interview with the politician, or her involvement with a major political initiative or scandal. However, a systematic connection between a mention of a politician in a tweet and the subsequent voting intention of a Twitter user is much less likely. The prognosis of election results based on tweets appears more problematic, therefore, than using tweets as indicators for objects of political attention by the users posting them.

A second precondition for the identification of statistical relationships is the number of observations. To determine a stable connection between independent and dependent variables, there must be a large number of observations. Again, for the detection and analysis of political events and their relationship to political mentions on Twitter, this precondition can be met. For analysis of the relationship between Twitter messages and voting intentions this is much harder. Elections on various levels of government happen only every couple of years. This necessarily leads to a rather limited number of observations which can serve as the basis for establishing a statistical relationship between Twitter messages and election results.

This limits the potential for establishing a valid statistical relationship between the two metrics (Diaz et al. 2014; Huberty 2013).

Unfortunately, most studies trying to establish links between metrics in digital trace data and political phenomena or events seldom discuss whether these preconditions are met, or—if not—how researchers tried to address contingent validity issues for their results. In lieu of such methodological reflections, there seems to be a heavy dose of scientific instrumentalism at work. One basic argument of researchers who were able to show for some political contests a statistical relationship between the number of tweets candidates received and their subsequent success at the polls, is that attention, measured by online chatter about a candidate, translates into somewhat better chances for the said candidate on election day. For example, Fabio Rojas claims in an op-ed based on his research:

> We believe that Twitter and other social media reflect the underlying trend in a political race that goes beyond a district's fundamental geographic and demographic composition. If people must talk about you, even in negative ways, it is a signal that a candidate is on the verge of victory. The attention given to winners creates a situation in which all publicity is good publicity. (Rojas 2013)

This reasoning clearly stands in the tradition of the scientific instrumentalists: we found a statistical relationship between two metrics, therefore, one metric can be used to predict the development of another. In the case of political opinion voiced online, the relationship between mention counts of politicians and their subsequent electoral success seems especially surprising. I have made the case elsewhere that the majority of political commentary online contains negative statements and explicit critique of political actors (Jungherr 2013). Even if a positive statistical relationship between messages predominantly voicing negative sentiment toward political actors and their respective electoral fortunes could be established, proponents of this approach—like Rojas—should be able to offer a mechanism leading to this surprising result. In their model, heavy opposition towards a political candidate would translate into increased chances for her to win on election day. This paradox has yet to be addressed by researchers proposing this model. In ignoring possible mechanisms producing these statistical relationships, proponents of using digital trace data to predict election results run the risk of falling victim to overnarrating the consequences of spurious statistical relationships.

There is another confounding factor for the prognosis of election results based on tweets. Not everyone who votes in elections voices support or critique of the running parties or candidates publicly. Any approach that exclusively focuses on public statements towards parties or candidates ignores opinions from members of the electorate who do not participate in public discourse but nevertheless intend to vote. The political opinions of non-vocal voters sometimes deviate from the opinions dominating public discourse. Using public statements to predict the electoral chances of parties might thus lead to a serious underestimation of parties whose supporters remain silent in public. This is known as the "spiral of silence" (Noelle-Neumann 1991). Similar patterns have been found with regard to political discourse on Twitter (Mustafaraj et al. 2011). It appears highly doubtful, therefore, that either the volume of political chatter offline or online stands in any meaningful or stable relationship with election results.

Even if constructing a connection between attention online and subsequent electoral success seems dubious, spikes in online attention to political actors might hold information on political events inspiring this attention. As such, spikes in the message volume mentioning political actors or pattern shifts in messages mentioning them can be used for the identification and analysis of political events. In this way, online trace data enable us to determine which events led to heavy activity by the users of an online service and which kind of political information was the focus of their attention.

The discussion above illustrates that online trace data do not offer a direct view of underlying social phenomena or events. Instead, they provide researchers with a view mediated through the behavior of individuals who reacted to a stimulus by interacting with an online service. The analysis of political phenomena and events especially requires us to address how this process might bias results, leading to a discussion about which kind of inferences on political phenomena based on digital trace data seem possible and which seem problematic. Understanding the consequences of this potentially biased representation of political reality through digital trace data is of paramount importance in understanding what these data can tell us about political phenomena.

3.5 A Mechanism Explaining the Publication of Tweets

An alternative to the analysis of social phenomena based merely on statistic relationships is offered by *Analytical Sociology* (Coleman 1990; Elster 2007; Hedström 2005; Hedström and Bearman 2009; Hedström and Swedberg 1998; Hedström and Ylikoski 2010), which:

> [...] seeks to explain complex social processes by carefully dissecting them and then bringing into focus their most important constituent components. (Hedström 2005, p. 1)

This approach is neither interested in universal laws, nor in mere statistical analysis; instead it focuses on the identification of social mechanisms that contribute to the phenomenon or process in question:

> [...] mechanisms can be said to consist of entities (with their properties) and the activities that these entities engage in, either by themselves or in concert with other entities. These activities bring about change, and the type of change brought about depends upon the properties of the entities and the way in which they are linked to one another. A social mechanism, as here defined, describes a constellation of entities and activities that are organized such that they regularly bring about a particular type of outcome. We explain an observed phenomenon by referring to the social mechanism by which such phenomena are regularly brought about. (Hedström 2005, p. 25)

This definition can easily be adapted for the formulation of a mechanism that explains under which circumstances users post messages on Twitter. Twitter users

3.5 A Mechanism Explaining the Publication of Tweets

are this mechanism's entities; their activity is the publication of messages, which in turn contain signals that allow us to infer some intentions of the users posting them. For example, an @message signals that the message was posted by a user to interact with another user; a retweet can be read as the result of a user's intention to pass on interesting, controversial, or simply funny information; the use of a hashtag signals that a user explicitly wanted to anchor her tweet in the context of an ongoing discussion and thus aimed to contribute to an issue public. These are only a few examples of how the content of messages allows us to infer possible motives that lead users to publish them.

By analyzing Twitter data, we see an aggregate of digital artifacts documenting individual actions, the publication of Twitter messages. Thus, we see macro-patterns produced by micro-behavior. By understanding the mechanism leading users to publish Twitter messages, we are able to identify and interpret patterns and pattern shifts in the aggregated data documenting individual behavior. This mechanism should account for an individual's propensity to tweet, since not every user utilizes Twitter with the same intensity; the temporal contexts during which a tweet was posted, as different time intervals such as hours of the day or days of the week have varying chances of tweets being posted; the influence of other Twitter users, as it is sensible to assume that Twitter users at least partially model their behavior on the behavior of other users; and external stimuli that might prompt users to post a message. For the moment, let us focus on the formal representation of a possible mechanism for the explanation of why users tweet. The identification of this mechanism provides the basis for any meaningful discussion of what data documenting public interactions of Twitter users in aggregate might tell researchers about social phenomena. Only if we know why and when users tend to tweet can we use their data traces for meaningful claims about the phenomena referred to in their messages.

Analytical Sociology offers not only an interesting perspective on digital data traces of human behavior on Twitter by focusing on the mechanism that leads people to tweet, but also a model of intentional human action that allows us to interpret data patterns in the aggregate of millions of single tweets. This model interprets intentional human action as the result of interplay between the *desires*, *beliefs*, and *opportunities* of people. Desires, in this context, are the goals, wants, and wishes of a person. Beliefs are the propositions a person holds to be true about the world. Opportunities are the options available to a person to fulfill her desires. Based on these elements, the model is sometimes also called DBO model. Various authors have discussed this model in detail and shown the potentials of this very basic approach to human action (Elster 2007; Hedström 2005; Hedström and Bearman 2009). If we adapt this model to the posting of Twitter messages, it offers a powerful perspective on the interpretation of the resulting data traces.

In various studies examining the uses and gratifications of Twitter use, a number of motives keep recurring. These include the expression of personal opinions, communicating with others, passing the time, finding and sharing information (Chen 2011; Liu et al. 2010; Parmelee and Bichard 2012). It seems safe to assume that the typical Twitter user tweets out of the desire to express opinion, gain recognition for it by her intended audience, and communicate with others, finding and linking to relevant information. The beliefs a Twitter user holds about the world, interesting events, or politics will influence the content of her messages. Her access to a device for updating Twitter within her waking hours will determine her opportunities to access the service. The desire of users to express their opinion and be recognized by other users, leads to the emergence of patterns in the aggregate of all messages that, in turn, allow for the detection of stimuli that led users to post about them or to change their usage behavior.

The following mechanism takes into account the social context within which a tweet is published, the context of the twittersphere's state directly before the publication, the influence of specific stimuli on the person posting the message, users' interest in larger topics connected with specific stimuli, and the propensity of the individual to post a message at all. The formula is not intended to be estimated on a data set. Instead, this formal representation shown below will illustrate the mechanism and its contributing elements.

$$Tweet_p = C + Tweets_{t-1} + S * I_{User} + \frac{\sum Tweets_{User}}{t_n} \qquad (3.1)$$

$Tweet_p$ stands for the probability of a user posting a message at t1; C stands for the social context of a tweet (e.g. day of the week, hour of the day); $Tweets_{t-1}$ stands for the state of the twittersphere in the time span directly preceding the publication of a tweet by identifying the number of Twitter messages that were posted at $t-1$ (this could alternatively be operationalized as the number of Twitter messages that were posted in the direct vicinity of the user's Twitter network at $t-1$); $S * I_{User}$ accounts for the chance of a stimulus to lead to a Twitter message adjusted by the interests of a Twitter user in the stimulus—this could for example be an event of personal relevance to the user or an event of relevance to a greater number of users; $\frac{\sum Tweets_{User}}{t_n}$ stands for the propensity of a user to post a Twitter message in the first place, which is measured by the sum of all Twitter messages the user has posted during the period under examination divided by the number of time slots under examination.

3.5.1 Social Context

The first element contributing to the probability of a Twitter message being posted is the social context within which it is posted. With this, I mean the influence of cultural conventions that structure the time of users sharing a cultural space. The two elements of social context discussed here are weekdays and weekends together with the division between waking and sleeping hours.

Before we can determine if these cultural conventions influence Twitter users to post messages on Twitter, we have to determine whether or not the data shows signs of being non-randomly distributed. If the number of Twitter messages during

3.5 A Mechanism Explaining the Publication of Tweets

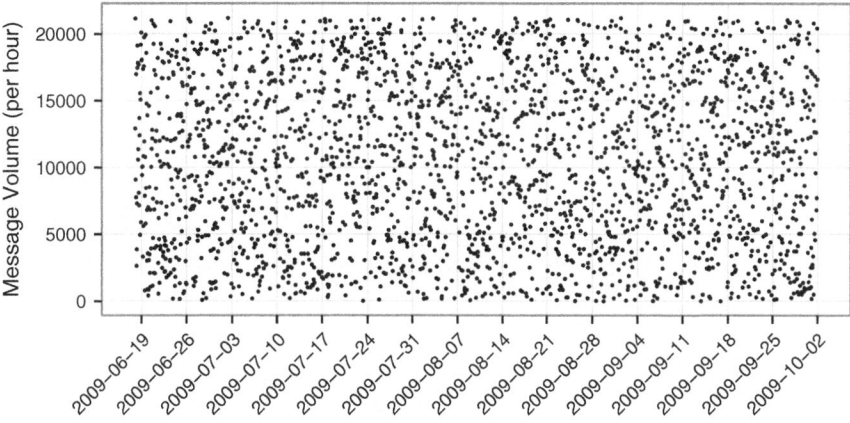

Fig. 3.4 Random volume of messages per hour over time

a given time interval would be fluctuating randomly, this would suggest that Twitter users post messages independently from other users and shared natural, social, or mediated phenomena. Figure 3.4 illustrates how such a random distribution might look. I used R (R Core Team 2014) to calculate 2544 random numbers between the values of one and 21,235. This corresponds to the empirical data on Twitter use from June 18 to October 2, 2009, which is the basis for the analyses in this book. Two thousand five hundred and forty four is the number of hours in this time span, for which the number of tweets can be calculated. The values one and 21,235 are the respective minimum and maximum counts of messages that were posted by the users in this data set during 1 h. In this figure each of the random values was assigned one of the hours during the given time span.

While Fig. 3.4 shows what a time series would look like if the number of Twitter messages per hour were fluctuating randomly, Fig. 3.5 shows the distribution of all messages that were posted during each hour between June 18 and October 2, 2009. The difference between the two figures is evident. Instead of randomly fluctuating message counts shown in Fig. 3.4 we see in Fig. 3.5 that the number of messages per hour cluster around specific values and fluctuate at regular intervals. We see that these regular patterns are broken during some hours, which showed much higher messages counts than the time intervals directly preceding and following them. Examples of this are found on June 18, the day of the Access Impediment Act's ratification, September 13, the day of a televised debate between the two leading candidates, and September 27, the day of the election. We thus see, that all hours showing exceptionally high message counts are connected to political events. These are hours during which the behavior of Twitter users clearly deviated from their regular behavior. It is sensible to assume, therefore, that a shared experience or common stimulus, led users to deviate from their regular behavior and respond to this stimulus by posting significantly more messages than during the hours lacking this stimulus. Later, I will address how these outliers, breaks in the regular pattern,

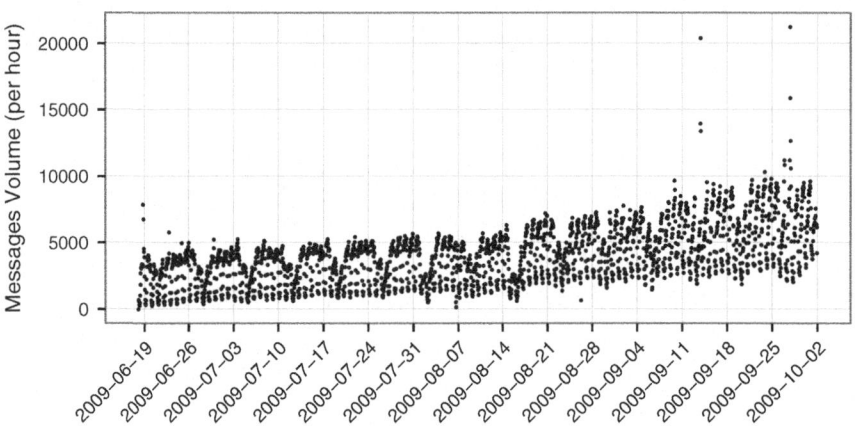

Fig. 3.5 Number of all messages per hour over time

can be reliably identified by quantitative analysis and what information they hold on political events. For the moment, though, I want to focus on the regularities in the time series of Twitter messages posted per hour and discuss what they can tell us about the processes and phenomena that lead Twitter users to tweet.

Figure 3.5 shows two types of patterns. First, we see that the volume of messages follows a weekly order. A rising hourly message volume from Mondays to Fridays is apparent, followed by a sharp decrease in message volume on Saturdays and Sundays. Second, we see that the hourly volume of messages also seems to fluctuate during the course of each day. Additionally, these patterns become less pronounced in the 2 weeks directly preceding the election. One reason for this could be that the behavior of users becomes more noisy and less regular in the run-up to the election, as users react more readily to various stimuli during the high phase of the campaign. The hourly volume of Twitter messages thus depends on the day of the week and the hour of the day. Let us have a closer look at these two types of patterns.

Boxplots in Fig. 3.6 show the total number of messages posted on each day during the time span of this analysis, grouped in accordance with the day of the week upon which they were posted. Thus, for example, the boxplot labeled *Monday* shows the distribution of the total number of messages that were posted on all Mondays in the data set.

The boxplots show that during weekdays, Mondays to Fridays, the median level of daily messages remains roughly stable at around 90,000. Figure 3.6 also shows that as the week passes, the total number of messages tends to rise somewhat. In contrast, we see that on Saturdays and Sundays the daily message volume tends to drop. One exception is Sunday, 27 September 2009, the day of the election, on which nearly 180,000 messages were posted. This pattern indicates that users tweet more often on weekdays than on weekends. One reason for this could be that many people spend their workday at a computer and thus have easy access to their Twitter-feeds. Another reason could be that during the course of the week media

3.5 A Mechanism Explaining the Publication of Tweets 53

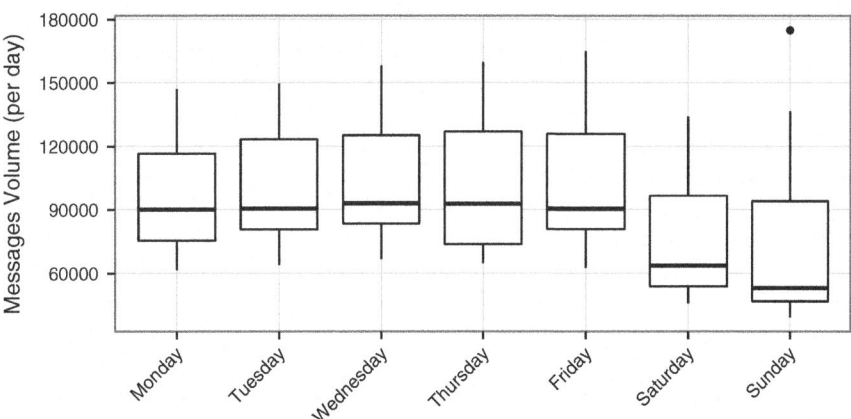

Fig. 3.6 Distribution of the message volume for each day of the week

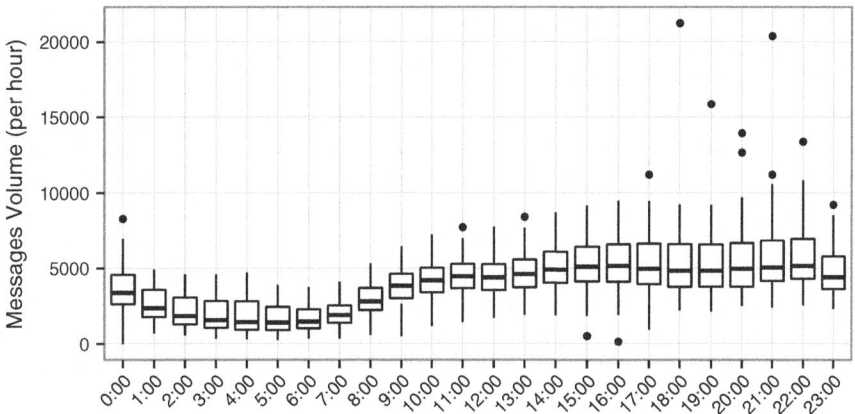

Fig. 3.7 Distribution of the message volume for each hour of the day

organizations regularly update their Internet presences with new content to which Twitter users react by linking or commenting. The reason for these shifts in the macro-patterns seems to lie with the regularities in social life, patterns of workdays and the publication of content by news organizations.

The second pattern, evident in Fig. 3.5, showed that the volume of hourly messages fluctuated during the course of a day. Figure 3.7 shows this pattern in greater detail. The boxplots show the distribution for the number of messages posted per hour. Thus, the boxplot *0:00* shows messages posted between 0:00 and 1:00 a.m. for each day in the dataset.

Figure 3.7 also shows that the number of messages per hour fluctuates according to the time of day. During the night from 11:00 p.m. to 6:00 a.m., the volume of messages per hour tends to fall. From 7:00 a.m. to 3:00 p.m. the number of messages per hour tends to rise again and remains somewhat stable until 11:00 p.m. This day-night pattern is easily explainable by the sleep-wake cycle of most users. This pattern corroborates findings by other studies (Golder and Macy 2011; Rios and Lin 2013). In comparison with Fig. 3.6, we see that the distribution of messages per hour is much more noisy than the distribution of messages per weekday, as evidenced by the higher number of outliers in the distribution. Again, these patterns can be connected to biological and social phenomena shared by a great number of users.

The patterns discussed above are visible in the count of all messages posted by politically vocal Twitter users during the course of the campaign in 2009. Although we are looking at an aggregate of politically relevant and non-relevant messages, we are able to identify outliers that are clearly connected with political events. Thus, although signals relevant to the analysis of political phenomena are diluted by the noise of irrelevant messages, we are still able to identify them—for instance exceptionally high tweet counts on days connected with protests by political activists, the TV-debate, and election day itself. If we can identify these signals among the noise of messages irrelevant to our analysis, we should be even more successful in interpreting pattern shifts of messages clearly referring to politics, the campaign, or specific political actors.

With regard to the bigger question, how does social context—such as the cultural conventions (e.g. weekdays and weekends, hours of the day)—influence the probability for tweets to be published? We clearly saw that they have a strong impact, as there is a regular fluctuation of the total number of tweets posted during each day of the week, and each hour of the day. It is important to note, though, that there are days and hours during which the expected pattern was broken, meaning that more or less messages were posted than would have been expected based on the regular user behavior. Thus, social context is a factor that influences but does not determine the probability of a message being posted during a given time span. Still, this is a factor, that has to be taken into account if one wants to assess the probability of a Twitter message being posted.

3.5.2 State of the Twittersphere

The second element of the mechanism contributing to the posting of Twitter messages is the state of the twittersphere directly before the message is posted. If there are many messages that have been posted in a given time span, the probability of other messages being posted increases. If the number is low, the probability decreases. An indicator for this process is given in Fig. 3.8.

Figure 3.8 plots the autocorrelation function for the time series of all posted messages in the data set, showing how strongly the number of the posted Twitter messages during any given hour correlates with the number of messages posted during preceding hours. The graphs show the two patterns discussed earlier. We see that the time series is heavily autocorrelated with a lag of 24; this is another way of quantifying the daily fluctuations of messages. The second plot shows a high

3.5 A Mechanism Explaining the Publication of Tweets

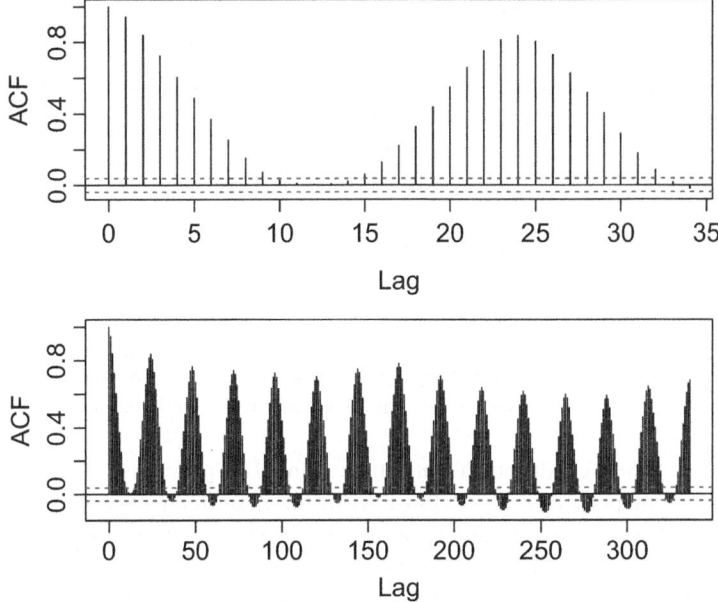

Fig. 3.8 Autocorrelation for time series of twitter messages per hour, for lags 0 to 35 and lags 0 to 336

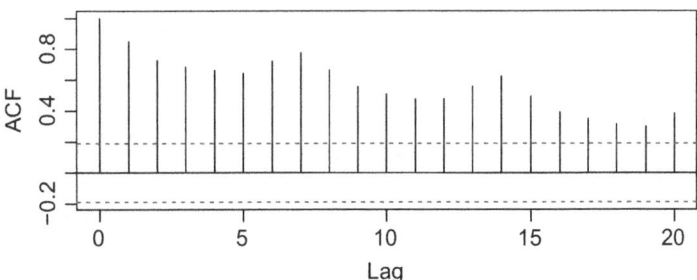

Fig. 3.9 Autocorrelation for time series of all twitter messages per day, for lags 0 to 20

autocorrelation with a lag of 168, accounting for the weekly fluctuations in the data set.

The element of Fig. 3.8 relevant to this argument is the strong autocorrelation of the time series at lag one. This is an indicator that the number of Twitter messages at any given point in time is highly dependent on the number of messages at the point in time directly preceding it. Figure 3.8 shows this pattern for hourly data, as Fig. 3.9 shows that this is also true if the number of messages is calculated in daily sums. The pattern thus seems to be stable irrespective of the time span used for the analysis.

3.5.3 External Stimuli

In the mechanism described above the third element allowing us to explain the publication of tweets comprises stimuli that users react to by tweeting. According to the evidence presented in Figs. 3.5, 3.6, and 3.7, we can see that the publication of messages on Twitter follows common patterns. Messages cluster during similar time frames and on specific occasions. This observation illustrates two elements of people's usage behavior on Twitter: people tweet during a shared time frame and in reaction to shared experiences—those they experience directly and those that they experience through media.

These observations are the basis for explaining the patterns in Figs. 3.5, 3.6, and 3.7. Thus, they offer us a deeper understanding of how we should interpret sudden spikes in the volume of Twitter messages published during a given time span.

People tend to tweet during the same time spans. This pattern is easily explicable: the majority of people—at least those living in countries having only one time zone—are asleep or awake during similar time spans, thus most messages cluster during these hours as per a biological pattern. That being said, culturally constructed time frames also influence user behavior on Twitter, which explains the patterns in Figs. 3.5, 3.6, and 3.7. Most messages are posted during work days, during the late afternoon and in the early evening. The cultural patterns of weekdays vs weekends and working hours vs personal time are clearly visible by fluctuations in the number of messages posted during the time spans corresponding with these cultural concepts. Based on these observations, we can differentiate between shared natural and shared cultural contexts that lead people to post tweets during similar time spans.

It is also important to note that these patterns are regularly reoccurring. Figure 3.5 shows that, although there are fluctuations, the median of the distribution of all messages posted on Saturdays and Sundays is much lower than the median of the distribution of all messages posted on a weekday. Similarly Fig. 3.7 shows that the median values of messages posted between 10 a.m. to 0:00 a.m. were clearly higher than of messages posted during the hours of 0:00 a.m. and 8:00 a.m. Again, the graph shows that the number of messages per hour fluctuates; still, the graph shows that there are fluctuations in the number of messages posted during given hours of the day that recurred during each day in the data set.

The second observation indicated that people tend to tweet in reaction to shared experiences. This phenomenon is shown in the figures by singular dots that are either far outside the clusters in the scatter plot or mark outliers in the boxplots. These dots mark hours during which the volume of posted tweets markedly exceeded (or in some cases fell below) the number of tweets typically to be expected during the respective day of the week or hour of the day. The dots thus mark times when the regular behavior of Twitter users was disrupted. One explanation for this might be that a large number of users experienced a shared event and posted tweets in reaction to it. This in turn brought about breaks in the pattern of the aggregated data, which

3.5 A Mechanism Explaining the Publication of Tweets

may enable us to conclude that the collective reaction to collectively experienced phenomena leads to clearly discernible pattern shifts in the data. One example for this is shown in Fig. 3.5 by the various dots on September 27, which mark times during which the hourly volume exceeded 15,000 and 20,000 messages. This was the day of the 2009 general election in Germany. This is only one example of an event—in this case a political event—that led a large group of Twitter users to post many more messages than during comparable time spans.

As before, we have to differentiate between recurrent events which create regularly returning spikes in message volume and single events which create only one spike. One example for a regularly recurring event would be soccer matches in Germany's premier league. Soccer games, their respective media coverage and Twitter messages using #bundesliga or hashtags representing prominent soccer clubs are regularly returning features of the German twittersphere on weekends during the soccer season. In contrast, there are singular events, such as natural disasters, that lead to one-off massive spikes in message volume.

It is also sensible to differentiate between types of phenomena and events to which people are reacting, such as natural phenomena and cultural phenomena. Tweets posted in reaction to natural disasters have already been mentioned. Other examples of reactions to natural phenomena are regular recurring tweets greeting a new morning (i.e. #gutenmorgen) or closing the day (i.e. #gutenacht). Furthermore, big cultural phenomena offline—such as games in Germany's premier soccer league (i.e. #bundesliga)—trigger clearly identifiable reactions on Twitter. Twitter users regularly post messages accompanying episodes of popular TV-series, such as Germany's premier crime series *Tatort* (i.e. #tatort). This would be an example of a case in which a cultural phenomenon that has its roots in traditional broadcast media is regularly accompanied by comments online. In this example, online media are reacting to offline cultural phenomena. But there are also cultural events leading users to deviate from their regular behavior. One such example is the *Follow Friday*, a usage convention established early in the spread of Twitter use. Users posted each Friday messages identified by the hashtag #ff in which they listed the names of Twitter users who might be of interest to their followers. What started in the early days of Twitter to foster the interconnectedness of users is still a cultural convention that is regularly used and which generates regular spikes in posted messages on Fridays.

Figure 3.10 shows the dynamics of three different hashtags mirroring reactions of Twitter users to cultural phenomena. The first graph shows the number of tweets referencing the German TV-show *Tatort* by using the hashtag #tatort. The red dots mark all days on which a new episode of the series premiered. The graph shows the biggest volume spikes on days on which episodes premiered. There is also another series of spikes with lower volumes that mark days during which reruns of the show aired.

The second graph shows the number of tweets referencing Germany's premier soccer league by using the hashtag #bundesliga. Red dots mark days on which games were scheduled. We see that most spikes in volume correspond with days

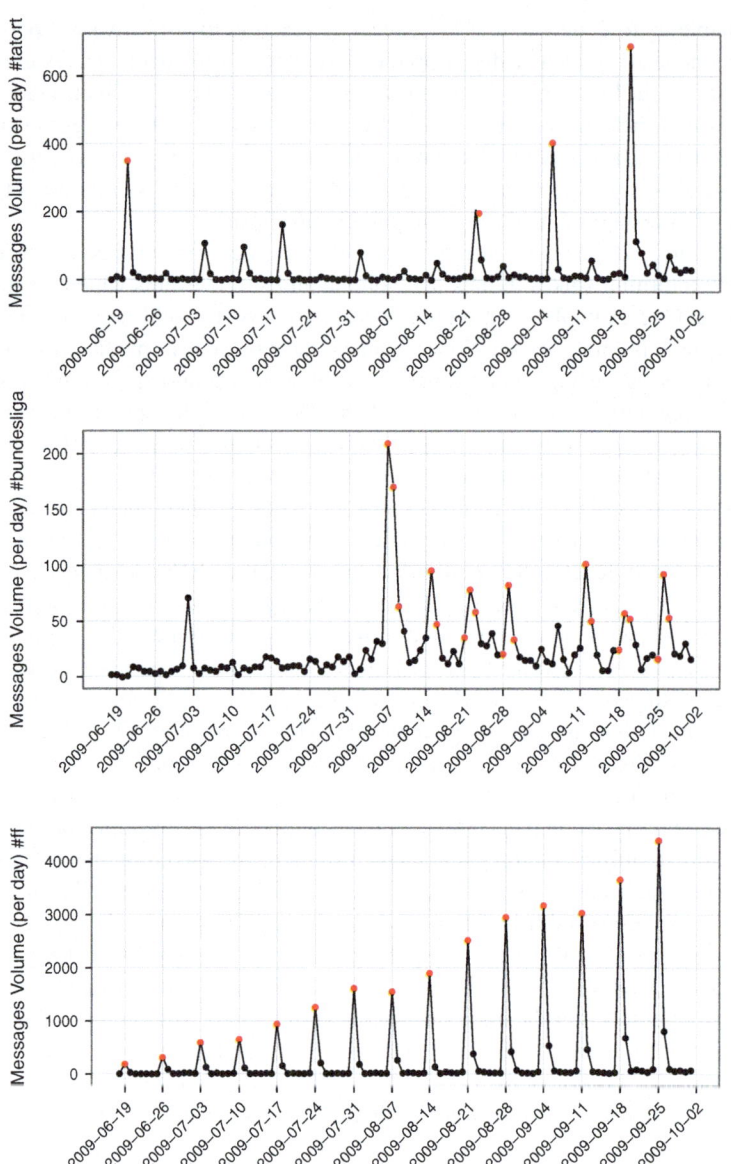

Fig. 3.10 Time series of hashtags referring to phenomena of media-, offline-, and online-culture

during which games took place. The biggest spike marks the first game of the season.

The third graph shows the number of tweets participating in the Twitter user convention *Follow Friday* by using the hashtag #ff. The graph shows the clearest

3.5 A Mechanism Explaining the Publication of Tweets

pattern yet. Spikes of the volume in tweets using the hashtag #ff appear predictably on Fridays.

Figure 3.10 serves to show that different cultural phenomena—be they anchored in offline culture, in media culture, or online culture—lead users to interact with Twitter, referencing connected stimuli in their messages. Thus, these events have online shadows.

Given the focus of this book, it is sensible to include a third category: political events. Twitter users accompanied the televised debate between the leading candidates of the CDU and the SPD, Angela Merkel and Frank-Walter Steinmeier, by heavy tweeting. Another example of a political event that generated heavy Twitter coverage comprised the protests against an infrastructure project in Stuttgart, Germany (Jungherr and Jürgens 2014b). Thus, traditional politics and political activism both have the potential to elicit heavy coverage on Twitter, which manifests itself in uncharacteristic spikes in the volume of Twitter messages during specific time intervals.

For singular and recurring events or phenomena to become visible in aggregated data, the events or phenomena either have to reach a large number of people directly—as for example large natural disasters do—or they have to be mediated to become visible to many Twitter users so they can tweet about them. It is thus also helpful to differentiate between those phenomena and events that were experienced directly by a large number of users and those that reached them through media coverage—be it mediated by traditional media (like TV or newspapers) or new media (like blogs, Facebook updates, or tweets). Since only few events and phenomena reach a large number of users directly, most tweets posted during a collective spike in messages were probably posted in reaction to mediated content (be it by coverage in traditional media, tweets, video streams, or links) of the event and not to the event itself. Mediated events, therefore, have the strongest chance of creating big online shadows. This is also true for unmediated events that people experience at the same time—such as natural disasters or earthquakes. The exceptions are events that are covered by participants live as they unfold and the coverage of which is in turn picked up by other Twitter users because of the resonance of their published messages, pictures, or links. Thus Twitter also has the potential to mediate events that would otherwise have been ignored by traditional media. This is of particular relevance for political activists (Jungherr and Jürgens 2014b).

Some of these cultural phenomena, be they singular events (such as the coverage of a political inauguration or a royal wedding) or regularly returning (such as the coverage of the soccer world cup or election night coverage), qualify as media events, which, in the words of Daniel Dayan and Elihu Katz, are

> (...) about the festive viewing of television. It is about those historic occasions—mostly occasions of state—that are televised as they take place and transfix a nation or the world (Dayan and Katz 1992, p. 1).

These are rituals that serve as moments of social integration that

> (...) viewers present themselves at the same time and in every place. All eyes are fixed on the ceremonial center, through which each nuclear cell is connected to all the rest. Social integration of the highest order is thus achieved via mass communication (Dayan and Katz 1992, p. 15).

Later, I will discuss in greater detail media events and their relationship with spikes in Twitter messages. At this point, it is important to note only that these types of events exist and can potentially lead users to deviate from their normal behavior to post messages commenting on these events as they unfold.

Table 3.2 shows the patterns described above with simple illustrating examples. Clearly, this account is not exhaustive regarding the phenomena leading to exceptional spikes in the volume of Twitter messages. Still, this account can serve as a basis for a discussion of mechanisms leading users to post messages, which give rise to highly clustered patterns in the aggregate of all posted messages.

Users thus react to events that are of personal relevance to them by posting messages on Twitter. Possible motives might be that they find them generally interesting, want to share or document them, or want to be seen to comment on them. Still, there remains an important caveat. For any stimulus leading a user to post a Twitter message referring to it, it has to arouse the user's interest. User interest in the stimulus is, therefore, an important moderator in its power to create reactions on Twitter. From a research point of view, user behavior becomes interesting once

Table 3.2 Examples for various types of events leading to spikes in Twitter messages

		Recurring events	Singular events
Natural phenomena	Direct experience	Day-and-night cycle (e.g. #goodmorning, #goodnight)	Natural disasters (#katrina)
	Mediated experience		Reactions to mediated coverage of disasters
Cultural phenomena	Direct experience	Cultural conventions offline such as working hours (e.g. #mittagspause, or #feierabend), or work days (e.g. #monday, or #weekend); cultural conventions online (e.g. #ff)	Audience participation at sporting events, or concerts
	Mediated experience	Sports events (e.g. #bundesliga) or popular TV shows (e.g. #tatort)	Coverage of the soccer worldcup final, or a royal wedding
Political phenomena	Direct experience	Election campaigns, or elections	Political protests, or high profile political speeces
	Mediated experience	Election night coverage, or TV-debates between candidates for high political offcr	Political protests; high-profile speeches in Parliament

3.5 A Mechanism Explaining the Publication of Tweets 61

several users start reacting to the same event. If an event is of relevance to a greater group of people and inspires them to post their reactions on Twitter, it becomes visible as an aberration in the aggregated data of all messages posted during a given time interval or of those contributing to a specific topic. The aggregated data on micro-behavior of users thus holds information on events that managed to capture the attention of a significant part of those users. Deviations in the behavior on the micro-level thus become visible on the macro-level, which makes Twitter a research tool with much more potential than simply documenting the fancies and mundane mores of its users.

3.5.4 A Person's Propensity to Tweet

The final element of the mechanism explaining the publication of Twitter messages is the propensity of each individual Twitter user to tweet. Not every user posts messages in equal frequency. Figure 3.11 shows all users, who between June 18 and October 1, 2009 posted at least one message, ranked by the total number of messages posted by them. The graph shows succinctly that the number of messages posted per user varied widely, with some users posting a lot of messages and most users posting only very few. Clearly, users are distinct with regard to their tweeting propensity.

The propensity of each individual Twitter user to post a message or not is an important element for the mechanism to take into account since it serves potentially as a multiplier—if a user tends to post a lot of messages, it is highly probable that she would react by posting a message if one or more of the mechanism's other elements were in play. In contrast, and given the same circumstances, if a user tends to post only a very low number of tweets, it is much less probable that she would react with a tweet.

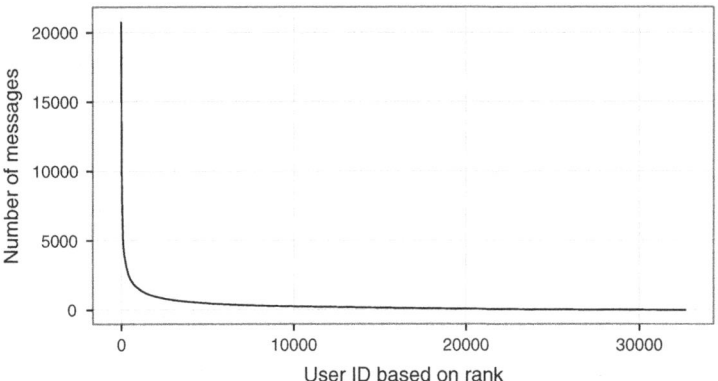

Fig. 3.11 Users ranked by total number of messages posted

To account for the total length of time that a user had the possibility of posting messages, the mechanism's formal statement divides the total number of messages a user posted during the time span under observation by the total number of time bins. If we observe the behavior of a Twitter user for a week and focus on her tweets per hour, the total sum of her tweets would be divided by 168, the number of hours during 1 week. If instead we focused on her tweets per day, the total sum of her tweets would be divided by 7, the number of days during 1 week.

3.5.5 What Does This Mechanism Enable Us to Do?

This mechanism helps us to understand the meaning of pattern shifts in the aggregated data. Social context, the state of the twittersphere, and an individual's propensity to tweet are three elements in the mechanism that can easily be measured and controlled. They are fairly steady patterns. It is, therefore, sensible to assume that if we see spikes in the volume of Twitter messages during a given time span, this is due to the fact that many users reacted to the same stimulus. Twitter thus becomes a sensor for foci and shifts in the attention of Twitter users and thereby a tool for the detection and analysis of events, objects of political attention, and political information.

It is important to note that Twitter, of course, documents only a part of social reality, namely that part of society stimulating the interest of vocal Twitter users. Thus, we cannot expect Twitter data to provide us with an unbiased sensor of social reality. This is especially true for politics.

3.6 A Framework for the Analysis of Social Phenomena with Twitter Data

This chapter has shown that digital trace data is best understood as offering a mediated reflection of reality. External stimuli are mediated by interest, attention, and intentions of users as well as by the technological design of the digital service before they leave marks in digital trace data. These mediating factors might lead the reflection of reality as seen in digital trace data to deviate from political reality at large.

This approach stands in stark contrast to the research practices currently dominating the field. At the moment, studies using digital trace data for the analysis of social or political phenomena predominantly seem to assume that these data offer a more or less true image of reality. Most studies comprise proof of concepts, in which some metrics developed based on digital trace data were shown to be somewhat connected with metrics of social or political reality.

These models, therefore, offer two competing hypotheses with regard to the use of digital trace data in the analysis of political phenomena. Following the mirror-hypothesis, we should expect digital trace data to offer a true image of political reality. In contrast, the mediation-hypothesis leads us to expect the reflection of political reality, found in digital trace data, to be biased in accordance with the underlying data generating processes. In the remainder of the book, I will test which of these models fits better when examining Twitter messages which commented on politics during the course of the 2009 federal election in Germany and their reflection of political actors, events, and campaign dynamics. For this analysis, I will focus on Twitter's reflection of political actors, political events, controversies, the interconnection with political coverage of traditional media, and the relative importance of political actors. In all cases, I will show that the patterns found on Twitter did not offer true reflections of the campaign but instead were heavily biased by users' interest, attention, and intentions.

Discussing the use of digital trace data in the social sciences, therefore, has to account for the mediated nature of digital trace data and show how these mediating factors might bias the analysis of social phenomena based on digital trace data. In this, various strands of mass communication research can offer templates, as here research in mediating factors influencing the construction of reality by media has long been a focus of research (Schulz 1976, 1989; Shoemaker and Reese 2014).

References

Anderson A, Huttenlocher D, Kleinberg J, Leskovec J (2013) Steering user behavior with badges. In: Schwabe D, Almeida V, Glaser H, Baeza-Yates R, Moon S (eds) WWW 2013: proceedings of the 22nd international conference on world wide web. International World Wide Web Conferences Steering Committee, Geneva, CH, pp 95–106

Aral S (2011) Identifying social influence in networks using randomized experiments. IEEE Intell Syst 26(5):91–96. doi:10.1109/MIS.2011.89

Aral S, Muchnik L, Sundararajan A (2009) Distinguishing influence-based contagion from homophily-driven diffusion in dynamic networks. Proc Natl Acad Sci USA 106(51):21544–21549. doi:10.1073/pnas.0908800106

Asur S, Huberman BA (2010) Predicting the future with social media. In: Huang XJ, King I, Raghavan V, Rueger S (eds) WI-IAT 2010: proceedings of the 2010 IEEE/WIC/ACM international conference on web intelligence and intelligent agent technology, vol 1. IEEE, Washington, DC, pp 492–499. doi:10.1109/WI-IAT.2010.63

Bakshy E, Hofman JM, Mason WA, Watts DJ (2011) Everyone's an influencer: quantifying influence on Twitter. In: King I, Nejdl W, Li H (eds) WSDM 2011: proceedings of the 4th ACM international conference on web search and data mining. ACM, New York, pp 65–74. doi:10.1145/1935826.1935845

Bastos MT, Raimundo RLG, Travitzki R (2013) Gatekeeping Twitter: message diffusion in political hashtags. Media Cult Soc 35(2):260–270. doi:10.1177/0163443712467594

Bollen J, Mao H, Zeng XJ (2011) Twitter mood predicts the stock market. J Comput Sci 2(1):1–8

Bond RM, Fariss CJ, Jones JJ, Kramer ADI, Marlow C, Settle JE, Fowler JH (2012) A 61-million-person experiment in social influence and political mobilization. Nature 489(7415):295–298. doi:10.1038/nature11421

Bruns A (2005) Gatewatching: collaborative online news production. Peter Lang Publishing, New York

Bruns A, Stieglitz S (2013) Towards more systematic Twitter analysis: metrics for tweeting activities. Int J Soc Res Methodol 16(2):91–108. doi:10.1080/13645579.2012.756095

Cha M, Haddadi H, Benevenuto F, Gummadi KP (2010) Measuring user influence in Twitter: the million follower fallacy. In: Proceedings of the 4th international AAAI conference on weblogs and social media (ICWSM). The AAAI Press, Menlo Park

Chaffee SH, Hochheimer JL (1985) The beginnings of political communication research in the United States: origins of the "limited effects" model. In: Rogers EM, Balle F (eds) The media revolution in America and in Western Europe. Ablex Publishing Corporation, Norwood, pp 267–296

Chakrabarti D, Punera K (2011) Event summarization using tweets. In: Nicolov N, Shanahan JG, Adamic L, Baeza-Yates R, Counts S (eds) ICWSM 2011: proceedings of the 5th international AAAI conference on weblogs and social media. Association for the Advancement of Artificial Intelligence (AAAI), Menlo Park, pp 66–73

Chen GM (2011) Tweet this: a uses and gratifications perspective on how active twitter use gratifies a need to connect with others. Comput Hum Behav 27(2):755–762. doi:10.1016/j.chb.2010.10.023

Choi H, Varian HR (2012) Predicting the present with Google trends. Econ Rec 88(Issue Suppl s1):2–9. doi:10.1111/j.1475-4932.2012.00809.x

Cioffi-Revilla C (2010) Computational social science. Wiley Interdiscip Rev Comput Stat 2(3):259–271. doi:10.1002/wics.95

Cioffi-Revilla C (2014) Introduction to computational social science: principles and applications. Springer, Heidelberg

Coleman JS (1990) Foundations of social theory. Harvard University Press, Cambridge

Conover MD, Ratkiewicz J, Francisco M, Goncalves B, Flammini A, Menczer F (2011) Political polarization on Twitter. In: Nicolov N, Shanahan JG, Adamic L, Baeza-Yates R, Counts S (eds) ICWSM 2011: proceedings of the 5th international AAAI conference on weblogs and social media. Association for the Advancement of Artificial Intelligence (AAAI), Menlo Park, pp 89–96

Conte R, Gilbert N, Bonelli G, Cioffi-Revilla C, Deffuant G, Kertesz J, V Loreto SM, Nadal JP, Sanchez A, Nowak A, Flache A, Miguel MS, Helbing D (2012) Manifesto of computational social science. Eur Phys J Spec Top 214(1):325–346. doi:10.1140/epjst/e2012-01697-8

Couldry N (2014) Inaugural: a necessary disenchantment: myth, agency and injustice in a digital world. Sociol Rev 62(4):880–897. doi:10.1111/1467-954X.12158

Crandall DJ, Backstrom L, Huttenlocher D, Kleinberg J (2009) Mapping the world's photos. In: Quemada J, León G, Maarek Y, Nejdl W (eds) WWW 2009: proceedings of the 18th international conference on world wide web. ACM, New York, pp 761–770. doi:10.1145/1526709.1526812

Dayan D, Katz E (1992) Media events: the live broadcasting of history. Harvard University Press, Cambridge

Diaz F, Gamon M, Hofman J, Kıcıman E, Rothschild D (2014) Online and social media data as a flawed continuous panel survey. Microsoft Res. http://research.microsoft.com/en-us/projects/flawedsurvey/

Dodds PS, Harris KD, Klouman IM, Bliss CA, Danforth CM (2011) Temporal patterns of happiness and information in a global-scale social network: hedonometrics and Twitter. PLoS One 6(12). doi:10.1371/journal.pone.0026752

Eagle N, Pentland A (2006) Reality mining: sensing complex social systems. Pers Ubiquit Comput 10(4):255–268. doi:10.1007/s00779-005-0046-3

Easley D, Kleinberg J (2010) Networks, crowds, and markets: reasoning about a highly connected world. Cambridge University Press, Cambridge

Elster J (2007) Explaining social behavior: more nuts and bolts for the social sciences. Cambridge University Press, Cambridge

Epstein JM (2006) Generative social science: studies in agent-based computational modeling. Princeton University Press, Princeton

Frank MR, Mitchell L, Dodds PS, Danforth CM (2013) Happiness and the patterns of life: a study of geolocated Tweets. Nat Sci Rep 3(2625). doi:10.1038/srep02625

Freelon D (2014) On the interpretation of digital trace data in communication and social computing research. J Broadcast Electron Media 58(1):59–75. doi:10.1080/08838151.2013.875018

Friedman M (1953) The methodology of positive economics. In: Friedman M (ed) Essays in positive economics. University of Chicago Press, Chicago, pp 210–244

Gayo-Avello D (2012) No, you cannot predict elections with Twitter. IEEE Internet Comput 16(6):91–94. doi:10.1109/MIC.2012.137

Gayo-Avello D (2013) A meta-analysis of state-of-the-art electoral prediction from Twitter data. Soc Sci Comput Rev 31(6):649–679. doi:10.1177/0894439313493979

Gilbert N (ed) (2010) Computational social science. SAGE Publications, London

Ginsberg J, Mohebbi MH, Patel RS, Brammer L, Smolinski MS, Brilliant L (2009) Detecting influenza epidemics using search engine query data. Nature 457:1012–1014. doi:10.1038/nature07634

Golder SA, Macy MW (2011) Diurnal and seasonal mood vary with work, sleep, and daylength across diverse cultures. Science 333(6051):1878–1881

Gomez-Rodriguez M, Leskovec J, Schölkopf B (2013) Structure and dynamics of information pathways in online media. In: Leonardi S, Panconesi A, Ferragina P, Gionis A (eds) WSDM 2013: proceedings of the 6th ACM international conference on web search and data mining. ACM, New York, pp 23–32. doi:10.1145/2433396.2433402

González MC, Hidalgo CA, Barabási AL (2008) Understanding individual human mobility patterns. Nature 453:779–782. doi:10.1038/nature06958

González-Bailón S, Borge-Holthoefer J, Rivero A, Moreno Y (2011) The dynamics of protest recruitment through an online network. Nat Sci Rep 1(197). doi:10.1038/srep00197

Gruhl D, Guha R, Kumar R, Novak J, Tomkins A (2005) The predictive power of online chatter. In: Grossman R, Bayardo R, Bennett K (eds) KDD 2005: proceedings of the 11th ACM SIGKDD international conference on knowledge discovery in data mining. ACM, New York, pp 78–87. doi:10.1145/1081870.1081883

Hedström P (2005) Dissecting the social: on the principles of analytical sociology. Cambridge University Press, Cambridge

Hedström P, Bearman P (eds) (2009) The Oxford handbook of analytical sociology. Oxford University Press, Oxford

Hedström P, Swedberg R (eds) (1998) Social mechanisms: an analytical approach to social theory. Cambridge University Press, Cambridge

Hedström P, Ylikoski P (2010) Causal mechanisms in the social sciences. Annu Rev Sociol 36:49–67. doi:10.1146/annurev.soc.012809.102632

Howison J, Wiggins A, Crowston K (2011) Validity issues in the use of social network analysis with digital trace data. J Assoc Inf Syst 12(12):767–797

Huberty ME (2013) Multi-cycle forecasting of congressional elections with social media. In: Weber I, Popescu AM, Pennacchiotti M (eds) PLEAD 2013: proceedings of the 2nd workshop politics, elections and data. ACM, New York, pp 23–30. doi:10.1145/2508436.2508439

Jackson MO (2008) Social and economic networks. Princeton University Press, Princeton

Jansen BJ, Zhang M, Sobel K, Chowdury A (2009) Twitter power: tweets as electronic word of mouth. J Am Soc Inf Sci Technol 60(11):2169–2188. doi:10.1002/asi.v60:11

Jasso G (1988) Principles of theoretical analysis. Sociol Theory 6(1):1–20. doi:10.2307/201910

Jungherr A (2013) Tweets and votes, a special relationship: the 2009 federal election in Germany. In: Weber I, Popescu AM, Pennacchiotti M (eds) PLEAD 2013: proceedings of the 2nd workshop politics, elections and data. ACM, New York, pp 5–14. doi:10.1145/2508436.2508437

Jungherr A, Jürgens P (2013) Forecasting the pulse: how deviations from regular patterns in online data can identify offline phenomena. Internet Res 23(5):589–607. doi:10.1108/IntR-06-2012-0115

Jungherr A, Jürgens P (2014a) Stuttgart's Black Thursday on Twitter: mapping political protests with social media data. In: Gibson R, Cantijoch M, Ward S (eds) Analyzing social media data and web networks. Palgrave Macmillan, New York, pp 154–196

Jungherr A, Jürgens P (2014b) Through a glass, darkly: tactical support and symbolic association in Twitter messages commenting on Stuttgart 21. Soc Sci Comput Rev 32(1):74–89. doi:10.1177/0894439313500022

Kalampokis E, Tambouris E, Tarabanis K (2013) Understanding the predictive power of social media. Internet Res 23(5):544–559. doi:10.1108/IntR-06-2012-0114

King G (2011) Ensuring the data-rich future of the social sciences. Science 331(6018):719–721

Kleinberg J (2003) Bursty and hierachical structure in streams. Data Min Knowl Discovery 7(4):373–397. doi:10.1023/A:1024940629314

Kleinberg J (2011) What can huge data sets teach us about society and ourselves. In: Brockman M (ed) Future science: essays from the cutting edge. Oxford University Press, Oxford, pp 73–87

Kolaczyk ED (2009) Statistical analysis of network data: methods and models. Springer, New York

Kwak H, Lee C, Park H, Moon S (2010) What is Twitter, a social network or a news media? In: Rappa M, Jones P, Freire J, Chakrabarti S (eds) WWW 2010: proceedings of the 19th international conference on the world wide web. ACM, New York, pp 591–600. doi:10.1145/1772690.1772751

Lane ND, Miluzzo E, Lu H, Peebles D, Choudhury T, Campbell AT (2010) A survey of mobile phone sensing. IEEE Commun Mag 48(9):140–150. doi:10.1109/MCOM.2010.5560598

Lazarsfeld PF, Berelson B, Gaudet H (1944) The people's choice. Sloan and Pearce, New York

Lazer D, Pentland A, Adamic L, Aral S, Barabási AL, Brewer D, Christakis N, Contractor N, Fowler J, Gutmann M, Jebara T, King G, Macy MW, Roy D, Alstyne MV (2009) Computational social science. Science 323(5915):721–723. doi:10.1126/science.1167742

Lin YR, Keegan B, Margolin D, Lazer D (2014) Rising tides or rising stars? Dynamics of shared attention on Twitter during media events. PLoS One 9(5):e94093. doi:10.1371/journal.pone.0094093

Liu IL, Cheung CM, Lee MK (2010) Understanding Twitter usage: what drive people continue to tweet. In: PACIS 2010: proceedings of the Pacific Asia conference on information systems. http://aisel.aisnet.org/pacis2010/92/

Mayer-Schönberger V, Cukier K (2013) Big data: a revolution that will transform how we live, work, and think. Houghton Mifflin, New York

McAfee A, Brynjolfsson E (2012) Big data: the management revolution. Harv Bus Rev 90(10):60–68

Metaxas PT, Mustafaraj E (2012) Social media and the elections. Science 338(6106):472–473. doi:10.1126/science.1230456

Miller TW (2014) Modeling techniques in predictive analytics: business problems and solutions with R. Pearson Education, Upper Saddle River

Miller JH, Page SE (2007) Complex adaptive systems: an introduction to computational models of social life. Princeton University Press, Princeton

Mitchell M (2009) Complexity: a guided tour. Oxford University Press, Oxford

Mitchell L, Frank MR, Harris KD, Dodds PS, Danforth CM (2013) The geography of happiness: connecting Twitter sentiment and expression, demographics, and objective characteristics of place. PLoS One 8(5). doi:10.1371/journal.pone.0064417

Muchnik L, Aral S, Taylor SJ (2013) Social influence bias: a randomized experiment. Science 341(6146):647–651. doi:10.1126/science.1240466

Mustafaraj E, Finn S, Whitlock C, Metaxas PT (2011) Vocal minority versus silent majority: discovering the opinions of the long tail. In: SocialCom 2011: the 3rd IEEE international conference on social computing. IEEE, Washington, DC

Newman MEJ (2010) Networks: an introduction. Cambridge University Press, Oxford

Noelle-Neumann E (1991) The theory of public opinion: the concept of the spiral of silence. In: Anderson JA (ed) Communication yearbook 14. SAGE Publications, Newbury Park, pp 256–287

O'Reilly Media (2012) Big data now: 2012 edition. O'Reilly Media, Sebastopol

Papacharissi ZA, de Fatima Oliveira M (2012) Affective news and networked publics: the rhythms of news storytelling on #egypt. J Commun 62(2):266–282. doi:10.1111/j.1460-2466.2012.01630.x

Parmelee JH, Bichard SL (2012) Politics and the Twitter revolution: how tweets influence the relationship between political leaders and the public. Lexington Books, Lanham

Pentland A (2008) Honest signals: how they shape our world. The MIT Press, Cambridge

R Core Team (2014) R: a language and environment for statistical computing. R Foundation for Statistical Computing, Vienna. http://www.R-project.org

Rios M, Lin J (2013) Visualizing the "pulse" of world cities on Twitter. In: Kiciman E, Ellison NB, Hogan B, Resnick P, Soboroff I (eds) ICWSM 2013: proceedings of the 7th international AAAI conference on weblogs and social media. Association for the Advancement of Artificial Intelligence (AAAI), Menlo Park, CA, pp 717–720

Rogers R (2004) Information politics on the web. The MIT Press, Cambridge

Rogers R (2013a) Debanalizing Twitter: the transformation of an object of study. In: Davis H, Halpin H, Pentland A, Bernstein M, Adamic L (eds) WebSci 2013: proceedings of the 5th annual ACM web science conference. ACM, New York, pp 356–365. doi:10.1145/2464464.2464511

Rogers R (2013b) Digital methods. The MIT Press, Cambridge

Rojas F (2013) How Twitter can help predict an election. Washington Post. http://articles.washingtonpost.com/2013-08-11/opinions/41299678_1_tweets-social-media-data-congressional-district

Romero DM, Meeder B, Kleinberg J (2011) Differences in the mechanics of information diffusion across topics: idioms, political hashtags, and complex contagion on Twitter. In: Sadagopan S, Ramamritham K, Kumar A, Ravindra MP, Bertino E, Kumar R (eds) WWW 2011: proceedings of the 20th international conference on world wide web. ACM, New York, pp 695–704. doi:10.1145/1963405.1963503

Sakaki T, Okazaki M, Matsuo Y (2010) Earthquake shakes Twitter users: real-time event detection by social sensors. In: Rappa M, Jones P, Freire J, Chakrabarti S (eds) WWW 2010: proceedings of the 19th international conference on the world wide web. ACM, New York, pp 851–860. doi:10.1145/1772690.1772777

Salganik MJ, Watts DJ (2008) Leading the herd astray: an experimental study of self-fulfilling prophecies in an artificial cultural market. Soc Psychol Q 71(4):338–355. doi:10.1177/019027250807100404

Salganik MJ, Watts DJ (2009) Web-based experiments for the study of collective social dynamics in cultural markets. Top Cogn Sci 1(3):439–468. doi:10.1111/j.1756-8765.2009.01030.x

Salganik MJ, Dodds PS, Watts DJ (2006) Experimental study of inequality and unpredictability in an artificial cultural market. Science 311(5762):854–856. doi:10.1126/science.1121066

Schoen H, Gayo-Avello D, Metaxas PT, Strohmaier M, Gloor P (2013) The power of prediction with social media. Internet Res 23(5):528–543. doi:10.1108/IntR-06-2013-0115

Schulz W (1976) Die Konstruktion von Realität in den Nachrichtenmedien: Analyse der aktuellen Berichterstattung. Alber, Freiburg, DE

Schulz W (1989) Massenmedien und Realität. Kölner Zeitschrift für Soziologie und Sozialpsychologie 30(Sonderheft):135–149. doi:10.1007/978-3-322-83571-0_9

Scott J (2013) Social network analysis, 3rd edn. SAGE Publications, London

Segerberg A, Bennett WL (2011) Social media and the organization of collective action: using Twittter to explore the ecologies of two climate change protests. Commun Rev 14(3):197–215. doi:10.1080/10714421.2011.597250

Shamma DA, Kennedy L, Churchill EF (2011) Peaks and persistence: modeling the shape of microblog conversations. In: Hinds P, Tang JC, Wang J, Bardram J, Ducheneaut N (eds) CSCW 2011: proceedings of the ACM 2011 conference on computer supported cooperative work. ACM, New York, pp 355–358. doi:10.1145/1958824.1958878 10.1145/1958824.1958878

Shoemaker PJ, Reese SD (2014) Mediating the message in the 21st century, 3rd edn. Routledge, New York

Siegel E (2013) Predictive analytics: the power to predict who will click, buy, lie, or die. Wiley, Hoboken

Ugander J, Backstrom L, Marlow C, Kleinberg J (2012) Structural diversity in social contagion. Proc Natl Acad Sci USA 109(16):5962–5966. doi:10.1073/pnas.1116502109

Verma S, Vieweg S, Corvey WJ, Palen L, Martin JH, Palmer M, Schram A, Anderson KM (2011) Natural language processing to the rescue? Extracting "situational awareness" tweets during mass emergency. In: Nicolov N, Shanahan JG, Adamic L, Baeza-Yates R, Counts S (eds) ICWSM 2011: proceedings of the 5th international AAAI conference on weblogs and social media. Association for the Advancement of Artificial Intelligence (AAAI), Menlo Park, pp 386–392

Wang W, Rothschild D, Goel S, Gelman A (2014) Forecasting elections with non-representative polls. Int J Forecast. doi:10.1016/j.ijforecast.2014.06.001

Wasserman S, Faust K (1994) Social network analysis: methods and applications. Cambridge University Press, Cambridge

Weber I, Garimella VRK, Borra E (2012) Mining web query logs to analyze political issue. In: Contractor N, Uzzi B, Macy M, Nejdl W (eds) WebSci 2012: proceedings of the 3rd annual ACM web science conference. ACM, New York, pp 330–334. doi:10.1145/2380718.2380761

Wu S, Hofman JM, Mason WA, Watts DJ (2011) Who says what to whom on Twitter. In: Sadagopan S, Ramamritham K, Kumar A, Ravindra MP, Bertino E, Kumar R (eds) WWW 2011: proceedings of the 20th international conference on world wide web. ACM, New York, pp 705–714. doi:10.1145/1963405.1963504

Yang J, Leskovec J (2011) Patterns of temporal variation in online media. In: King I, Nejdl W, Li H (eds) WSDM 2011: proceedings of the 4th ACM international conference on web search and data mining. ACM, New York, pp 177–186. doi:10.1145/1935826.1935863

Zeitzoff T (2011) Using social media to measure conflict dynamics: an application to the 2008–2009 Gaza conflict. J Confl Resolut 55(6):938–969. doi:10.1177/0022002711408014

Chapter 4
Twitter as Political Communication Space: Publics, Prominent Users, and Politicians

4.1 The Political Communication Space

Twitter has become a widely used element in political campaigns around the world. The posts and interactions of political elites, journalists, and the general public constitute a political communication space. This communication space is deeply interconnected with other spaces built by media coverage and campaign communication. This interconnection does not necessarily extend to shared dynamics. Instead, political communication on Twitter follows dynamics specific to the platform's technology and users' cultural usage practices.

I use the term *communication space* to refer to all Twitter messages contributing to one topic—in this case, politics—by using topically relevant hashtags (e.g. #cdu, #zensursula, or #btw13) on one Internet service—in this case Twitter. As such, the term is clearly different from the use of the term *sphere*, which focuses on all communication from a device or service (Rogers 2013) and the term *issue public*, which could refer to communication on a given topic on multiple devices or services.

In this chapter, I will focus on the usage patterns of three user groups—publics, prominent users, and politicians—which have been the focus of most research examining political uses of Twitter (Jungherr 2014b). Focusing on these usage patterns allows us to develop inferences on the underlying mechanism linking political phenomena to political references in Twitter messages, allowing us to check whether the patterns found in the data correspond with assumptions of the mirror- or the mediation-hypothesis.

4.2 Data Collection and Preparation

The analyses in this book are based on data collected through the Twitter application programming interface (API) from mid-June to early October 2009, the months directly preceding the 2009 federal election in Germany. These data have been collected in close collaboration with Pascal Jürgens from the University of Mainz.

For our Twitter sample, Pascal and I decided to include all Twitter users' messages who had posted messages referring to politics or the campaign during the months directly preceding the federal election of 2009. We thus queried the Twitter API regularly for messages containing one of 19 politically relevant hashtags (see Table 4.1 for the complete list of hashtags used to identify politically vocal users). We then identified the users who had posted messages containing these hashtags and collected all their previous and future messages. This process established a self-updating panel containing all messages of users who were politically vocal—i.e. who had posted at least one message containing one of our listed hashtags. We did this, on the one hand to be able to assess the role politics plays in relation to all other messages, and on the other hand to capture potentially politically relevant messages that did not happen to contain one of the political hashtags identified by us. We kept a list of all users who had utilized at least one of our predefined hashtags during the months before the election and queried the Twitter API regularly for new messages posted by them. In addition to their messages, we also downloaded politically vocal

Table 4.1 Hashtags used to identify politically vocal users

Hashtag	Type
cdu	Partyname
csu	Partyname
union	Partyname
spd	Partyname
fdp	Partyname
gruene	Partyname
grüne	Partyname
linke	Partyname
linkspartei	Partyname
piraten	Partyname
npd	Partyname
bundestagswahl	Campaign
btw09	Campaign
wahl	Campaign
sst	Campaign
tvduell	Campaign
petition	Activism
zensursula	Activism
politik	General

4.2 Data Collection and Preparation

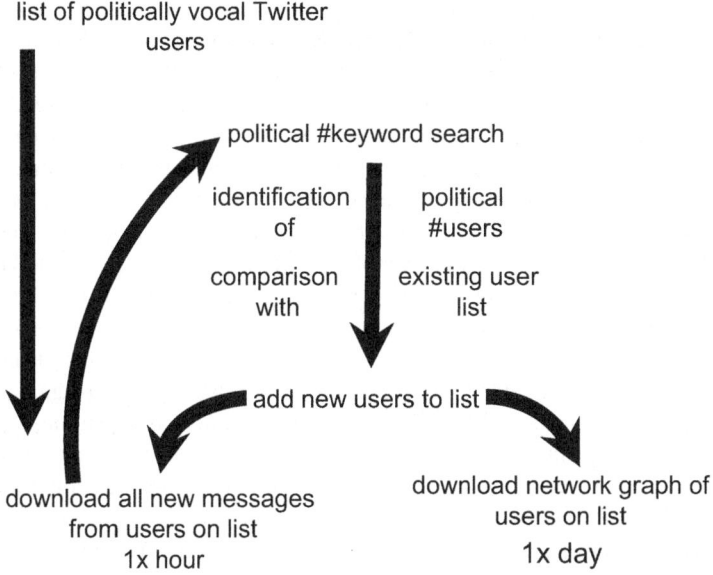

Fig. 4.1 Data acquisition process

Twitter users' network graphs (i.e. the lists of their *friends* and *followers*). This process of data acquisition is schematically documented in Fig. 4.1.

Thirty-two thousand seven hundred and thirty one users included one or more of these hashtags in messages posted between June 18 and October 1, 2009. In this time span these users posted in total 10,085,982 messages. To determine the politically relevant messages—i.e. the political communication space on Twitter— I identified 500 hashtags that were used most often in combination with each of the hashtags listed in Table 4.1. I then identified the politically relevant hashtags in this list. This resulted in a list of 787 additional politically relevant hashtags. Based on this list that included the names of political parties, candidates, political issues, and terms relevant to the campaign, I further collected all hashtags that were connected to the hashtags in this list. The criteria for this secondary selection included spelling variations, obvious spelling mistakes, abbreviations for terms, and extensions for abbreviations, which resulted in a final list of 2629 hashtags. The sum of all messages that contained at least one of the original hashtags or one hashtag of the extended list constitute the *political communication space* on Twitter for the federal election of 2009 in Germany (the list of all hashtags used to identify messages contributing to the political communication space can be found online[1]). Between June 18 and October 1, 2009 there were 930,371 messages that contained at least one of those hashtags. This means that roughly 9 % of the messages in

---

[1] http://andreasjungherr.net/wp-content/uploads/2014/08/political_communication_space.txt.

the data set referred to the campaign of 2009 in some way. Concentrating only on messages using at least one of the original 19 hashtags would have created a much smaller political communication space. Only 359,275 messages, or 3.6 % of all messages, in the data set used one of the original 19 hashtags. Extending the political communication space by including more hashtags thus seems necessary to gain a comprehensive understanding of political communication on Twitter.

Furthermore, I differentiated between messages in support of parties or candidates and messages in opposition. To do this, I chose a simple approach enabled by a special feature of the German twittersphere. Starting early in 2009, the German communication consultant Sascha Lobo introduced the service *Wahlgetwitter.de*. This site is now defunct and was rebranded *Twitterbarometer*[2] for the 2013 federal election. The website tracked the use of parties' names and the suffixes + and − in hashtags. The name of a party followed by a plus sign was meant to signal support for a party (e.g. #piraten+), while the name of a party followed by a minus sign was meant to signal opposition (e.g. #piraten-). The website calculated the total sums of positive and negative mentions of a party per day. This tool was communicated widely on the Web and in traditional media, which led to the growing adoption of the usage convention during the campaign of 2009. In the dataset, 11,212 users posted messages with a #partyname followed by a + or −, which led to a total of 223,551 messages in which these conventions were used. Roughly 24 % of all messages in the political communication space were commenting explicitly—either positively or negatively—on one of the established political parties. Nearly 35 % of all users in our sample used the #partyname+ or #partyname- convention at least once. The convention was thus widely adopted and can serve as an indicator for political sentiment in users' messages and political affiliations.

Various analyses in this book address the use of popular usage conventions in messages posted by Twitter users. These are @messages, retweets, and URLs. In 2009, the Twitter API did not consistently identify these conventions through specific meta-tags in the data it returned. To identify usage conventions in the message-bodies included in the data set, we used automated text analysis. The appearance of specific character chains in messages were identified as usage conventions in a message. We chose to follow Twitter's technological imperatives as closely as possible, counting only messages that started with "@user" as directed messages. Retweets were captured by Twitter's "in_reply_to_user_id" field as well as the conventions "RT", "retweet", "from", and "via" followed by a username. All messages containing the character string "http://" followed by a valid URL were identified as containing URLs. This might exclude some atypical, idiosyncratic, or individual ways some users marked messages as interactions with other users or retweets. Still, these character strings cover typical usage practices.

---

[2]http://twitterbarometer.de.

4.3 Publics

The political uses of Twitter by politically vocal publics during campaigns has been a focus of researchers examining political phenomena with data collected on Twitter (Jungherr 2014b). In discussing online use, the term *publics* has gained popularity. With this term researchers describe a fragmentation of the mass media audience into many interest-based sections of the public—*publics*. The increasing popularity of Internet services through which people can connect, based on their online profiles and interests, has led to the rise of the term *networked publics* (Papacharissi and de Fatima Oliveira 2012). In the case of political Twitter use, publics can be regarded as all users who posted messages with politically relevant hashtags or keywords or those users who followed the accounts of politicians or parties. Thus, this term encompasses the activities of all politically interested and vocal Twitter users.

Here, I understand all Twitter users to be part of political publics who posted messages containing politically relevant hashtags—such as party names or politically relevant terms. Through the explicit reference of politics in hashtags, their messages are seen as contributing to the political communication space on Twitter. The analysis of these messages allows us to examine the political behavior—and potential behavioral shifts—of users during the course of a campaign. This potentially allows for a deepening in our understanding of political communication, as for the first time we have access to comprehensive data sources documenting the behavior of non-elites during election campaigns.

4.3.1 Publics: Message-Centric Analysis

Let us start by examining basic underlying patterns in the messages posted by politically vocal users during the campaign of 2009. Since the data set contains all messages posted by users who had used at least one of 19 politically relevant hashtags at least once, it is possible to compare patterns in all messages posted by them with those in messages referring to politics and the campaign—their contributions to the political communication space.

Between June 18, and October 1, the 32,731 users in the data set posted a total of 10,085,982 messages. In the same time period, 31,766 users posted 930,371 messages containing one of the 2629 hashtags contributing to the political communication space. So, roughly one tenth of all messages posted by politically vocal users during the course of the campaign referred to politics. For the comparison of usage conventions in both contexts, the analysis of absolute counts shown in Table 4.2 is of only limited use. A more meaningful indicator is the share that messages containing @messages, retweets, or hyperlinks have on the total messages counts. These shares are shown in Table 4.3.

Table 4.2 Conventions used in all messages and the political communication space between June 18, and October 1, 2009

Usage convention	All messages	Pol. comm. space
Messages	10,085,982	930,371
Messages containing neither @messages, retweets, or URLs	4,982,058	287,881
@messages	1,680,942	125,439
Retweets	582,992	219,711
Messages with URLs	3,911,007	551,011
Users	32,731	31,766

Table 4.3 Message to convention ratio

Message to convention ratio	All messages	Pol. comm. space
% messages containing neither @messages, retweets, or URLs	49.4	30.9
% @messages	16.7	13.4
% retweets	5.8	23.6
% messages with URLs	38.8	59.2
Average no. of daily messages per user	2.9	0.3

Table 4.4 Message to convention ratio reported in other studies

Message to convention ration	Java et al. (2007)	Honeycutt and Herring (2009)	Boyd et al. (2010)
% @messages	12.5	31	36
% retweets	–	–	3
% messages with URLs	13	–	22

Table 4.3 shows that messages contributing to the political communication space contained @messages, retweets, or hyperlinks more frequently than general messages. This difference seems largely to be driven by the higher shares of retweets and messages containing hyperlinks in the political communication space than in all messages. Compared with the total number of messages, those messages containing political hashtags thus are posted much more frequently in reaction to outward stimuli be they content on the Web or tweets posted by other users on Twitter.

Table 4.4 shows the share of @messages, retweets, and messages containing hyperlinks reported in other studies. In 2007, Akshay Java and colleagues collected messages appearing in Twitter's public stream and analyzed them with a focus on user behavior (Java et al. 2007). Courtenay Honeycutt and Susan C. Herring sampled messages posted on Twitter's public stream on January 11, 2008 (Honeycutt and Herring 2009). Finally, Danah Boyd and colleagues analyzed a random sample of messages posted on Twitter's public timeline between January and June 2009 (Boyd et al. 2010). These studies are highly referenced papers on general uses of Twitter and thus offer a valuable basis for comparison with the patterns found in this data set.

4.3 Publics

Politically vocal users in Germany posted significantly fewer @messages than users contained in the samples of Honeycutt and Herring (2009) and Boyd et al. (2010). Their messages also contained more hyperlinks than the messages included in the samples of Java et al. (2007) and Boyd et al. (2010). Other differences appear in the comparison of the messages containing retweets. While the retweet share of all messages posted by politically vocal users is roughly comparable to that reported by Boyd et al. (2010) the retweet share in messages contributing to the political communication space was much higher.

These findings corroborate the impression gained from comparison of the total number of messages posted by politically vocal users and those contributing to the political communication space. Users in Germany interacted much less through @messages than users whose messages were analyzed in comparable studies. Additionally, messages containing politically relevant hashtags were posted much more frequently in reaction to outside stimuli—such as content on the Web or Twitter messages posted by other users—than was the case with messages not referring to politics or messages sampled from Twitter's public feed.

4.3.2 Publics: Dynamics Over Time

The analysis of message aggregates and convention use has already offered some perspective on the nature of Twitter's use by politically vocal Twitter users. Nevertheless, an analysis of the dynamics of these metrics over time offers an even closer look.

Figure 4.2 shows the number of users who posted at least one message with a politically relevant hashtag from June 18, to October 1, 2009. After a relative spike in the number of active users on June 18—the day of a controversial piece of

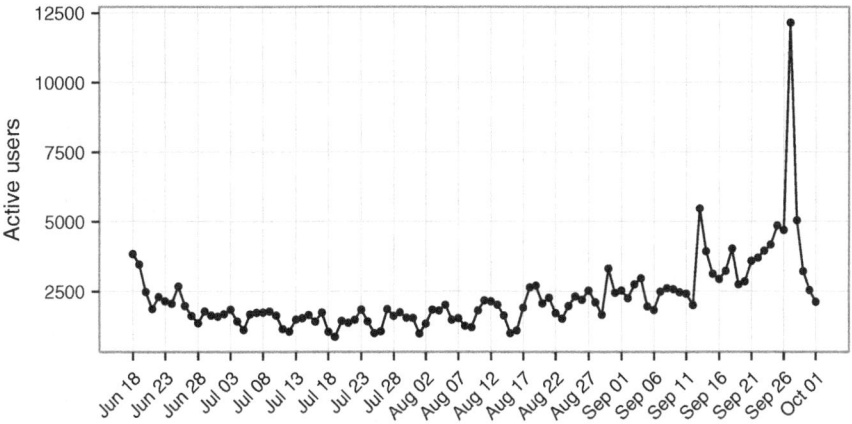

Fig. 4.2 Number of active users per day

Internet regulation's ratification—the number of users posting at least one message with a politically relevant hashtag fluctuates by around 2500 users. This changes, starting on September 13—the day of the televised candidate debates. The number of active users reaches its absolute peak of nearly 12,500 users on September 27— election day. Between September 13 and September 27, the volume of active users rises continuously. This pattern speaks of a cognitive activation by Twitter users who during the course of the campaign very likely reacted to an increased number of political stimuli—be it through increasing media coverage of politics and the campaign or the campaigning activities of parties themselves—by posting a steadily increasing number of messages referring to politics or the campaign. The spikes on days connected with mediated political events show that these events focused the collective attention of Twitter users which led to significantly higher counts of users commenting on politics than on other days.

Another possibility for assessing the growing political activation of Twitter users through the course of the campaign exists through analysing the average number of messages posted by users per day. This dynamic is shown in Fig. 4.3. From June 18, to September 12, the average number of messages per user fluctuates somewhere between two and four. This pattern is broken on 3 days—June 18, the day of the Access Impediment Act's ratification; August 8, a day of protests against election proceedings in Iran; and August 30, the day of important state elections. The average number of messages reaches its maximum at some six messages per user on the day of the televised candidate debate. Having fallen back immediately after this spike, from this day on, the average number of messages per user rises until election day without quite reaching the level of the televised debate. Again, this pattern corresponds with the concept of cognitive activation through the run of a campaign as well as activation through mediated political events.

Another way to analyze dynamics in the use of conventions is through the analysis of Twitter messages containing neither @messages, retweets nor hyper-

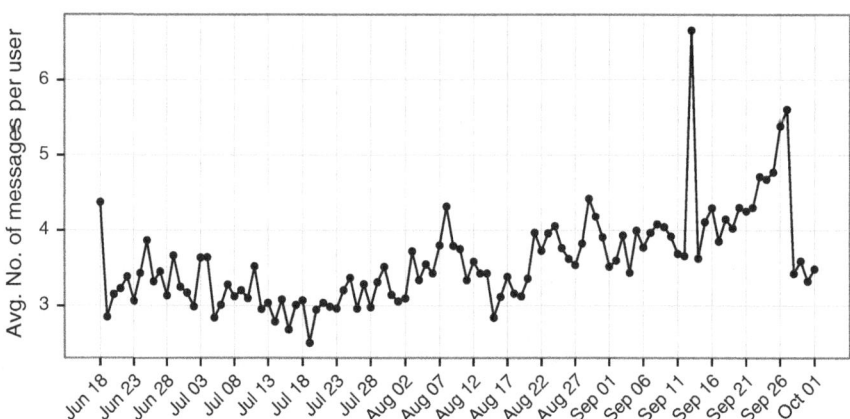

Fig. 4.3 Average number of messages per user

4.3 Publics

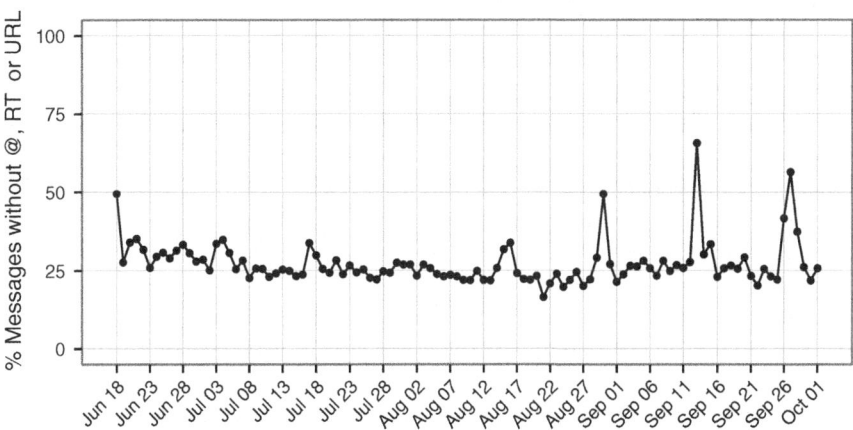

Fig. 4.4 Share of messages containing neither @messages, retweets, or URLs (in percent)

links. Researchers have found that users tend to interact less by @messages or retweets and post fewer messages containing hyperlinks during mediated political events (Lin et al. 2014). This is also shown here in Fig. 4.4. The share of messages containing neither @messages, retweets, or URLs spiked on days of mediated political events—such as coverage of the Access Impediment Act's ratification on June 18; election night coverage on August 30; the day of the televised debate on September 13 and election night coverage on September 27. These shifts were driven largely by decreases in the number of messages containing hyperlinks and only marginally by shifts in the share of @messages or retweets.

This pattern corroborates the mechanism explaining the publication of tweets presented above. Fluctuations in the volume of Twitter messages mentioning political actors appear to reflect attention shifts by users. The relatively high share of URLs in messages containing political hashtags illustrates that users tend to post messages referring to politics once they received a stimulus—in this case a stimulus by content on the Web. In moments of significant drops in the share of messages containing URLs, the locus of political stimuli changed towards television coverage of political events. This shows that a large share of messages posted by politically vocal Twitter users documented their attention towards political topics or events in other media—either online or in traditional media. Following this logic, sudden drops in the share of messages containing neither @message, retweets, or URLs referring to a given topic might indicate the appearance of a televised event related to that topic resulting in an attention shift by Twitter users away from content on the Internet towards media coverage of the event itself.

4.3.3 Publics: User-Centric Analysis

While the preceding sections focused on the analysis of messages posted by Twitter users during the course of the 2009 campaign, this section focuses on the user as a unit of analysis. A recurrent finding of studies examining Twitter is that users show widely diverging usage patterns, with very few tweeting extensively and most tweeting much more sparingly, if at all (Jungherr 2014b). This general pattern is replicated through analysis in the behavior of users posting messages during the campaign.

Table 4.5 offers a first glance in the behavior of the users in this data set. If we compare the maxima and minima in the use of various elements of Twitter—such as messages posted, messages contributing to the political communication space, accounts followed, accounts followed by, posted @messages, received @messages, posted retweets, and received retweets—we see very wide spreads. For instance, the user contributing most intensively to the political communication space posted 17,093 messages during the period under examination while the user contributing the least to the political communication space posted no messages at all. Similar patterns emerge across all usage conventions.

Comparing the average and median values of convention use offers yet another indicator for divergent usage practices. For instance, the average user had 172 followers on election day while the median user had only 43 followers. This spread between average and median values indicates a heavily skewed distribution. In this case, very few users had very high follower counts—thereby raising the average of all users—while most users had only few followers—as shown by the median value, which indicates that half of all users in the data set had 43 or fewer followers. This spread between average and median values is found for all elements of Twitter use, thus indicating widely skewed distributions in the use of all conventions.

Only a handful of users posted more than 1000 messages during the period of analysis, while the overwhelming majority posted 500 or less. The account which posted the most messages, incidentally, was an automated account posting links to pictures posted online. This very uneven participation skews even more once we examine contributions to the political communication space, with only

Table 4.5 User statistics aggregated between June 18, and October 1, 2009

Usage convention	Max.	Min.	Avg.	Median
Messages	20,802	1	309	135
Political communication space	17,093	0	20	4
Followers on election day	68,750	0	172	43
Followers on election day	62,421	0	156	45
@messages, posted	9244	0	51	9
@messages, received	16,232	0	51	7
Retweets, posted	7736	0	18	3
Retweets, received	15,534	0	18	2

few users posting more than 100 messages while the overwhelming majority of users were posting less than 100. Half of all users posted less than four messages contributing to the political communication space. This shows that most politically vocal Twitter users were referring only sparingly to the campaign, while a minority was posting very actively. This pattern has already been shown in other studies (e.g. Mustafaraj et al. 2011) and poses a serious challenge for researchers trying to use Twitter messages as proxy for public opinion. Simply counting messages mentioning political actors will lead to a significant oversampling of contributions by a very small and very active minority of Twitter users.

Only very few users had more than 1000 followers or followed more than 1000 accounts. Roughly a third of all users had less than 100 followers or followed less than 100 accounts. This shows that the attention on Twitter focuses on only a small minority of users who could boast high follower counts. This finding is mirrored by the analysis of posted and received @messages. Very few users posted or received more than 500 @messages. Less than a third of all users posted or received more than 100 @messages, while nearly a sixth of all users posted and received no @message at all. These findings again emphasize that attention on Twitter—this time measured by received @messages—focuses on a very small share of users. An analysis of posted and received retweets offers a similar pattern. The overwhelming majority of users posted or received less than 100 retweets. Nearly a third of all users posted and received no retweets at all. This share is even higher than the share of those users who posted or received no @messages.

These findings show two characteristics of Twitter's use. First, the intensity is highly skewed among different users, with few users using the service—and various conventions—very intensively and most users using it only sparingly. Second, the attention on Twitter—measured by follower counts, received @messages, and received retweets—focuses on only a minority of users, thereby rendering Twitter a far from egalitarian medium.

4.3.4 Publics: Political Support and Opposition

During the campaign, users commented frequently on political parties by mentioning them in hashtags. Later, I will focus on the relationship between the relative importance of political parties as measured by their mention shares on Twitter and their subsequent vote share. For the moment, I want to focus on the number of users who used hashtags to refer to political parties. During the federal-election campaign, users posted messages with three different types of hashtags referring to parties: those containing some variation of party names (e.g. #spd), others containing some variation of a party name followed by a plus sign (e.g. #spd+), and some containing some variation of a party name followed by a minus sign (e.g. #spd-). These two conventions should allow users to mark their messages explicitly either in support of or in opposition to a given party. This usage convention allows researchers to assess the political leanings of a large number of politically vocal users based on their own behavior.

In this section, I will focus on the number of users who were mentioning one of six political parties using hashtags.[3] To do this, I produced a list of the most prominent hashtags referring to one of the six parties either neutrally,[4] positively[5] or negatively.[6] I then calculated the number of users who had used one of these hashtags at least once between June 18, and October 1. I also calculated the sums for all users who had used either a neutral, positive, or a negative hashtag in reference to either of the six parties. Table 4.6 documents the results.

Between June 18 and October 1, 2009, 19,258 users posted messages containing neutral hashtags mentioning one of the six parties included in this analysis. There were roughly three levels of user activity with regard to political parties. The Pirate Party was referred to by 11,747 users. CDU/CSU, SPD, and FDP were mentioned by somewhere between 6500 and 7000 users respectively. The Greens and the Left were mentioned by 3823 and 2514 users. This quick overview already shows that the count of users mentioning political parties does not correspond neither to their size or their electoral chances.

Of the 11,212 users who either used positive or negative hashtags referring to parties, 8723 users posted messages with positive hashtags while 8254 users posted

---

[3]The parties selected for this comparison are five parties that gathered enough votes to enter the German Parliament (i.e. CDU/CSU, SPD, FDP, Bündnis 90/Die Grünen, Die LINKE) and the *Piratenpartei*. The Pirate Party was included in the analysis, despite its subsequent failure to enter Parliament, since it dominated the political online-sphere and received extensive media coverage in the run-up to the election.

[4]The following hashtags were collected to calculate neutral mentions: CDU/CSU: #cdu, #cducsu, #csu; SPD: #spd; FDP: #fdp; Bündnis 90/Die Grünen: #buendnis90, #bündnis, #bündnis90, #bündnis90diegrünen, #bündnis90grüne, #bündnisgrüne, #bündnisgrünen, #die_gruenen, #die_grünen, #diegrünen, #gruene, #grüne, #grünen; Die LINKE: #die_linke, #dielinke, #linke, #linkspartei; Piratenpartei: #piraten, #piratenpartei; Angela Merkel: #angie, #merkel, #angie_merkel, #angelamerkel, #angela_merkel; Frank-Walter Steinmeier: #steinmeier, #fws, #frank_walter_steinmeier, #steini, #frankwaltersteinmeier, #frank_steinmeier. This collection might still exclude some more exotic or more ambiguous spelling variations of the political actors in question. Still, it should account for the vast majority of the hashtags and should thus offer a comprehensive view of the dynamics between them.

[5]The following hashtags were collected to calculate positive mentions. CDU/CSU+: #cdu+, #cducsu+, #csu+; SPD+: #spd+; FDP+: #fdp+; Bündnis 90/Die Grünen+: #diegrünen+, #gruene+,#gruenen+, #grüne+, #grünen+; Die LINKE+: #dielinke+, #linke+, #linkspartei+; Piratenpartei+: #piraten+, #piratenpartei+. This list diverges somewhat from the hashtags collected in the neutral or negative mentions. This is because not all that were used to identify parties were used in combination with plus signs.

[6]The following hashtags were collected to calculate negative party mentions CDU/CSU-: #cdu-, #cducsu-, #csu-; SPD-: #spd-; FDP-: #fdp-; Bündnis 90/Die Grünen-: #die_gruenen-, #gruene-, #gruenen-, #grüne-, #grünen-; Die LINKE-: #die_linke-, #dielinke-, #linkspartei-; Piratenpartei-: #piraten-, #piratenpartei-. This list diverges somewhat from the hashtags collected in the neutral and positive mentions. This is because not all that were used to identify parties were used in combination with minus signs.

4.3 Publics

Table 4.6 User counts explicitly supporting and opposing parties using hashtags

Party	No. of users, neutral hashtags	No. of users, supporting hashtags	No. of users, opposing hashtags	Ratio + vs. −
CDU/CSU	6679	621	6218	0.09
SPD	7155	1012	4975	0.2
FDP	6694	974	3334	0.29
Grüne	3823	1119	2129	0.52
Linke	2514	514	1680	0.3
Piraten	11,747	6777	1544	4.39
total	19,258	8723	8254	1.05

messages with negative hashtags. While this suggests a balanced use of the hashtags, a closer look at the mentions of political parties shows significant differences in the use of positive and negative hashtags referring to parties. By far the most users—6777—referred to the Pirate Party with the use of positive hashtags. All other parties are mentioned positively by much fewer users—somewhere between 500 and 1000 users. This pattern changes once we look at the negative mentions of parties. More than 6000 users referred negatively to the CDU/CSU—the party of the then and future chancellor Angela Merkel. SPD and FDP are also mentioned negatively by many more users than the Greens, the Left and the Pirates but clearly by fewer users than the CDU/CSU.

Calculating the ratio between users mentioning each party positively and negatively allows us to gain a more systematic view of the reactions of the support and opposition each party encountered among the publics on Twitter. The Pirate Party holds the best ratio here, with roughly four users posting positive hashtags for each user who posted negative hashtags. The ratios for the other more established parties are much worse, with the Greens having two users referring to the party with negative hashtags for each user who used positive hashtags and the CDU/CSU having nearly ten users mentioning the party negatively for each user mentioning the party positively. This shows, that for all parties—except the Pirate Party—most users on Twitter were referring to them using negative hashtags.

4.3.5 Publics: Patterns in the Use of Twitter

A number of observations emerged from analyzing the aggregated behavior of politically vocal publics in the German twittersphere during the campaign for the federal election of 2009. German users interacted less through @messages than users whose messages were analyzed in comparable studies. Beyond that, messages containing politically relevant hashtags were posted much more frequently in reaction to outside stimuli—such as content on the Web or Twitter messages posted by other users—than was the case with messages not referring to politics or messages sampled from Twitter's public feed.

Users shifted their behavior in reaction to mediated events. For instance, the total volume of messages commenting on politics increased after highly promoted events, such as the televised candidate debate. During these events, users also interacted less amongst one another and referred less to other content on the Web than at other times. Sudden drops in the share of messages containing @messages, retweets, or URLs on the total volume of messages posted might thus serve as an indicator for the appearance of mediated events of high social importance and collective attention.

The intensity of Twitter use was highly skewed, with few users using Twitter—and various usage conventions—very intensively and most users using Twitter only sparingly. The attention on Twitter—measured by follower counts, received @messages, and received retweets—also focused only on a minority of users, thereby again rendering Twitter a far from egalitarian medium.

During the campaign of 2009, politically vocal publics were composed of users who referred to political parties predominantly using neutral hashtags. Of the users who used hashtags to support or oppose a party publicly, the Pirate Party found the strongest support. While there were users who referred to the established parties positively, their number was vastly dwarfed by the number of users referring to political parties negatively. Thus, political publics on Twitter were sympathetic towards the Pirate Party and highly critical of the established parties.

These findings can be seen as supporting the mediation-hypothesis. Skewness of activity, high dependence on external stimuli, and distorted levels of political support all point to Twitter communication about politics being highly mediated. Based on these mediating factors, it seems plausible that Twitter data might serve as an indicator of attention shifts by Twitter users with regard to political information but hold little information on public opinion at large.

The analysis of convention use over time showed that large shares of messages were posted which contained links to content on the Web and thereby emerged in reaction to political information received by the authors of the messages. Additionally, days on which the shares of messages containing URLs dropped significantly were all days on which mediated political events caught the attention of Twitter users. Again messages were posted in reaction to political information only this time the information was not received by Twitter users online but through televised coverage. This goes to show that many Twitter messages containing political hashtags were posted in direct response to political information and thereby document the attention of their authors towards political information from various sources.

In contrast, it could be shown that only a small minority of Twitter users were posting very high numbers of messages containing politically relevant hashtags. Any message-based approach towards the calculation of public opinion would, therefore, oversample the contributions of this very small group of users significantly. This raises a non-trivial challenge for researchers interpreting Twitter mentions of political actors in Twitter messages as proxies for political opinion.

4.4 Prominent Users

Which actors exert influence over others is one of the most interesting questions with regard to Twitter use, the answer to which is far from simple. The problem starts with the definition of the term *influential*. Is a user influential if her messages are potentially seen by many users? Or is she influential if her messages are retweeted by many users? In which case, is it enough if one of her messages is retweeted many times or does this have to occur regularly before we want to label her influential? What is more, influence could be understood as the ability of users to move other users to action—be it to retweet a message, click on an URL, or donate money. Another metric of influence could be the position of an actor in a network of

Table 4.7 Interpretations and operationalizations for influence on Twitter

Interpretation of influence	Operationalization	Examples
Attention received	Total number of received @messages/@mentions	Jürgens and Jungherr (2011), Jürgens and Jungherr (2015), Dubois and Gaffney (2014), Wu et al. (2011), Subbian and Melville (2011), Sousa et al. (2010), González-Bailón et al. (2013), and Cha et al. (2010)
Information distribution, potential	Various network metrics	Jürgens et al. (2011), Dubois and Gaffney (2014), Subbian and Melville (2011), Lee et al. (2010), Rattanaritnont et al. (2012), González-Bailón et al. (2013), and Bakshy et al. (2011)
Reach	Total number of received retweets	Jürgens and Jungherr (2011), Jürgens and Jungherr (2015), Subbian and Melville (2011), Lee et al. (2010), Cha et al. (2010), and Dang-Xuan et al. (2013)
Reach, potential	Total number of followers	Dubois and Gaffney (2014), Wu et al. (2011), Subbian and Melville (2011), Lee et al. (2010), González-Bailón et al. (2013), and Cha et al. (2010)
Reach to influencers	Qualitative/quantitative case studies of whose tweets are picked up by journalists and the media	Chadwick (2011), Chadwick (2013), and Ausserhofer and Maireder (2013)
Relevant information posted by users	Analysis of tweet content or URLs	Dubois and Gaffney (2014)

interactions between users. The more central a user is in a network, the more important her role is for the distribution of information through the network.

Already these observations show the multitude of possible interpretations of influence on Twitter and the varying operationalizations connected to them. Table 4.7 shows a short list of possible interpretations as to what constitutes influence on Twitter with corresponding operationalizations and studies following these approaches. As it stands, the jury is still out on how these metrics vary within the types of accounts they identify, also because—with few exceptions (Dubois and Gaffney 2014; Lee et al. 2010)—researchers tend to make a choice without systematically comparing the results of different operationalizations. The question of influence on Twitter becomes even more complicated, when we factor in that influence on Twitter is probably highly interconnected with influence and information on other online services—such as blogs, news platforms, forums, or Facebook (Gomez-Rodriguez et al. 2013).

4.4 Prominent Users

For the purposes of this analysis, I decided to focus on two intuitive metrics of influence on Twitter—the number of incoming @messages/@mentions and the number of retweets a user received. Thus, this analysis focuses on *prominent* users, not necessarily *influential* ones. This operationalization might miss some finer points of influence among politically vocal Twitter users. Still, it offers a very intuitive assessment of users who featured prominently in the messages posted by others and their behavior on Twitter during the campaign.

@messages, @mentions, and retweets serve as indicators that Twitter users found specific accounts relevant to their interests and either decided to interact with these accounts or to distribute their content further. If we calculate the total amount of incoming @messages, @mentions, and received retweets for each user, we can rank them by their relative prominence in the messages posted by others. Focusing on the most interacted with users allows us to identify the actors whom other users thought to be of relevance to their interest. These ranked lists can be seen as results of a collective curating process, to which each user posting an @message, @mention, or retweet contributed unwittingly. This curating process allows us to focus on the users who were deemed most relevant by the Twitter community.

4.4.1 Prominent Users: General Observations

To identify the most prominent users, for each I calculated the total amount of @messages, @mentions, and retweets received between June 18, and October 1, 2009. Following this, I ranked users separately, based on their @message and @mention count and their retweet counts. I then identified the 100 users with the highest @message and @mention counts and the 100 users with the highest retweet count. Based on this, I identified 166 unique users. Forty-four users appeared on both top 100 lists. The top 100 ranked users based on @messages and @mentions received from 16,232 to 1443 during the campaign. The top 100 users ranked based on retweets received from 15,534 to 634.

One question often asked by researchers is whether digital services benefit new political actors or whether traditional political actors end up dominating the online sphere, as they are dominating other areas of political communication. This has become known as the normalization vs transformation debate (Chaffee and Metzger 2001; Margolis and Resnick 2000; Schweitzer 2011). For Twitter, the results have remained mixed. In studies based on evidence from Scandinavian countries, the most active users tended to be part of established political elites (Larsson and Moe 2012). Other studies from Germany showed high rates of interaction for new political actors—such as bloggers, communication consultants, and supporters of new political parties (Dang-Xuan et al. 2013; Jungherr 2014a; Jürgens and Jungherr 2015). Some researchers argue that Twitter has changed the political process in a way that has empowered non-traditional political actors. They base this assessment on the fact that messages by some Twitter users are picked up by traditional political elites or the media, thereby gaining access to the traditional political communication sphere (Ausserhofer and Maireder 2013; Chadwick 2013). Table 4.8 shows the shares that users, who could be categorized as either traditional or new political actors, had among the top 100 lists based on the @messages, @mentions, and retweets they received.

Table 4.8 shows that between June 18 and October 1, among the 100 users who received the most @messages and @mentions were 13 who could be characterized as traditional political actors. These were campaigners, parties, and politicians (4), accounts of traditional media—such as TV-stations, TV-programs, or newspapers—(6), journalists (2) and political activists without party affiliation (1). Seventy-one users could be characterized as new political actors. These were bloggers (29), social media professionals, or programmers (16), political supporters of parties who mentioned their affiliation in the biography or on linked websites (8), users with other stated professions (6), and Twitter users with no further specification (12). There was also one satirical account amongst the 100 most interacted with accounts and 15 accounts whose account holders could not be identified by the time of the analysis, as they had been shut down. It is likely that these 15 accounts for the most part would have contributed to the share of new political actors, as they appear to be largely the accounts of normal Twitter users who had either stopped tweeting since the campaign, switched their accounts, or had their accounts shut down.

The shares between traditional and new political actors were somewhat different with regard to the 100 accounts that received most retweets. Here we find 31 accounts belonging to traditional political actors. This difference is largely caused by the higher number of political activists among the 100 retweeted accounts (14) and the somewhat higher number of accounts belonging to traditional media (10). The share of campaigners, parties, politicians (4), and journalists (3) resembled their shares of the 100 most interacted with users very closely. Another difference was the number of accounts which could not be identified (1).

These findings indicate that new political actors were clearly more prominent among the most interacted with and the most retweeted accounts than traditional political actors. Nevertheless, it is important to note that neither type of political actor was dominating the top 100 lists completely. During the campaign of 2009, Twitter, therefore, was a medium in which both traditional and new political actors were prominent. However, it is striking that only four accounts belonged to professional campaigners, parties, or politicians and that only six of the most mentioned and ten of the most retweeted accounts belonged to traditional media. Attention on Twitter thus clearly focused on actors who were expanding the sphere of political communication.

4.4.2 Prominent Users: Message-Centric Analysis

Let us move to the analysis of basic patterns in Twitter use by the most prominent users during the course of the campaign. Table 4.9 shows the direct comparison

4.4 Prominent Users

Table 4.8 New and traditional political actors among the most prominent Twitter users

User type		Share of users who received most @messages (in %)	Share of users who received most retweets (in %)
Traditional political actors	Activists	13	31
	Campaigners/Parties/Politicians	1	14
	Journalists	4	4
	Traditional media	2	3
		6	10
New political actors	Bloggers	71	66
	Non-traditional news platforms/news aggregators	29	13
	Political supporters (party mentioned in bio or on linked website)	–	5
	Social media professionals/Programers	8	9
	Twitter users (no further specification)	16	21
	Other professions	12	11
		6	7
Satire		1	2
Not identifiable		15	1

Table 4.9 Conventions used in all messages and the political communication space posted by the most prominent users between June 18, and October 1, 2009

Usage convention	All messages	Pol. comm. space
Messages	404,365	56,513
Messages containing neither @messages, retweets, or URLs	136,782	11,041
@messages	178,154	10,240
Retweets	37,415	17,628
Messages containing URLs	118,790	38,459
Users	166	165

Table 4.10 Message to convention ratio for the most prominent users

Message to convention ratio	All messages	Pol. comm. space
% messages containing neither @messages, retweets, or URLs	33.8	19.5
% @messages	44	18
% retweets	9.3	31.2
% messages with URLs	29.4	68.1
Average no. of daily messages per user	23	3

between all messages posted by the most prominent users and their messages contributing to the political communication space.

Between June 18, and October 1, 2009, the 166 most prominent users in the data set posted a total of 404,365 messages. 0.5 % of all users in the data set thus posted 4 % of all messages. Hundred and sixty five of the most prominent users contributed to the political communication space by posting 56,513 messages. Thus, 0.5 % of all users contributing to the political space posted 6 % of all messages contributing to the political communication space. Although the most prominent users posted a disproportionally large share of messages—overall and contributing to the political communication space—these ratios show the most messages were contributed by other users. Fourteen percent of all messages posted by the most prominent users contributed to the political communication space. This compares with 9 % of the messages posted by all users. Prominent users were thus more actively contributing to the political communication space than all users.

Table 4.10 shows that, as with all users, messages contributing to the political communication space contained more retweets and hyperlinks than all messages posted by prominent users. Again, this can be seen as an indicator that tweets commenting on politics were more frequently posted in reaction to content on the Web or on Twitter than messages overall. Compared to the usage patterns of all users, prominent users were posting more messages containing @messages and retweets. Beyond that, the average number of daily messages posted by users was significantly higher than the average number of daily messages calculated for all users.

In general, the patterns found in the Twitter use of prominent users resemble those found with all users. Again, messages referring to politics in reaction to outside stimuli—either Twitter messages that were retweeted or Web content that was linked to—were posted more frequently than messages overall. In contrast to all users, prominent users interacted much more frequently with other users than normal users. Still, these interactions happened predominantly in messages not contributing to the political communication space. This higher interaction rate and the generally higher activity on Twitter, as shown by the average number of daily messages posted by users, are the only two major differences in the behavior of prominent users when compared with the behavior of all users.

4.4.3 Prominent Users: User-Centric Analysis

The previous section illustrated that the behavior of all users varied widely with regard to their use of Twitter generally and in the intensity with which they employed usage conventions. This finding is replicated when examining the 166 prominent users.

Table 4.11 offers a first overview of prominent Twitter users' behavior. We see that the by now familiar spread between average and median values in the use of various conventions is also apparent in the use of Twitter by prominent users. This is an indicator that in this population usage intensity also varied widely, with a few users raising the average values based on their heavy use of Twitter. In general, prominent users were clearly among the most active users in the sample. If you compare their usage behavior with that of all users, we see that the median prominent user was posting more messages, contributed more strongly to the political communication space, had more followers and followees on election day, had posted and received more @messages, and more retweets than the median user in general. The strong showing in received @messages and retweets is clearly no surprise, as the users were selected based on their strong performance in these metrics. Nevertheless, between the median values of prominent users and users

Table 4.11 Usage statistics for most prominent users, aggregated between June 18, and October 1, 2009

Usage convention	Max.	Min.	Avg.	Median
Messages	15,393	54	2438	1810
Political communication space	6194	0	224	51
Followers on election day	65,301	10	2192	965
Followers on election day	6940	1	743	312
@messages, posted	9244	3	1074	569
@messages, received	16,232	147	1926	1569
Retweets, posted	2484	0	225	100
Retweets, received	15,534	54	1001	708

in general in all other categories the number of differences is striking. The most prominent users were thus clearly among the most active users during the campaign.

During the course of the campaign, ten prominent users posted more than 5000 messages. Twenty users posted less than 500 messages. The majority of prominent users posted somewhere between 5000 and 1000 messages. This stands in stark contrast to the findings of the message volume posted by all users. There, we saw that the overwhelming majority of all users had posted less than 500 messages during the 3 months under examination. Thus, the overwhelming majority of users, who were the focus of attention by other users, as manifested in interaction and retweet counts, were among the most active users with regard to the volume of messages posted by them. A similar but more moderate picture emerges once we examine their contributions to the political communication space. Nine prominent users had posted more than 1000 messages contributing to the political communication space. While a total of 56 prominent users had posted 100 messages or more, contributing to the political communication space. Thirty-six prominent users had posted ten messages or less. This stands somewhat in contrast to the behavior of all users. We recall that the overwhelming majority of all users posted less than 100 messages contributing to the political communication space, with half of all users posting only four messages or less. Thus, prominent users contributed more strongly to the political communication space than normal users.

The differences between prominent users and users in general becomes even more apparent once we examine their follower and followee counts. Eighty-two of the prominent users had more than 1000 followers on election day, while only 12 had less than 100 followers. This offers an extreme contrast to the follower counts of all users, of whom roughly a third had less than 100 followers. Thus, users who were highly interacted with and highly retweeted tended to be among the most followed users in the data set. These findings are mirrored by the ranking of users based on the number of accounts followed by them—their number of followees. Thirty-eight prominent users followed more than 1000 accounts. While only 25 prominent users followed less than 100 accounts. This is a striking contrast to the median user, who followed 45 accounts, a contrast that indicates how prominent users tended not only to be followed by more accounts than normal users but also to follow more accounts.

The analysis of incoming and posted @messages reinforces the previous findings that prominent users tended to use Twitter more intensively than normal users. Sixty-four prominent users posted more than 1000 @messages, while only 25 prominent users posted less than 100 @messages. In comparison, half of all users posted nine @messages or less. This shows that the users who received most @messages during the course of the campaign were more likely to interact with other users than users in general. To see prominent users as heavy recipients of incoming @messages comes as no surprise, because this was one of the criteria for identifying prominent users. Fifty-five prominent users received more than 2000 @messages, while only 17 users received less than 500 @messages. In comparison, the median user received only seven @messages during the run of the campaign.

These findings are mirrored by the analysis of retweets posted and received by prominent users. Seven prominent users posted more than 1000 retweets during

4.4 Prominent Users 91

the course of the campaign, while only 12 users posted less than ten retweets. In comparison, half of all users posted three retweets or less. These numbers are significantly lower than the volume of posted @messages. Still, so far as the intensity of this feature's use is concerned, the difference between all users and prominent users remains stable. Examining prominent users based on the number of retweets they received also gives rise to no surprise, as this was the second criterion by which prominence was determined. Fifty-one prominent users received more than 1000 retweets, while only 11 prominent users received less than 100 retweets. Again, this is in striking contrast to the distribution of received retweets among all users, where half received two retweets or less.

These findings illustrate two characteristics of Twitter as a political communication space. First, the skewness in the distribution of activity, attention, and convention use, which had been found in the analysis of all users' behavior is also apparent in the behavior of prominent users—although, to a slightly lesser degree. User behavior on Twitter thus appears to be far from stable, no matter which population of users is under examination. Second, the users identified by their prominence in two categories—received @messages and received retweets—were also in every other category much more active or received much more attention than the average or the median user. This could be an indicator that prominence in one metric might also lead to prominence in another.

4.4.4 Prominent Users: Political Support

Of the 166 most prominent users in the data set, 74 used hashtags referring to parties followed by a plus, thereby signalling their support for the political party. The use of these hashtags allows us to assess the strength of political parties' support among the most prominent users in the data set. Table 4.12 shows the number of users who referred to either party by a supporting hashtag.

A quick glance at Table 4.12 shows already that the share of support for political parties by prominent Twitter users did not mirror the support these parties had on election day. The Pirate Party had by far the strongest support among prominent

Table 4.12 Political support by prominent users

Party	No. supporting users
CDU/CSU	20
SPD	24
FDP	17
Bündnis 90/Die Grünen	27
Die LINKE	9
Piratenpartei	54
Total	74

Twitter users, followed at some distance by the Greens, the SPD, the CDU, and the FDP. Only nine users posted hashtags supporting the Leftists.

4.4.5 Prominent Users: Patterns in the Use of Twitter

Analyzing the behavior of prominent users offered a series of observations on the nature of Twitter as a political communication space. It could be shown that a mixture of traditional and new political actors were among the most prominent users. Traditional political actors were somewhat more prominent among the top 100 retweeted accounts, while new political actors were somewhat more prominent among the top 100 interacted with accounts. It is important, though, to note that neither type of political actor was dominating the top 100 lists. During the campaign of 2009, Twitter, therefore, was a medium in which both traditional and new political actors were prominent. However, it is striking that, as was the situation earlier, only four accounts belonged to professional campaigners, parties, or politicians and that only six of the most mentioned and ten of the most retweeted accounts belonged to traditional media. Attention on Twitter thus clearly focused on actors who were expanding the sphere of political communication.

The patterns found in prominent Twitter users' behavior roughly resembled patterns found in the analysis of behavior by all users. Again, in reaction to outside stimuli—either Twitter messages that were retweeted or Web content that was linked to—messages referring to politics were posted more frequently than messages overall. In contrast to all users, prominent users interacted much more frequently through @messages. Still, these interactions happened predominantly in messages not contributing to the political communication space.

Political parties had similar levels of support by prominent Twitter users and by all politically vocal Twitter users. German Twitter users tended to support the Pirate Party most strongly on Twitter, followed by the Greens. These levels of support were thus clearly different from those in the general population.

The skewness in the distribution of activity, attention, and convention use, which had been found in the analysis of the behavior of all users is also apparent—although, to a slightly lesser degree—in the behavior of prominent users. User behavior on Twitter thus appears to be far from stable, no matter which user population is under examination. Furthermore, the users identified by their prominence in two categories—received @messages and received retweets—were also in every other category much more active or received much more attention, than the average or the median user, which might indicate that prominence in one metric might also lead to prominence in another. In total, these findings thereby further support the mediation-hypothesis.

4.5 Politicians

4.5.1 Politicians: General Observations

After analyzing the usage behavior of all users and the behavior of prominent users, the behavior of politicians is of obvious further interest. Unfortunately, there is no list of Twitter accounts for all candidates running in the federal election of 2009. Instead, I collected the accounts of all members in the 17th Parliament—elected in 2009—and checked if they were active during the campaign. In this way, I was able to identify 90 politicians who were successful in securing a parliamentary seat during the election of 2009 and who used Twitter during the course of the campaign. Identifying this core group limits the following analysis to accounts of politicians who were successful in their campaign. Accordingly, I ignore candidates who were unsuccessful. As a consequence, candidates representing the Pirate Party are missing from this section, although supporters of the party were a major factor in the analyses from previous sections.

Table 4.13 lists the accounts of politicians belonging to the five parties represented in the *17th Bundestag*. As the table shows, the shares of politicians representing parties did not mirror the shares of seats these parties had collected in the election. In Germany, politicians of small parties—the FDP and the Greens—were more likely to be using Twitter than politicians representing bigger parties. The German Conservatives especially were underrepresented on Twitter, compared with their share of seats in Parliament. This finding corresponds with the available literature on adoption patterns of politicians in the USA where politicians belonging to opposition parties appear to be using the service more frequently than politicians from parties in government (Golbeck et al. 2010; Peterson 2012).

There are two possible explanations for these different adoption patterns. First, candidates for parties with an older voter base—such as CDU/CSU, SPD, Die LINKE—might be using Twitter less enthusiastically than politicians of parties with a younger voter base—such as FDP or Bündnis 90/Die Grünen. Second, it could also be that candidates of smaller parties have more trouble gaining media attention with smaller campaign budgets and thus might be using Twitter to offset this disadvantage. With the limitation of the existing data set, it is not possible to test these competing hypotheses.

Table 4.13 Count of politicians who were using Twitter

Party	No. of politicians	% accounts	% seats 2009	Diff.
CDU/CSU	19	21	38	−17
SPD	22	24	23	1
FDP	25	27	15	12
Bündnis 90/Die Grünen	19	21	11	10
Die LINKE	5	6	12	−6
Total	90			

4.5.2 Politicians: Message-Centric Analysis

Let us start with the analysis of basic patterns in politicians' Twitter use during the course of the campaign. The comparison of these patterns with the behavior of all users and the behavior of prominent users enables us to assess Twitter use by politicians. Table 4.14 shows the messages posted and the usage conventions employed by politicians between June 18, and October 1, 2009.

The 90 successful candidates included in this sample posted 16,475 messages during the course of the campaign. Of these, 4261 messages, roughly 26%, contributed to the political communication space. This compares with 14% of all messages posted by prominent users and 9% of messages posted by all users. Thus, unsurprisingly, politicians were the user group most likely to contribute to the political communication space.

Table 4.15 shows that by far most messages posted by politicians contained neither @messages, retweets, or URLs. The share of these messages amongst all posted by them is much greater than the share of these messages for all users and for prominent users. Politicians especially posted much fewer messages containing URLs than all users. This clearly shows that their Twitter activity was less dependent on outside stimuli—such as content published on the web. The average number of daily messages posted by politicians was also somewhat lower than the average number of daily messages posted by all users.

Table 4.14 Conventions used in all messages and the political communication space posted by politicians between June 18, and October 1, 2009

Usage convention	All messages	Pol. comm. space
Messages	16,475	4261
Messages containing neither @messages, retweets, or URLs	10,083	2645
@messages	2569	308
Retweets	499	233
Messages containing URLs	4203	1335
Users	90	75

Table 4.15 Message to convention ratio for politicians using Twitter

Message to convention ratio	All messages	Pol. comm. space
% messages containing neither @messages, retweets, or URLs	61.2	62.1
% @messages	15.6	7.2
% retweets	3	5.5
% URLs	25.5	31.3
Average no. of daily messages per user	1.7	0.5

4.5.3 Politicians: User-Centric Analysis

The previous sections have shown that users diverged widely in the intensity of their Twitter use, various usage conventions and the attention that they received on Twitter. This skewness in the behavior is also to be expected in the use of Twitter by politicians. Table 4.16 offers an overview of Twitter's use by politicians.

This table shows that the gap between average and median values is also visible in the usage of Twitter by politicians. Again, this is an indicator that the intensive use of Twitter, various usage conventions, and the attention some of them received shifted average values to a higher degree than median values. Politicians tended to be much less active Twitter users than the prominent users. Only five politicians posted more than 500 messages between June 18, and October 1, 2009, whilst 40 posted less than 100 messages. Thus, the majority of politicians posted somewhat fewer messages than the average and the median user. Even the most active politicians were not among the most active politically vocal Twitter users during the campaign. This impression is reinforced once we examine politicians and their contributions to the political communication space, where only six politicians posted more than 100 messages, while 40 politicians posted less than five, of which 18 posted none. Thus, politicians tended to contribute to the political communication space by posting significantly fewer messages than prominent users, but by somewhat more messages than normal users. Again, politicians proved themselves to be far from the most active politically vocal Twitter users during the campaign.

We find a similar picture once we look at the number of followers and followees of politicians on election day. Nine politicians had more than 1000 followers on election day, while 27 had less than 100. The median politician had 181 followers, compared with the median prominent user, who had 965 followers on election day, a number which appears rather small. Compared with the median users, who had 43 followers on election day, the number of followers of the median politician appears a bit higher. Even politicians with the highest following on Twitter did not reach the levels of the most actively followed politically vocal users. Still, politicians tended to have more followers than normal users. A similar picture emerges once we examine the number of accounts followed by politicians. Only seven politicians followed

Table 4.16 Usage statistics of politicians aggregated between June 18, and October 1, 2009

Usage convention	Max.	Min.	Avg.	Median
Messages	1226	5	175	111
Political communication space	469	0	30	7
Followers on election day	3722	6	375	181
Followers on election day	2452	0	250	79
@messages, posted	431	0	26	5
@messages, received	792	0	106	39
Retweets, posted	53	0	5	1
Retweets, received	282	0	34	12

more than 1000 accounts, whilst 51 politicians followed less than 100 accounts, of which ten followed ten or fewer accounts. The median politician followed 79 accounts on election day. This compares with 312 accounts followed by the median prominent users and 45 accounts followed by the median user. With regard to online attention received and online attention paid, politicians were again far from the most active of the politically vocal Twitter users in the data set. Still, in contrast to the volume of messages posted by politicians, they were also clearly more prominent than the median user with regard to the number of users who followed them and the number of users they themselves followed.

The direct comparison between @messages posted and received by politicians offers a somewhat different picture. Politicians clearly posted less @messages than prominent users. Even in comparison with all users, politicians showed a lower propensity to post @messages. Only seven politicians posted more than 100 @messages, 58 posted 10 or fewer messages, while 19 posted no @message at all. The median politician posted five @messages. Compared with 569 @messages posted by the median prominent users and nine @messages posted by the median user, this shows that politicians used Twitter less frequently than other user groups to interact with other users. While politicians tended to be among the users posting comparably few @messages, they tended to receive more @messages than normal users. Four politicians received more than 500 @messages, while 17 received ten or fewer @messages. The median politician received 39 @messages. These were fewer than the median prominent user, who received 1569 @messages, but also clearly more than the median user, who received seven @messages during the same time span. Although politicians by comparison tended to interact seldom with other users, they themselves were more often than general users the focus of interaction attempts.

The analysis of retweets posted and received by politicians offers a similar picture. Only 17 politicians posted ten or more retweets, 43 posted no retweet at all, whilst the median politician posted one retweet. This compares to three retweets posted by the median user and 100 retweets posted by the median prominent users, leading us to conclude that politicians tended to post retweets less frequently than users overall. As was the case with @messages, politicians tended to be more often interacted with than interacting with other people through retweets. Thirteen politicians received more than 100 retweets, while 42 politicians received ten retweets or less. Only eight politicians received no retweets at all, while the median politician received 12 retweets. This ratio compares with two retweets received by the median user and 708 retweets received by the median prominent user. Again, politicians were not among the most popular users with regard to retweets received, but they were clearly more retweeted than normal users. Although politicians tended to pay little attention to the messages of other users—at least if you measure attention in retweets—their messages received more attention than the tweets of normal users.

These findings illustrate various characteristics in the use of Twitter by successful candidates in the campaign for the 2009 federal elections. First, the skewness in the distributions of individual activity, attention, and conventions use, which we have already found for all politically vocal users and for prominent users, was also apparent for the use of Twitter by politicians. A few politicians used Twitter intensively during the course of the campaign, received considerable attention by other users and interacted with them strongly. In contrast, most politicians used Twitter only moderately, received limited attention, and interacted only sparingly with other users.

Second, politicians were far from the most active users of Twitter during the run of the campaign. For most metrics examined here, usage patterns of politicians conformed roughly with the median values of these metrics for all users. Only with regard to the @messages and retweets did the usage behavior of politicians diverge from that of all users' median. Politicians tended to post fewer @messages and retweets than users in general, but tended to receive more @messages and retweets. This is an indicator that politicians used Twitter only sparingly to interact with other users. Still, through their function as candidates for Parliament, they received somewhat more attention online than other users. Never did politicians come close to the metrics characterizing prominent users.

4.5.4 Politicians: Content

A number of studies have analyzed the content of messages posted by politicians. These focused on determining whether or not there exist any underpinning empirical patterns for politicians' usage of Twitter across various countries and election cycles. Nearly all studies used different coding schemes, thus making the direct comparison between them rather difficult. Nevertheless, a number of observations about the use of Twitter by politicians appear to be stable across most studies. For instance, politicians across countries and election cycles tended to use Twitter predominantly to post information on their campaign activities, policy statements, and links to their own websites. Explicit calls for action to their supporters—such as get out the vote mobilizing or fundraising requests—were much less frequent. Interactions with other users on Twitter were also very infrequent and if present mostly directed at other politicians or journalists (Jungherr 2014b).

One of the most elaborate coding schemes of Twitter messages posted by politicians was proposed by Graham et al. (2013) for the UK. I will use this coding scheme as a template to examine the Twitter messages posted by 87 candidates for Parliament who were using Twitter during the campaign of 2009. I follow the original coding scheme in differentiating between the function of a tweet (e.g. being an update from the campaign trail, call to vote, or a reference to a media report) and its content, or primary topic, (e.g. commenting on campaign & party affairs, opponents, or specific political issues). In deciding on categories for coding, I largely followed the original coding scheme but adapted it somewhat for the specifics of German politics. For example, the original coding scheme used a category for tweets commenting on animal rights, a topic of little prominence in German politics. In contrast, it lacked a category for tweets referring to energy supply, a topic—especially in the context of nuclear and regenerative power—of great importance in Germany. Still, the backbone of the coding scheme remained very much based on the original study.

To understand how German politicians used Twitter during the campaign, I analyzed the content of messages posted on the accounts, which I could link to candidates running for the 2009 federal election. For my content analysis, I focused on all messages posted between July 3, and 9—the last week before the election when Parliament was still in session—and September 20–26—the last week of the campaign. This choice allows for a comparison between Twitter activities of candidates at the very beginning and at the height of the campaign, thus allowing for an assessment of whether the behavior on Twitter by politicians changed or remained fundamentally the same. Following these selection criteria, I coded 2528 messages by hand, which were posted by 87 candidates. In the following analysis, I will present the aggregated results for all politicians and, following this, also differentiated for politicians of different parties, to identify potential party-specific behavioral patterns.

In a first step—following Graham et al. (2013)—I coded all messages based on a tweet's function. I differentiated between four general categories of functions that tweets posted by politicians could fulfil. Politicians might post tweets informing their followers about elements of the campaign. Within this category, I differentiated between tweets in which politicians acknowledged the work of others (individuals or institutions) or thanked their supporters, tweets in which they promoted their campaign or their profiles on other online services, messages promoting the party stance, messages announcing personal political positions, those referencing media reports or reports by non-traditional sources as well as those messages updating their followers about the campaign trail or parliamentary work. Politicians might also use Twitter to interact with others. Within this category, I differentiated between messages in which politicians actively critiqued or argued with stances taken by political actors; messages that were part of a public exchange between politicians and other users; and messages in which politicians actively requested public input on various matters. Also, politicians might use Twitter to mobilize their followers. Within this category, I differentiated between messages that were calls to action and calls to vote. Finally, I collected informal messages posted by politicians, either containing humor or personal comments and information. Table 4.17 shows the percentage of messages posted by politicians during 2 weeks of the campaign of 2009 corresponding with these categories.

The table reveals that most tweets posted by politicians contained information about politics or the campaign, followed by a wide margin with messages in which politicians interacted with other users and those in which they used an informal tone. It is significant here that only a negligible amount of messages were geared towards mobilizing followers. German politicians predominantly posted tweets containing factual information. Interactions geared towards integrating users in the campaign by mobilizing them and messages constituting conversational interaction with other users were comparatively few and far between. It also seems noteworthy that there are only minor shifts in the content of messages posted by politicians during the

4.5 Politicians

Table 4.17 Functions in tweets posted by politicians

Function	Usage practice	% (July 3–9)	% (September 20–26)
Informing		74.4	76.8
	Acknowledgment of others	0.9	1.1
	Campaign promotion	2.1	4
	Party stance	0.7	1.2
	Position taking	7.7	6.5
	Reference to media report	5.8	8
	Reference to non-traditional source	13.4	0.7
	Update from campaign trail	38	54.9
	Update from parliamentary work	5.8	0.4
Interacting		14.3	17
	Critiquing/arguing	1.5	3.4
	Public exchange	12.7	13.4
	Requesting public input	0.1	0.2
Mobilizing		0.6	2.5
	Call to action	0.5	0.5
	Call to vote	0.1	2
Informal		10.7	3.2
	Humor	0.1	0.6
	Personal	10.6	2.6
Other		0.1	0.6
Total no. messages		861	1667
Total no. users		70	87

beginning and during the last week of the campaign. We do find less informal messages and somewhat more tweets that try to mobilize followers. While the total amount of messages posted nearly doubles, there are only minor shifts in the content posted by politicians.

Of all messages posted by politicians, I identified those contributing to a specific topic—either the campaign, political issues, or world events—and coded them in line with the topic to which they were contributing. I grouped all campaign-related messages into those generally commenting on the campaign and party affairs, the electoral system, the horse-race, and political opponents. Among the messages commenting on general political issues, I furthermore differentiated between those commenting on the distinct issues of civil rights, consumer protection, defense, economy, education, energy, environment, Europe, family policy, the financial crisis, foreign policy, health, homeland security and police, immigration, infrastructure, Internet policy, social welfare, and taxes. Beyond that, I also coded messages in which politicians commented on world events unrelated to the campaign, for example the death of Michael Jackson or the human rights situation in Iran. Table 4.18 shows the percentage of messages corresponding with these categories that were posted by politicians during the 2 weeks included in the analysis.

Table 4.18 Primary topic of tweets posted by politicians

Primary topic of tweet		% (July 3–9)	% (September 20–26)
Campaign		9.9	43.6
	Campaign & party affairs	1.4	16.2
	Electoral system	1.4	1.4
	Horse-race	1.1	5.3
	Opponents	6	20.7
Issues		54.8	55.2
	Civil rights	0.6	2.7
	Consumer protection	3.4	1
	Defense	5.7	2.2
	Economy	8	8.4
	Education	2.9	4.3
	Energy	8	8
	Environment	4.9	1.6
	Europe	1.4	0.6
	Family policy	0.9	0.2
	Financial crisis	2.9	0.8
	Foreign policy	0.6	1
	Health	0.6	0.8
	Homeland security/police	1.4	6.5
	Immigration	0.3	0.8
	Infrastructure	1.4	1.8
	Internet policy	5.2	4.3
	Social welfare	1.7	5.1
	Taxes	4.9	5.1
World events		35.1	1
Total no. messages		348	489
% topical messages		40.4	29.3

When interpreting these results, it is important to keep in mind that the high share of messages contributing to world events during the week of July 3–9 is almost exclusively due to roughly 100 messages posted by Omid Nouripour (Bündnis 90/ Die Grünen)—a German politician with Iranian roots—who posted a large number of messages commenting on the human rights situation in Iran. This value is probably best treated as an incident-based outlier. The shifts in the percentages of messages commenting on topics between July 3–9 and September 20–26 are thus not entirely due to a potential shift in overall Twitter behavior by the majority of politicians during the campaign, but instead originated from Omid Nouripour's shift to posting more campaign focused messages.

The first observation has to be that tweets contributing to specific topics were in the minority during the campaign. Between 60 and 70 % of all messages posted by politicians during these 2 weeks were general updates or exchanges without a clear topical context. When we focus on topically relevant messages, we see that during the course of the campaign messages directly commenting on the campaign increased in volume. This can be linked to the overall increase in messages commenting on their own campaign or party or addressing the performance of opponents. When analyzing political issues mentioned by politicians, we see that no single issue dominates within the political twittersphere. In the week of the election, messages mentioning the economy, education, as well as homeland security and police dominate somewhat but not extraordinarily so.

These results show that politicians did not use Twitter during the campaign predominantly as a tool to communicate about political issues. Instead, most messages seemed to be posted as contributing to non-issue specific updates about the campaign or the politician's schedule. During the time in question here, Twitter seems to have been assigned only symbolic purpose by political actors because it is not consistently utilized for the promotion of political issues or the mobilization of supporters. These patterns remained largely stable across various parties, although politicians of the SPD, FDP, and Die LINKE were somewhat more active in commenting on political issues emphasized by the general campaigns of their parties, indicating that Twitter might serve in some cases as a source to measure campaign agendas. Still, it is important to note that roughly only a fourth to a third of all messages posted by politicians were referring to specific issues.

4.5.5 Politicians: Patterns in the Use of Twitter

Analyzing the behavior of politicians using Twitter offered a series of observations allowing for the assessment of Twitter's role in German political communication. Candidates belonging to small parties with comparatively young supporters used Twitter disproportionately more often than candidates of bigger parties with comparatively older supporters.

Politicians tended to post fewer messages containing usage conventions than normal users. The overwhelming majority of messages posted by politicians contained neither @messages, nor retweets, nor URLs. Amongst all messages posted by politicians, the share without usage convention is far greater than the share by both all and prominent users. Politicians in particular posted considerably fewer messages containing URLs than other users. This discrepancy shows that Twitter activity by politicians is clearly less dependent on outside stimuli—such as content published on the Web. Additionally, the average number of daily messages posted by politicians was somewhat lower than the average number of daily messages posted by all users.

The skewness in the distributions of individual activity, attention, and conventions use which we have already found for all politically vocal users and for prominent users was also apparent in politicians' use of Twitter. Thus, a few politicians used Twitter intensively during the run of campaign, received considerable attention by other users, and interacted with them strongly. In contrast, most politicians used Twitter only moderately, received limited attention, and interacted only sparingly with other users. Politicians were also far from the most active users of Twitter during the course of the campaign.

For most metrics examined here, usage patterns of politicians conformed roughly with the median values of these metrics for all users. In regard only to the @messages and retweets did the usage behavior of politicians diverge from that of the all users' median. Politicians tended to post less @messages and retweets than users in general, but tended to receive more @messages and retweets. This is an indicator that politicians used Twitter only sparingly to interact with other users, albeit receiving more attention than other users due to the public exposure they received in their role as candidates running for national Parliament. However, politicians never came close to the metrics characterizing prominent users.

The use of Twitter by politicians during the campaign of 2009 resembled the use of Twitter by politicians in other countries. German politicians tended predominantly to post messages containing information on the campaign while interacting with other Twitter users only sporadically. Twitter was, therefore, used much more strongly as a broadcasting medium than a medium for public dialogue. In contrast to findings from studies in other countries, German politicians posted significantly fewer messages geared towards mobilizing their followers to act or to vote. This restrictive usage pattern may be read as an indicator that candidates considered Twitter a less viable means to garner grass-roots support for their campaigns than politicians in other countries. Alternatively, we may also interpret this behavior as a further case of online services being used by German candidates more as a symbol for campaign activities than in substantial support of their campaigns (Jungherr 2012; Jungherr and Schoen 2013). The findings indicate that candidate activities remained pretty much focused on documenting personal campaigning activities. Politicians used Twitter predominantly to summarize, log, and symbolize their general campaign activity rather than as a grass-roots communication tool to mobilize supporters and interact with potential voters.

4.6 Publics, Prominent Users, and Politicians in Their Use of Twitter

The findings in this chapter showed that while many users posted Twitter messages referring to politics, only a comparatively small group posted many messages. Half of all users in this data set posted four or fewer messages contributing to the political communication space while the most active user posted 17,093. Thus while Twitter is clearly a medium for political references and interaction, most politically vocal users do not use it as such very frequently and when they do it is usually in reaction to big mediated political events. Their tweets can be seen as reaction to a stimulus they received, thus documenting their attention toward politics at that moment. This reading is further supported by the finding that nearly 60% of all messages

4.6 Publics, Prominent Users, and Politicians in Their Use of Twitter

contributing to the political communication space contained URLs. A clear majority of messages referring to politics thus were posted in reaction to outside stimuli—be they politically relevant content on the Web or the coverage of mediated political events. The analysis of Twitter messages accordingly promises insights into what kind of political information caught the attention of politically vocal Twitter users during the campaign. On the other hand, the skewness of the activity and political support of users makes it doubtful that Twitter allows valid inferences on the relative strength of political actors. Both these observations support the mediation-hypothesis.

The attention of Twitter users focused on a very small set of other users. This could be shown by the distribution of @messages and retweets that all users included in the data set received during the period under analysis. Half of all users received seven or fewer @messages and two or fewer retweets while the top ranked users received 16,232 @messages and 15,534 retweets. Twitter can be seen, therefore, as a far from egalitarian communication space with few users receiving most attention—measured in interactions—and most users receiving almost no attention at all.

Among users who were most interacted with—be it through @messages or retweets—new political actors—, such as social media professionals, bloggers, and normal Twitter users—had a very strong presence. Traditional political actors—such as politicians or journalists—were somewhat less visible. Thus, at least in 2009, traditional political actors did not achieve high levels of prominence in the political communication space on Twitter. It will be interesting to see if this finding remains stable through different election cycles. Once politicians and journalists gather experiences with their professional personae online and put more effort into their Twitter presence, they might increasingly become the focus of interactions by other Twitter users. This could be seen as a process of political normalization on Twitter, with traditional political actors growing more central in the interactions of Twitter users and thereby potentially gaining influence. In contrast, it is also possible that the early advantage of normal Twitter users over traditional political actors might continue if they continue to remain central to the interactions of other Twitter users. More generally, it will be interesting to compare different metrics of *influence* on Twitter with regard to the stability of and systematic differences between their results.

Analyzing the behavior of politicians who were active on Twitter showed that they did not tend to be among the most active users in the data set. That said, the behavior of politicians on Twitter was equally skewed as the behavior of all users. There was a small group of politicians who used Twitter frequently and a large group of politicians who used Twitter only sparingly. Politicians tended predominantly to post messages containing information on the campaign while only interacting with other Twitter users sporadically. As such, Twitter was used much more strongly as a broadcasting medium than a medium for public dialogue. There was only little evidence of messages in which politicians actively tried to mobilize their followers to vote or to volunteer in their campaigns. Again, it will be interesting to see whether or not these findings are stable across various election cycles. It might be that they are less indicative of Twitter's use by German politicians in general. Instead, these findings might relate to an early state of politicians' Twitter use that could evolve over time once politicians grow more comfortable in their use of the microblogging service.

The analyses presented in this chapter are based on digital trace data, so while the results are compelling they are also limited. The biggest potential for researchers interested in the effects of digital tools on political communication lies in the combination of digital trace data and survey data on characteristics, attitudes, and opinions of Twitter users producing these data. To date, little is known about the ways in which specific types of users can be linked to specific types of usage behavior or political support. Without establishing this connection, it might be difficult for researchers to advance the understanding of political Twitter use meaningfully or learn how to use data collected on Twitter for the analysis of more fundamental political topics.

In general, the findings presented in this chapter indicate that we should be careful in expecting aggregates of Twitter messages to mirror political phenomena correctly. Especially, the high skewness of users' activity and the strong dependence on outside stimuli indicate that Twitter activity referring to politics follows mediation processes potentially skewing the image of reality emerging from aggregates of messages.

References

Ausserhofer J, Maireder A (2013) National politics on Twitter: structures and topics of a networked public sphere. Inf Commun Soc 16(3):291–314. doi:10.1080/1369118X.2012.756050

Bakshy E, Hofman JM, Mason WA, Watts DJ (2011) Everyone's an influencer: quantifying influence on Twitter. In: King I, Nejdl W, Li H (eds) WSDM 2011: proceedings of the 4th ACM international conference on web search and data mining. ACM, New York, pp 65–74. doi:10.1145/1935826.1935845

Boyd D, Golder SA, Lotan G (2010) Tweet, Tweet, Retweet: conversational aspects of retweeting on Twitter. In: Jr RHS (ed) HICSS 2010: proceedings of the 43rd Hawaii international conference on system science, IEEE. IEEE Computer Society, Washington, DC, pp 1–10. doi:10.1109/HICSS.2010.412

Cha M, Haddadi H, Benevenuto F, Gummadi KP (2010) Measuring user influence in Twitter: the million follower fallacy. In: Proceedings of the 4th international AAAI conference on weblogs and social media (ICWSM). The AAAI Press, Menlo Park

Chadwick A (2011) The political information cycle in a hybrid news system: the British Prime Minister and the "Bullygate" affair. Int J Press/Politics 16(1):3–29. doi:10.1177/1940161210384730

Chadwick A (2013) The hybrid media system: politics and power. Oxford University Press, Oxford

Chaffee SH, Metzger MJ (2001) The end of mass communication? Mass Commun Soc 4(4):365–379. doi:10.1207/S15327825MCS0404_3

Dang-Xuan L, Stieglitz S, Wladarsch J, Neuberger C (2013) An investigation of influentials and the role of sentiment in political communication on Twitter during election periods. Inf Commun Soc 16(5):795–825. doi:10.1080/1369118X.2013.783608

Dubois E, Gaffney D (2014) The multiple facets of influence: identifying political influentials and opinion leaders on Twitter. Am Behav Sci 58(10):1260–1277. doi:10.1177/0002764214527088

Golbeck J, Grimes JM, Rogers A (2010) Twitter use by the U.S. Congress. J Am Soc Inf Sci Technol 61(8):1612–1621. doi:10.1002/asi.21344

Gomez-Rodriguez M, Leskovec J, Schölkopf B (2013) Structure and dynamics of information pathways in online media. In: Leonardi S, Panconesi A, Ferragina P, Gionis A (eds) WSDM 2013: proceedings of the 6th ACM international conference on web search and data mining. ACM, New York, pp 23–32. doi:10.1145/2433396.2433402

González-Bailón S, Borge-Holthoefer J, Moreno Y (2013) Broadcasters and hidden influentials in online protest diffusion. Am Behav Sci 57(7):943–965. doi:10.1177/0002764213479371

Graham T, Broersma M, Hazelhoff K, van 't Haar G (2013) Between broadcasting political messages and interacting with voters: the use of Twitter during the 2010 UK general election campaign. Inf Commun Soc 16(5):692–716. doi:10.1080/1369118X.2013.785581

Honeycutt C, Herring SC (2009) Beyond microblogging: conversation and collaboration via Twitter. In: Jr RHS (ed) HICSS 2009: proceedings of the 42nd Hawaii international conference on system sciences. IEEE Press, Los Alamitos, pp 1–10. doi:10.1109/HICSS.2009.89

Java A, Song X, Finin T, Tseng B (2007) Why we Twitter: understanding microblogging usage and communities. In: Zhang H, Mobasher B, Giles L, McCallum A, Nasraoui O, Spiliopoulou M, Srivastava J, Yen J (eds) WebKDD/SNA-KDD '07: proceedings of the 9th WebKDD and 1st SNA-KDD 2007 workshop on web mining and social network analysis. ACM, New York, pp 56–65. doi:10.1145/1348549.1348556

Jungherr A (2012) Online campaigning in Germany: the CDU online campaign for the General Election 2009 in Germany. Ger Polit 21(3):317–340. doi:10.1080/09644008.2012.716043

Jungherr A (2014a) The logic of political coverage on Twitter: temporal dynamics and content. J Commun 64(2):239–259. doi:10.1111/jcom.12087

Jungherr A (2014b) Twitter in politics: a comprehensive literature review. Soc Sci Res Netw. http://papers.ssrn.com/sol3/papers.cfm?abstract_id=2402443

Jungherr A, Schoen H (2013) Das internet in Wahlkämpfen: Konzepte, Wirkungen und Kampagnenfunktionen. Springer VS, Wiesbaden

Jürgens P, Jungherr A (2011) Wahlkampf vom Sofa aus: Twitter im Bundestagswahlkampf 2009. In: Schweitzer EJ, Albrecht S (eds) Das Internet im Wahlkampf: Analysen zur Bundestagswahl 2009. VS Verlag für Sozialwissenschaft, Wiesbaden, pp 201–225. doi:10.1007/978-3-531-92853-1_8

Jürgens P, Jungherr A (2015) The use of Twitter during the 2009 German national election. Ger Pol. Forthcoming.

Jürgens P, Jungherr A, Schoen H (2011) Small worlds with a difference: new gatekeepers and the filtering of political information on Twitter. In: Roure DD, Poole S (eds) WebSci 2011: proceedings of the 3rd international web science conference. ACM, New York, p 21. doi:10.1145/2527031.2527034

Larsson AO, Moe H (2012) Studying political microblogging: Twitter users in the 2010 Swedish election campaign. New Media Soc 14(5):729–747

Lee C, Kwak H, Park H, Moon S (2010) Finding influentials based on the temporal order of information adoption in Twitter. In: Rappa M, Jones P, Freire J, Chakrabarti S (eds) WWW 2010: proceedings of the 19th international conference on the world wide web. ACM, New York, pp 1137–1138. doi:10.1145/1772690.1772842

Lin YR, Keegan B, Margolin D, Lazer D (2014) Rising tides or rising stars? Dynamics of shared attention on Twitter during media events. PLoS One 9(5):e94093. doi:10.1371/journal.pone.0094093

Margolis M, Resnick D (2000) Politics as usual: the cyberspace "revolution". SAGE Publications, Thousand Oaks

Mustafaraj E, Finn S, Whitlock C, Metaxas PT (2011) Vocal minority versus silent majority: discovering the opinions of the long tail. In: SocialCom 2011: the 3rd IEEE international conference on social computing. IEEE, Washington, DC

Papacharissi ZA, de Fatima Oliveira M (2012) Affective news and networked publics: the rhythms of news storytelling on #egypt. J Commun 62(2):266–282. doi:10.1111/j.1460-2466.2012.01630.x

Peterson RD (2012) To tweet or not to tweet: exploring the determinants of early adoption of Twitter by House members in the 111th Congress. Soc Sci J 49(4):430–338. doi:10.1016/j.soscij.2012.07.002

Rattanaritnont G, Toyoda M, Kitsuregawa M (2012) Characterizing topic-specific hashtag cascade in Twitter based on distributions of user influence. In: Sheng QZ, Wang G, Jensen CS, Xu G (eds) Web technologies and applications. Lecture notes in computer science, vol 7235. Springer, Heidelberg, pp 735–742. doi:10.1007/978-3-642-29253-8_71

Rogers R (2013) Digital methods. The MIT Press, Cambridge

Schweitzer EJ (2011) Normalization 2.0: a longitudinal analysis of German online campaigns in the national elections 2002–9. Eur J Commun 26(4):310–327. doi:10.1177/0267323111423378

Sousa D, Sarmento L, Rodrigues EM (2010) Characterization of the Twitter @replies network: are user ties social or topical? In: Cortizo JC, Carrero FM, Cantador I, Troyano JA, Rosso P (eds) SMUC 2010: proceedings of the 2nd international workshop on search and mining user-generated contents. ACM, New York, pp 63–70. doi:10.1145/1871985.1871996

Subbian K, Melville P (2011) Supervised rank aggregation for predicting influence in networks. In: PASSAT 2011: IEEE 3rd international conference on privacy, security and trust. IEEE Computer Society, Los Alamitos, pp 661–665. doi:10.1109/PASSAT/SocialCom.2011.167

Wu S, Hofman JM, Mason WA, Watts DJ (2011) Who says what to whom on Twitter. In: Sadagopan S, Ramamritham K, Kumar A, Ravindra MP, Bertino E, Kumar R (eds) WWW 2011: proceedings of the 20th international conference on world wide web. ACM, New York, pp 705–714. doi:10.1145/1963405.1963504

Chapter 5
Sensor of Attention to Politics

5.1 Connecting Politically Relevant Events to Spikes in the Volume of Twitter Messages

In the previous chapters, I showed that during the campaign for the 2009 federal election in Germany the microblogging service Twitter was used by politicians, campaigners, political supporters as well as the general public to voice their opinions about the campaign and to communicate about politics. Many of the messages contributing to the political communication space were posted in reaction to outside stimuli—be it mediated political events, such as the televised leaders' debates, or content on the Web. This strong connection between external stimuli raises the question of whether or not Twitter messages can be used to detect crucial events during the run of the campaign. Do shifts in the attention of politically vocal Twitter users, identified by sudden changes in the dynamics of Twitter messages commenting on politics, signify key moments during the campaign? And do the events thus identified offer a comprehensive account of key-points during the course of the campaign?

Underlying this question is an implicit assumption about the mechanism connecting spikes in Twitter messages with politically relevant events. Figure 5.1 shows the schematic of a potential mechanism explaining this connection based on the link between macro-phenomena (i.e. politically relevant events), patterns in aggregates of data (i.e. sudden spikes in Twitter mentions using hashtags referring to politics, specific political actors, or controversies), and individual behavior on the micro-level (i.e. posting a Twitter message using politically relevant hashtags), which was outlined in Chap. 3. This mechanism can easily be tested by checking if spikes in the volume of politically relevant message reliably coincide with events connected to the campaign.

The first question of interest will, therefore, be if spikes in the volume of topical Twitter messages can be connected with specific events leading to the focus of collective attention. Following this, it has to be shown how the events

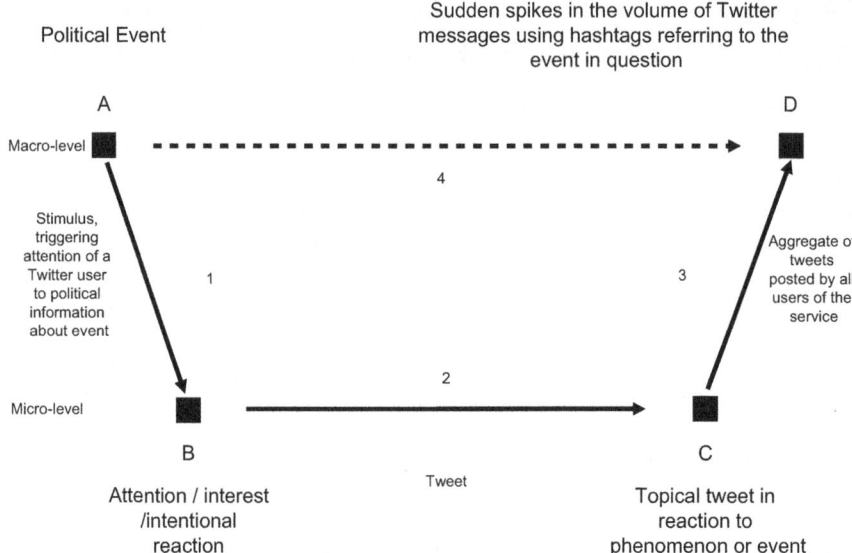

Fig. 5.1 Mechanism linking political events to shifts in the behavior of Twitter users

thus identified connect with the campaign. Evidence from messages accompanying collective action in Germany indicates that messages may spike in reaction to events of crucial importance for related campaigns, but also to rather trivial events that lend themselves to scandal, ironic commentary, or visualization (Jungherr and Jürgens 2014b). It is, therefore, far from certain that identified events reliably represent key-events during the campaign. Alternatively, they might be frivolous episodes which through their characteristics sparked the interest or mirth of politically vocal Twitter users. We also have to examine the flip side of this argument. While spikes in the volume of topical Twitter messages might indeed reliably point to politically relevant events, not all relevant events might reliably produce message spikes.

Before we begin this analysis, we have to decide which hashtags will enable us to identify messages referring to political topics. In fact, it could be argued that the use of hashtags to identify relevant messages already constitutes too strict a criterion for the selection of relevant messages. An alternative, therefore, could be a selection dependent on whether or not politically relevant keywords are present. A concentration on hashtags might lead us to focus exclusively on messages by Twitter-savvy users proficient in the communication conventions of the medium. While this is a reasonable argument, the use of keywords such as *wahl* (election), *kampagne* (campaign), *linke* (left), and others is not restricted to messages commenting on the campaign. Thus, the conception of the political communication space on Twitter based on keywords may produce a high number of false positives—messages identified by the selection criteria but not actually relevant to the research object.

In order to avoid this type of data dilution, I decided on using politically relevant hashtags to identify messages contributing to the political communication space. The decision to focus in this way does not completely solve the problem including false positives in the data set but mitigates it considerably. For example, the use of the term *linke* preceded by a hashtag indicates a user's intentional contribution to the topic *#linke*—the abbreviation for the party Die LINKE. However, the use of the adjective *linke*—German for left—could also apply to a non-political context, such as *die linke Spur ist gesperrt* (the left lane is blocked). Unfortunately, at present there are no systematic studies addressing potential biases based on the decision to use hashtags or keywords for the identification of politically relevant messages. Hence my decision to proceed this way is purely a subjective one.

In the following analyses, I compare events identified by examining various different constitutions of the political communication space on Twitter. First, I analyze the dynamics in the time series of all messages using at least one of 2629 politically relevant hashtags. As this relatively high count makes the ad hoc analysis of political communication spaces unwieldy, I compare the results of this analysis with the results of the analysis of the time series of messages using one of 42 politically relevant hashtags, selected for their overall significance to the campaign—such as party names, candidate names, political issues et al. This selection of highly relevant political hashtags I will call *index of political relevance* with reference to Lin et al. (2014). Following this, I also analyze the time series of messages commenting on specific political actors—be they political parties or candidates—to determine whether or not their mentions allow for the identification of events specific to the actor's respective role during the campaign, events which might have remained undetected by the analysis of the wider political communication space.

5.2 How to Detect Spikes in Data Streams?

A user's Twitter feed functions as a sensor for all things of interest to her, be it the lifelogging of mundane details, which might be of interest only to followers closest to her or be it her reactions to a social event, which might not only be of interest to her immediate social circle but also to Twitter users, who might not be following her but who might be interested in the event on which she is commenting. When aggregated, Twitter data thus promise a birds-eye view of social events that received attention from Twitter users. In fact, research shows that Twitter has become a platform for users to post and receive reactions to public events. An analysis of search queries entered on Twitter shows that they refer more often to unfolding events than search queries used on regular search engines (Teevan et al. 2011).

Recently, researchers have begun to examine the possibility of using Twitter data to detect major events (Jungherr and Jürgens 2013, 2014a). The basic idea behind this research is that each Twitter user can be seen as a sensor who documents her observations about reality in the form of tweets. While most of these messages might document mundane details of her daily activities, some might address a social event in which the user might participate (e.g. a sport event seen on television) or an event she accidentally witnessed (e.g. police action during a protest). For events with high popular appeal (e.g. television shows or the death of a celebrity) or social relevance (e.g. protests or natural disasters), it is reasonable to assume that many Twitter users post their reactions or observations. In the process of formulating their individual perceptions of unfolding events, they necessarily code their subjective impressions in a common vocabulary, sometimes independently converging in the use of common terms, sometimes following wording-queues by media coverage or political elites. These perceptions thus become automatically identifiable as signals describing the same phenomenon. Sudden increases in messages referring to a specific event or topic produce patterns which can be automatically identified, since these messages typically share attributes in semantic structure, vocabulary, hashtags, time stamps, or linked content. Thus, social events leave an imprint in Twitter data through clearly identifiable clusters of similar messages, which can be identified automatically.

Various research communities with different objectives have approached event detection through Twitter data. Some researchers have tried to detect events as they were unfolding as an early warning system—such as the early detection of earthquakes (e.g. Sakaki et al. 2010)—or to increase situational awareness in emergencies or humanitarian missions (e.g. Verma et al. 2011). Researchers also tried to use Twitter messages to determine the structure of big broadcast events based on the dynamics and persistence of spikes in the use of event specific terms (e.g. Shamma et al. 2010). Other researchers work on event detection algorithms in the hope of improving real-time search results with Twitter data (e.g. Becker et al. 2011; Chakrabarti and Punera 2011; Petrović et al. 2010; Weng and Lee 2011).

In the social sciences, text-based event detection is most prominently used in the research of international politics (Schrodt 2010; Schrodt and Yonamine 2012) and public opinion (Landmann and Zuell 2008). The underlying assumption in event detection is that crucial events within a field of study or topic of interest leave detectable traces in texts. If researchers were able to connect patterns in texts to events automatically, this would enable them automatically to build timelines documenting events of interest. If, for example, a reliable method could be developed, identifying political actors, time, and topics based on official documents, researchers of international politics would be able to establish an accurate map of treaties and conflicts, and perhaps would even be able to model their dynamics (Brandt et al. 2011). By the same token, if researchers of public opinion were able to detect events in media coverage automatically, this would go a long way in being able to model their impact on public opinion dynamics precisely.

At present, most research has focused on using official documents or newspaper articles for the detection of events (Allan 2002; Kleinberg 2003). These structured texts allow researchers to analyze a pre-filtered textual corpus, focusing on elements of events deemed relevant by officials or journalists, thereby raising the signal-to-noise ratio in the available data sets. But through their structure and form of publication these data keep researchers one level removed from the events

5.2 How to Detect Spikes in Data Streams?

themselves. Event detection based on newspaper articles documenting a campaign may provide a researcher with data about who campaigned when and where, but the unfolding events during the campaign itself will remain hidden. For researchers interested in large-scale social phenomena following regular dynamics—such as conflicts or treaties—this might seem a reasonable trade-off. Still, in political communication research these data might obscure important micro-events which contribute to a campaign and thereby hold crucial information for understanding the underlying dynamics of a campaign. This illustrates potential for the analysis of texts less distant from the events themselves. These data can increasingly be found in the digital data traces documenting interactions with digital services.

Most public interactions on digital services come in the shape of time-coded textual status updates lending themselves to automated computer-assisted analysis. Still, the benefits from the direct connection of textual record and event is diluted by the noise surrounding it. Most users of digital services do not intend to document unfolding socially relevant events impartially; most social media users post updates on mundane details of their lives. They do not act as objective chroniclers or journalists; instead they act as passers-by and participants in social events with their public interactions partially documenting elements of these events. Thus, each user becomes an unwitting sensor of her environment. For researchers, the challenge is how to cut through the noise of digital trace data and to identify those pieces of text that hold meaning.

The automatic identification of topics in large corpora of data—topic modeling—has long been a prevalent area in data mining research (e.g. Blei 2012; Blei and Lafferty 2009). Various researchers have tried to adapt topic modeling approaches to data collected on Twitter. Although there are interesting case studies illustrating the general potential of this approach (e.g. Hong and Davison 2010; Hong et al. 2011; Petrović et al. 2010; Ramage et al. 2010; Ritter et al. 2012; Zhao et al. 2011), there remain challenges that arise from the nature of Twitter messages (Atefeh and Khreich 2013). Tweets are relatively short messages, revealing little about the context or teleology behind the information provided. Was it an ironic commentary? Did it contain a serious statement or substantial information? This leads some researchers to use hashtags for the establishment of a tweet's topical context (e.g. Romero et al. 2013). A further challenge for real-time analyses is that data collected on Twitter are being streamed live. The comments on a given topic or event are constantly evolving over time, so the associated prominent hashtags or keywords might continue to change. Spikes in attention to a topic, event, hashtag, or keyword during a given time interval might be dwarfed when compared to bigger spikes in the future. Thus analysts interested in the real-time detection of events have to use quantitative methods accounting for this characteristic of streaming data (e.g. Kleinberg 2003, 2015; Yao et al. 2009).

Fortunately, for the purposes of this chapter, simpler approaches for the analysis of shifts in the attention of Twitter users during the campaign suffice. First, the data consist of messages referring to a topic which had been concluded at the time of the analysis, namely the campaign for the federal election of 2009. Hence, problems connected with the analysis of streaming data can be safely disregarded. Second, as the campaign has finished, it is possible to focus the analysis on various hashtags that referred to the campaign, events, or political issues. This eliminates the need to identify hashtags referring to the topic of interest automatically.

Given these specific circumstances, I will use a series of differently constructed hashtag sets to build time series of messages using these hashtags. I will then check if unusual peaks in the occurrences of messages, using these politically relevant hashtags, can be connected with events relevant to the ongoing campaign for the federal election of 2009 in Germany. The use of politically relevant hashtags should make it possible to cut through the noise of messages referring to mundane topics or those unrelated to politics. Following Kleinberg (2003), unusual peaks might be considered as the results of specific events leading to a sudden concentration of attention by Twitter users. To check the validity of this assumption, I will analyze the content of Twitter messages posted during days of sudden increases in messages using politically relevant hashtags in determining to which political event or which set of events they were referring. This will show if messages contributing to these volume spikes were indeed commenting on events relevant to the campaign or just happened to cluster on a given day.

It is also important to decide which patterns in the time series of Twitter messages might potentially be helpful in identifying politically relevant offline events. Fluctuations in a time series are natural. Data points falling outside these normal fluctuations are outliers. Approaches to the detection of outliers in data fall between very simple approaches—for example, designating each data point that falls beyond two standard deviations in the distribution of all values as outlier—to more advanced models (for overviews on different approaches to the identification of outliers see Aggarwal 2013; Barnett and Lewis 1994). In analyzing the time series of Twitter messages commenting on politics, I decided on the use of boxplots to detect outliers and inspect the overall distribution of data points. While this may not be the most sophisticated detection approach, it has the distinct benefit of offering an intuitive account of the data which in turn makes possible the interpretation of the patterns found.

5.3 Identifying Politically Relevant Events

While quantitative time series analysis might provide us with a list of dates on which users changed their behavior by posting significantly more messages than usual, the collection of a politically relevant list is much more uncertain. This list hinges on the question of what makes an event politically relevant. Is it the attention by the public or the media or is it the identity of the actor initiating the event, such as campaigners or the media?

Topologies of political events and their coverage by the media have a rich tradition in communication science. Early research tried to develop a scheme to differentiate between genuine events—events of true political importance independent of their media coverage or political spectacle—and events that were of no

5.3 Identifying Politically Relevant Events

political importance, except for the media coverage they might create—so called pseudo events (e.g. Boorstin 1961; Kepplinger and Habermeier 1995). Beyond these routinely covered events, Dayan and Katz introduced the term *media events*. The term refers to extraordinary events of high social importance—such as televised candidate debates, royal marriages, or high profile sporting occasions. Dayan and Katz maintain that mass media allowed the audience to participate in these events and thus be part of an ongoing negotiation of meaning between the producers of the events, participants, and the media covering them (e.g. Couldry et al. 2010; Dayan and Katz 1992).

One of the most prominent approaches to the question of which events or issues make it into the news is to assess their *newsworthiness*. This approach is based on content analysis of news items and interviews with editors to assess characteristics they deem important in an event to make it newsworthy—so called *news values* (e.g. Schulz 1976; Shoemaker and Cohen 2006). Researchers have levelled criticism against this approach since the field came to understand the news not as a true, if reduced, mirror of reality, whose selection criteria were based on objective criteria. Instead, researchers increasingly interpret news coverage as a process of social construction between actors promoting events, journalists, editors, and the public. Researchers following this approach, therefore, focus much more strongly on actors who produce and promote events, the rhythms of scheduled events, and routine interactions between journalists and political actors, than on any objective criteria of events or news items (e.g. Molotch and Lester 1974).

For the following analysis, I used a selection of political events informed by this literature. To assess which types of events led to the increased coverage of political actors in traditional media and on Twitter, I differentiated between four types of events: independent events, these are events that are not connected with the campaign and the media (e.g. international talks between heads of government about the financial crisis or a political scandal); campaign-initiated events (e.g. presentation of an election manifesto or a party convention); media-initiated events (e.g. broadcast of an interview with a leading candidate or an investigative report); and media events, scheduled broadcasts of high profile political occasions (e.g. the televised leaders' debate or election day coverage).

Based on this typology, I collected key-events during the course of the campaign for the federal election. This provided me with a set of dates on which politically relevant events took place and which I could compare with the list of events as provided by the analysis of spikes in the volume of Twitter messages. This approach also allowed me to interpret potential deviations between my list of political events and the list produced by the analysis of Twitter data. If, for example, spikes in the mentions of political actors on Twitter would predominantly arise in reaction to independent events, one could see this as an indicator that users discuss politics at least somewhat independently from the biases of traditional news. In this case Twitter data could serve as a *true* mirror of political reality. If spikes, for instance, were to arise in reaction to campaign-initiated events, we could read this as indicating that users react strongly to the inputs of political elites. In this case Twitter data could serve as a sensor for the campaigning activities of political elites.

If instead spikes arise largely in reaction to media-initiated events, we would have to interpret Twitter as a medium largely reactive to traditional media coverage and thus also mirroring the various biases of news coverage. In this case, Twitter data could serve as a mirror of political news coverage. Spikes in reaction to media events are a different matter, because they do not necessarily show the dependence of Twitter on media coverage. Instead, spikes in the volume of messages commenting on political actors, posted in reaction to media events, might be considered as indicators for Twitter having become a channel on which users negotiate the social meaning of events they are watching. Thus, Twitter becomes, at least for some, a channel through which they can extend the negotiation of media events' meaning from their original negotiating tables, described by Dayan and Katz—namely the commentary track accompanying live coverage of the event, the living room, and the water cooler at work (Dayan and Katz 1992). In this case, the analysis of Twitter data would allow for insights into a part of public reactions to important political events that, until now, has remained hidden from social scientists.

The campaign for the federal election of 2009 in Germany was rather uneventful. The two biggest parties, CDU/CSU and SPD, governed Germany from 2005 to 2009 in a grand coalition. Both leading candidates, Angela Merkel and Frank-Walter Steinmeier respectively, had to campaign against the other following 4 years of political cooperation. This led to a campaign lacking drama, in which the main political actors neither attempted to nor succeeded in polarizing the electorate (Krewel et al. 2011). Although the campaign lacked drama, there was a series of events either independent of the campaign, or initiated by the campaign, or initiated by the media, and media events that focused public attention between July and October 2009. Table 5.1 shows a selection of crucial events during the course of the campaign.

Although the campaign was rather uneventful, there was a series of significant events dominating the months preceding the election. On August 30, there were state elections in Saarland, Thüringen, Sachsen, and local elections in Nordrhein-Westfalen. The results of these bellwether elections were widely discussed, mainly because these elections were seen as foreshadowing the upcoming federal elections. Furthermore, in late August the grand coalition in the state of Schleswig-Holstein was dissolved and state elections were scheduled for September 27, the day of the federal election. Additionally, the ongoing financial crisis was a constant topic during the campaign. Symbolically, this topic culminated in Angela Merkel's participation in the G20 Pittsburgh summit. Besides various state elections and the financial crisis, a series of controversies arose that coincided with the campaign: one of these involved Germany's then minister of health, Ulla Schmidt (SPD), whose official car was stolen under mysterious circumstances in Spain while she was vacationing there. Turmoil also ensued in the media after reports that the then minister for the economy, Karl-Theodor zu Guttenberg (CSU), had outsourced the drafting of future legislation concerning the financial sector to a private law firm. The final and probably biggest controversy during the campaign arose after media reports that chancellor Angela Merkel (CDU) had held a birthday reception for

5.3 Identifying Politically Relevant Events 115

Table 5.1 Key events during the campaign for the federal election of 2009 in Germany

Date	Description	Type
2009-06-17	SZ interview Frank-Walter Steinmeier (FWS)	Media initiated event
2009-07-16	ZDF summer interview FWS	Media initiated event
2009-07-17	Birthday of Angela Merkel (AM)	Independent event
2009-07-17	CSU party convention	Campaign initiated event
2009-07-23	Break of governing coalition in Schleswig-Holstein	Independent event
2009-07-26	Controversy, theft of Ulla Schmidt's car in Spain	Independent event
2009-07-30	SPD presents shadow cabinet	Campaign initiated event
2009-08-03	SPD presents its campaign program, the *Deutschlandplan*	Campaign initiated event
2009-08-04	First leg of summer press tour of FWS	Campaign initiated event
2009-08-11	RTL summer interview AM	Media initiated event
2009-08-12	Controversy, outsourcing of the drafting of legislation for bank bailout	Independent event
2009-08-13	Second leg of summer press tour of FWS	Campaign initiated event
2009-08-14	Minister Guttenberg presents concept for industrial policy	Campaign initiated event
2009-08-16	RTL Townhall FWS	Media initiated event
2009-08-17	Leading candidates of the Greens' start their campaign tour	Campaign initiated event
2009-08-23	ARD summer interview FWS	Media initiated event
2009-08-24	Controversy, birthday dinner in Chancellory	Independent event
2009-08-29	ARD/ZDF summer interview AM	Media initiated event
2009-08-30	State elections in Saarland, Sachsen, and Thüringen	Media event and independent event
2009-08-31	Party convention SPD	Campaign initiated event
2009-09-02	RTL summer interview FWS	Media initiated event
2009-09-03	Governor of Thüringen resigns	Independent event
2009-09-03	Party convention FDP	Campaign initiated event
2009-09-04	Air strike of *Bundeswehr* against tanker in Kunduz, Afghanistan	Independent event
2009-09-04	Campaign convention Die Linke	Campaign initiated event
2009-09-06	Party convention CDU	Campaign initiated event
2009-09-07	ARD Wahlarena AM	Media initiated event
2009-09-08	ARD Wahlarena FWS	Media initiated event
2009-09-12	SZ Interview AM	Media initiated event

(continued)

Table 5.1 (continued)

Date	Description	Type
2009-09-13	TV leaders' debate	Media event
2009-09-14	TV leaders' debate, small parties	Media initiated event
2009-09-15	Campaign tour AM *Rheingold-Express*	Campaign initiated event
2009-09-19	SZ Interview FWS	Media initiated event
2009-09-20	Party convention FDP	Campaign initiated event
2009-09-24	Party convention Die Grünen	Campaign initiated event
2009-09-25	G20-summit Pittsburgh	Independent event
2009-09-25	Party convention SPD & Linke	Campaign initiated event
2009-09-26	Party convention CDU & CSU & FDP	Campaign initiated event
2009-09-26	TV total election special	Media initiated event
2009-09-27	Election night	Media event and independent event

the CEO of the *Deutsche Bank*, Josef Ackermann, in the official rooms of the chancellery.

Besides these independent events, there was also a series of events initiated by the campaigns that attracted attention during the months preceding the election, which included a series of national party conventions. Specifically there were staged campaign events, such as the launch of the SPD's campaign program—the *Deutschlandplan*—, a press tour through Germany by Frank-Walter Steinmeier early in the campaign and Angela Merkel's press tour on the train *Rheingold Express*.

When looking at media coverage of the campaign, we find it dominated by two distinct formats. Three of the major television stations in Germany—ARD, ZDF, and RTL—produced prominently advertised individual interviews with the leading candidates of each party. In Table 5.1 the dates of the interviews with Angela Merkel and Frank-Walter Steinmeier are listed. Additionally, ARD produced two programs in which Angela Merkel and Frank-Walter Steinmeier discussed their respective positions with selected audience members in a town-hall setting. These programs were called *Wahlarena*. Two other media-initiated events are listed in the table: the televised debate between the leading candidates of FDP, Guido Westerwelle, Bündnis 90/Die Grünen, Jürgen Trittin, and Die LINKE, Gregor Gysi, on September 14 as well as the election special of *TV-total*, a widely watched comedy program aimed at young voters on September 26, the evening before the election.

During the run-up to the federal election of 2009, three events fit Dayan and Katz (1992) concept of *media events*: the election night coverage of the state elections in Saarland, Thüringen, Sachsen, and the local election in Nordrhein-Westfalen on August 30, 2009; the televised debate between the candidates of the two leading parties CDU/CSU and SPD, Angela Merkel and Frank-Walter Steinmeier on September 14; and the election night coverage of the federal election and the state election in Schleswig-Holstein on September 27. The following analysis illustrates the extent to which these events caught the attention of politically vocal Twitter users and thereby left traces in the dynamics of Twitter messages commenting on politics.

5.4 Political Events and Their Shadows on Twitter

Plotting the daily volume of Twitter messages in a time series offers an intuitive view of the dynamics in the communication space at any given point in time. Let us start this analysis by examining a collection of simple time series documenting the daily volume of Twitter messages posted during the run-up to the election.

In Fig. 5.2 we see the time series of all messages collected in the data set between June 18, and October 1, 2009. This time series shows all messages posted by all users who, during the run of the analysis, posted at least one Twitter message containing at least one of the 19 predetermined politically relevant hashtags, that were documented in Table 4.1. Black dots represent the number of messages that were posted on weekdays while red dots mark the number of messages that were posted on weekends. During the timespan under consideration, a cursory glance at the plot already shows that the time series has a clear upward trend, with a steady increase in messages that were posted each day. In addition, we also see a strong seasonality in the time series. Each Saturday and Sunday the amount of posted messages dropped rapidly. People used Twitter much more actively on weekdays than on weekends. Similar seasonal patterns in Twitter time series were discussed

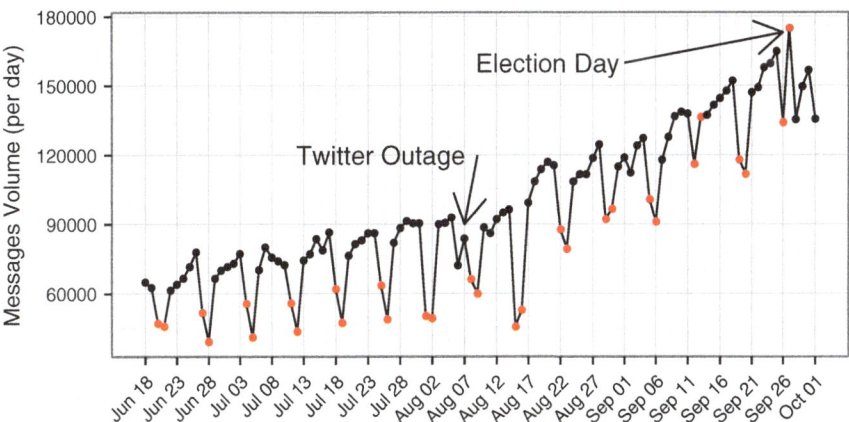

Fig. 5.2 All messages between June 18, and October 1, 2009

in detail during Chap. 3 and have also been shown by Golder and Macy (2011) who identified regular day-night patterns by regular drops in messages volume.

Another interesting feature of the time series is that some drops and increases in the daily volume of posted messages do not correspond with dynamics of either trend or seasonality. Two of these deviating data points are marked in the plot by arrows. The first arrow marks an unexpected drop in messages volume on August 6. On this day, the total volume of Twitter messages fell well below the expected value for a Thursday. This was due to an unscheduled outage of Twitter because of a politically motivated hacker attack (Stone 2009). The second arrow marks the day of the federal election, September 27. On this day, users posted the highest amount of Twitter messages during the course of the analysis. This is especially significant since elections in Germany are held on Sundays and thus, focusing only on trend and seasonality dynamics, we should have expected a much more moderate message volume. Both breaks in the patterns of digital trace data are clearly connected to specific offline events. This illustrates the potential to identify politically relevant events by pattern shifts in digital trace data. It is especially interesting to note that the day of the federal election is clearly identifiable by users' increased activity on Twitter, even in this data set which represents Twitter messages in their highest aggregate.

Although some events relevant to the campaign led to visible shifts in the time series dynamics of all messages per day, a closer look at the time series of only those messages actually referring to politics promises better results. As described in Chap. 4 earlier, I identified 2629 politically relevant hashtags, followed by all messages that were using at least one of these hashtags between June 18, and October 1, 2009. These messages constitute the *political communication space* on Twitter.

In Fig. 5.3 we see a time series for all messages that were identified as part of the political communication space. The time series shows striking differences to Fig. 5.2. The two elements that dominated Fig. 5.2—a strong upward trend and heavy seasonalities on weekends—are much weaker in Fig. 5.3. Instead of a clear upward trend we see three distinct phases in the data that are interrupted by a series of strong outliers. During the first phase—lasting from June 19, roughly to September 12, the televised candidate debate—the number of daily messages fluctuates somewhat stably between 4000 and 9000 messages. During the second phase—lasting from September 13 to election night—we see a strong increase in the daily volume of messages. The last week of the campaign was thus covered very intensely on Twitter. The third phase—from election night to October 1—shows a steep decline in messages contributing to the political communication space with the daily volume of messages quickly falling back to levels seen before the televised debate.

These patterns are interrupted by four heavy outliers—June 18 (ratification of the Access Impediment Act), August 30 (elections in the states Saarland, Sachsen, and Thüringen), September 12 (televised leaders' debate) and September 27 (election day). Three of these four events are clearly connected with the campaign. The other, the ratification of the Access Impediment Act by Parliament, was a very

5.4 Political Events and Their Shadows on Twitter 119

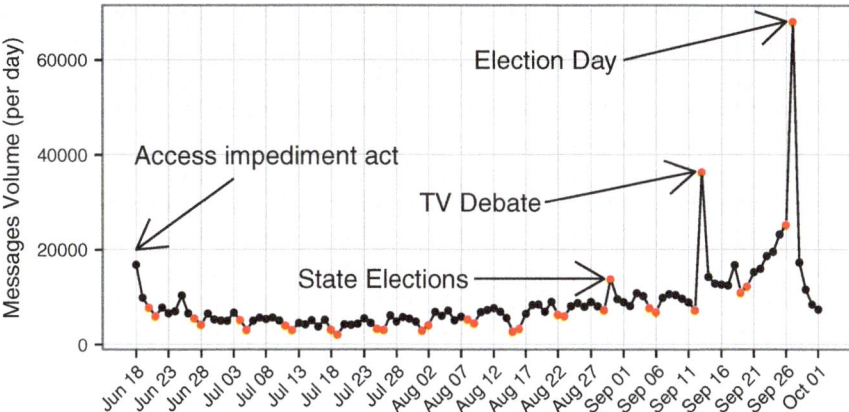

Fig. 5.3 Messages contributing to the political communication space between June 18, and October 1, 2009

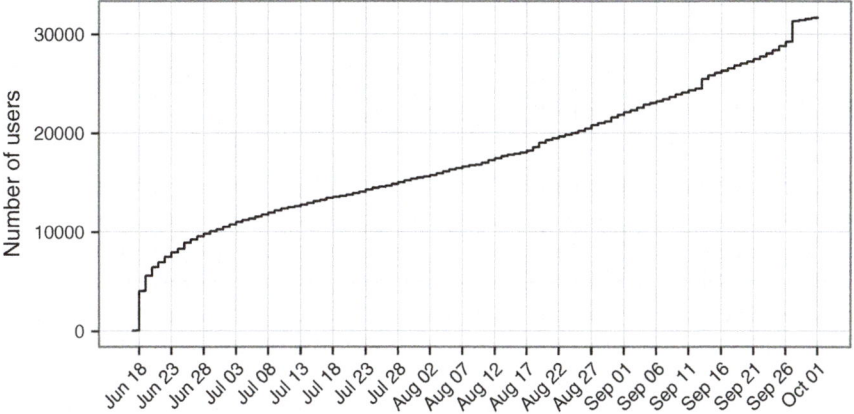

Fig. 5.4 Cumulative number of users who had contributed to the political communication space at any given hour

controversial policy issue. Thus, of the events that led to outliers, three were media events (state elections, leaders' debate, and election day) while one was an independent event (ratification of the Access Impediment Act).

Another interesting characteristic of a communication space is its growth. When do people decide to participate for the first time? Does the number of participants rise steadily over time or do they join predominantly during specific time spans, maybe in reaction to an event related to a topic of interest within the communication space? Figure 5.4 shows the cumulative number of users that had contributed to the communication space during any given hour. At the beginning of the time series we see a bursty pattern, followed by a predominantly steady increase. Only on September 12, and September 27—the dates of the televised leaders' debate and election day respectively—do we see a greater number of users contributing to the communication space for the first time than on other days. We thus see that some mediated events indeed led to a larger than usual amount of people joining the communication space. Other than that, we see a largely gradual activation of users during the course of the campaign.

Already these cursory visual analyses show promise in detecting potentially relevant days during which users deviated from their usual behavior by posting significantly more or less messages than should be expected based on their past behavior. With a more robust assessment of outliers we might find a more rigorous indicator for days during which events or processes led users to change their behavior. Examining the raw data, as for example in Fig. 5.2, has only limited potential in the detection of meaningful outliers. The time series is dominated by regular dynamics, that have to be accounted for in making sure that values that seem to be outliers based on their total volume are indeed so and not just products by regular dynamics of the time series. In the following sections, I will introduce two quantitative approaches that promise to offer a better understanding of these time series.

5.4.1 Event Detection by Differencing

As discussed above, the volume of messages contributing to the political communication space is dominated by two regular dynamics. We have seen a steady—if modest—trend over the time that the daily volume of messages increased. In addition, we see that the volume of messages per day is highly dependent on the day of week. The most obvious pattern is that on Saturday and Sunday the volume of Twitter messages regularly drops drastically. Other less obvious patterns might also be present in the dynamics of the daily message volume posted on other weekdays. These obvious and not so obvious, but highly regular dynamics in the time series of message volume per day make it hard to determine meaningful outliers in the data by just examining the graph. Some very basic techniques of time series analysis may help us to transform the data so that it becomes easier to spot obvious strays.

Most analysis techniques depend on the time series being stationary. This means, that the series have to remain stable in their mean value over time. Also, their autocorrelation function, the amount of how much the value of a variable at a given time depends on the values of the same variable at earlier stages, has to decrease steadily towards zero. Since most time series, as the one shown in Fig. 5.2, do not correspond to this prerequisite, statisticians have developed tools to transform time series in a way that maintains their underlying dynamics but strips them of some of their regular fluctuations. Two of these techniques are the differencing of time series and the detrending based on a regression model. Below, I explore both approaches to identify potentially meaningful days during the course of the campaign on which users deviated from their regular behavior.

5.4 Political Events and Their Shadows on Twitter

By calculating the difference between two variables, that are taken to be statistically dependent, one can transform a time series so that it becomes stationary by losing its trend and seasonal components while still keeping other dependencies and dynamics intact (Shumway and Stoffer 2011, pp. 59–63):

$$x_t - x_{t-1} \tag{5.1}$$

In the case of the time series documenting messages contributing to the political communication space, we have to transform the original time series to account for a trend component and a seasonal component. In a first step, because of the highly skewed distribution of the data, I performed a logarithmic transformation so as to avoid the influence of potential scale effects in the following analyses. I then calculated the first difference of the time series to account for the trend component in the data. Following this, I calculated the seventh difference so as to account for the seasonal dependency in the data.

$$log(x_t) - log(x_{t-1}) - (log(x_{t-7}) - log(x_{t-8})) \tag{5.2}$$

The resulting time series of the first and seventh differences in the original time series, is shown in Fig. 5.5. The volatility of the series increases over time. We can identify two volatility regimes. The first, one of rather stable volatility, lasts from the start of the time series up until lag 67. The other, one of high volatility, lasts from lag 67 until the end of the time series. Other than was the case with the time series of all messages, the phases of increased volatility coincide with the intensifying phase of the campaign.

Due to the fact that we see two volatility regimes, I decided to determine outliers during these phases by calculating box-and-whisker plots for both. Developed by John Tukey (Tukey 1977), these plots are helpful in visualizing the distribution of data based on their quantiles. A box-and-whisker plot has four elements: a rectangular box, a black line, two dashed lines, and potentially a number of circles. The edges of the rectangular box are determined by the lower and upper quantiles of the distribution; the median is shown by the thick black lines splitting the rectangular box in two parts; the dashed lines are called whiskers and end at 1.5 times the spread

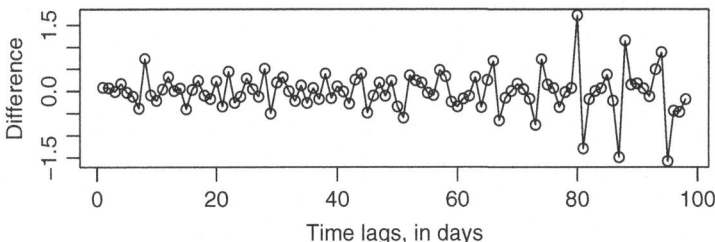

Fig. 5.5 First and seventh differences of the political communication space

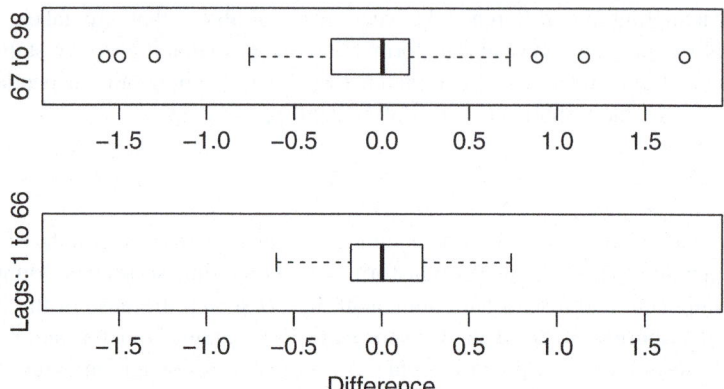

Fig. 5.6 Boxplots of two volatility regimes in differenced time series of political communication space

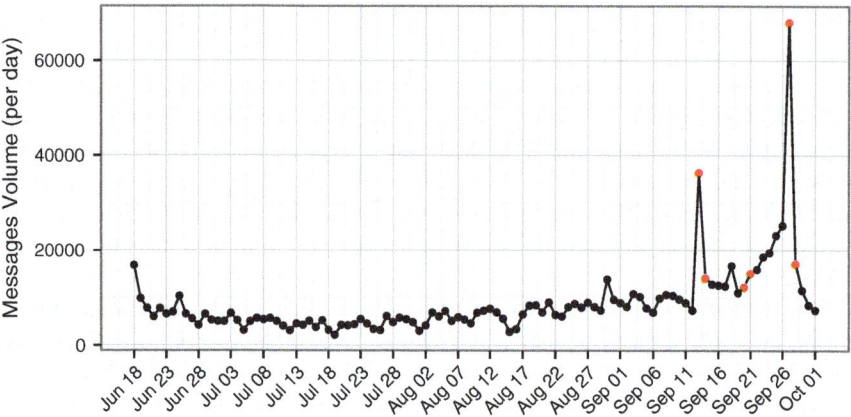

Fig. 5.7 All messages of the political communication space over time with outliers based on differencing

between the lower and upper quantiles; values that lie beyond these borders are outliers and indicated by circles in the graph (Keen 2010, pp. 95–104). Figure 5.6 shows that although there are fluctuations during the first volatility regime, we see that none qualify as outliers, whereas in the second regime we find three pairs of outliers.

In Fig. 5.7 red dots mark the dates on which the outliers fell, while Table 5.2 identifies the corresponding events. It is noteworthy that outliers come in pairs. Because the approach uses data that document the relationship of a data point at any given time to the data point directly preceding it and the data point preceding it by 7 days, the approach identifies not only the day on which users deviated from their usual behavior but also the following day, when users switched back to their

5.4 Political Events and Their Shadows on Twitter

Table 5.2 Days identified by differencing and corresponding events in the political communication space

Date	Event	Direction	Type
September 12/13, 2009 (Sunday)	TV debate	Positive/negative	Media event
September 21, 2009 (Monday)	n.a.	Positive	n.a.
September 27/28, 2009 (Sunday)	Election day	Positive/negative	Media event

usual routine. This produces a second outlier in the opposing direction. We see the first pair of outliers being the day of the televised leaders' debate. The third pair of outliers is also clearly connected to the campaign. It identifies the day of the federal election. The second pair of outliers falls on September 21 and 22. Again, these dates are not related to the campaign.

It turns out that the analysis of outliers in differenced time series offers some potential to identify significant political events. But it has to be said, that this appears to be a very coarse measure that produced false positives—days during which nothing significant for the campaign happened—and correctly indicated only two high profile campaign events while missing many others.

5.4.2 Event Detection by Regression Models

The discussion above showed that although the detection of potentially significant events during the course of the campaign by the analysis of outliers based on differenced time series is straight forward, the results are only partially meaningful. How does event detection based on a regression model of the time series perform?

As we have seen, the time series documenting the political communication space shows three dominant dynamics. First, it has a trend component—albeit a moderate one—over time. Second, there are small shifts in message volume between weekdays and weekends. Third, the outliers on the days of the televised debate and the election dominate the time series. These dynamics have to be accounted for in the regression term. I chose a linear model with four coefficients: one accounting for the weak but perceptible exponential trend by regressing the squared number of messages on itself over time[1]; the second being a dummy variable that accounts for each day being a weekday or a day during the weekend[2]; the third and fourth coefficients are dummy variables for the dates of the televised debate and the

---

[1] As an alternative, I fitted a model that regressed the time series on its first difference. The adjusted R^2 value of the resulting model was inferior so this simpler model was chosen.

[2] I fitted alternative models that built dummy variables for each day of the week or that differentiated between weekdays, Saturdays and Sundays. As the coefficients of these additional variables did not prove to be significant and the adjusted R^2 values of the resulting models did not show much improvement I chose the simpler model.

election day.[3] This results in a simple regression term, in which x stands for the number of messages posted per day, w documents whether or not a given value of the time series falls on a weekday or a weekend, t stands for the value on the day of the televised debate, e stands for the value on election day and z stands for the expected messages per day.

$$z_t = \beta_0 + \beta_1 x_i^2 + \beta_2 w_i + \beta_2 t_i + \beta_2 e_i + \epsilon_i \tag{5.3}$$

x = number of messages posted per day
w = weekend or weekday (dummy variable)
t = TV debate (dummy variable)
e = election day (dummy variable)
z = number of messages expected by the model

Table 5.3 shows the model diagnostics. This model seems to be appropriate as the p-value of the F statistic indicates high significance. The adjusted R^2 value indicates that this model accounts for 85 % of the variance in the empirically measured values. The coefficients also point in the right direction. The positive coefficient of x indicates a strong increase of messages over time, while the negative coefficient for w indicates some decreases in messages on weekends while the t and e values indicate the steep increase of messages on the days of the TV debate and the election. This simple regression model thus accounts for much of the time series dynamics.

Figure 5.8 further corroborates the appropriate model fit. The figure shows the fitted values of the regression model (the black line in the plot) compared with the actual values (the red dots in the plot). Visual inspection shows that the model seems reasonably close to the actual values. Despite a few exceptions, we see that the model generally performs quite well. Initially, the model somewhat

Table 5.3 Regression model of time series political communication space

	Coefficients	p-Value
x (number of messages)	$9.180e - 01$	$< 2e - 16$***
y (weekend or weekday, dummy)	$-1.551e + 03$	0.0189*
t (TV debate, dummy)	$2.598e + 04$	$9e - 14$***
e (election day, dummy)	$5.520e + 04$	$< 2e - 16$***
Adjusted R^2: 0.85		
F statistic: 157.6 on 4 and 101 DF		$< 2e - 16$***

*p-Value between 0.01 and 0.05; ***p-value between 0 and 0.001

---

[3]I ran the model with and without these dummy variables. Without the variables the regression model overestimated the number of messages on all weekends based on the values of the two outliers. This is an obvious misfit that had to be accounted for by the inclusion of the dummy variables.

5.4 Political Events and Their Shadows on Twitter

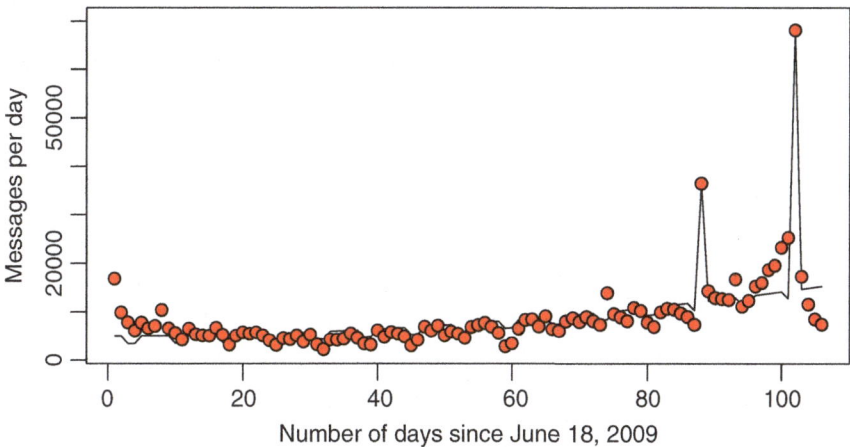

Fig. 5.8 Fitted values of regression model compared with actual message volume political communication space

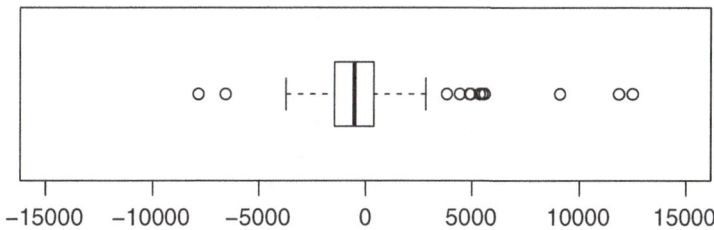

Fig. 5.9 Outliers in the residuals of the regression model political communication space

underestimates the number of messages following the day of the Access Impediment Act's ratification. During the following months, the model misses only a few outliers until closer to the election when it again systematically underestimates the number of messages leading up to election day. During the final days of the analysis, the model overestimates the number of messages per day, no doubt influenced by the rising trend in message number leading up to election day. We thus see, that the model is vulnerable to sudden shifts in user behavior.

In Fig. 5.9 we see that most residuals of the model cluster around zero. Still, we find 13 values that lie outside 1.5 times the spread between the lower and upper quantiles. A negative value in this graph indicates that the value expected by the model is bigger than the value that was actually measured in the data set, while a positive value would suggest the opposite. As we have seen in the event detection by differencing, the event detection with regression models also shows that most unexpected values in the data set undershoot the expectation based on regular dynamics.

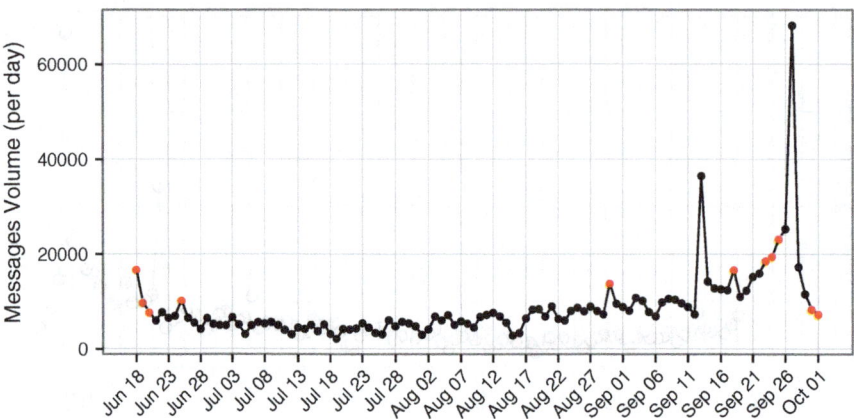

Fig. 5.10 Political communication space over time with outliers based on regression models

Both Fig. 5.10 and Table 5.4 identify different dates in the time series than the event detection approach using the differenced time series. We also see that this approach clearly identifies more dates that were meaningful for the campaign than the approach based on differencing the time series. Still, this approach is also far from certain to deliver meaningful results. On the one hand, we again find dates on which the volume of messages was overestimated by the model based on high message counts on the preceding days, for instance September 30, and October 1. On the other hand, we also find dates on which the volume of messages was higher than estimated by the model. Nevertheless, on those days, September 18, 23, and 24, no specific event was responsible for the rise in Twitter activity; instead they seem part of a general increased level of Twitter activity in the run-up to the election. Additionally, the spike on June 19, arose in reaction to an event the day before—the ratification of the Access Impediment Act—and not events on the day. These observations show that rises in daily mentions on Twitter do not necessarily indicate that relevant events happened on the respective days. Instead, Twitter behavior seems to change gradually in reaction to preceding or upcoming events.

However, some shifts in the dynamics of Twitter messages containing political hashtags did indeed happen on days of relevant political events. The spike on June 18 was produced by messages commenting on the Access Impediment Act's ratification—a piece of legislation trying to introduce measures for blocking access to websites offering child pornography. The spike of June 20 was dominated by messages referring to protests against the Access Impediment Act organized by Germany's Pirate Party. Tweets celebrating the fact that the Pirate Party was included in a popular online poll of party mentions on Twitter produced a considerable spike in volume on June 25. On August 30 tweets anticipating and reacting to the results of the state elections produced a volume spike. On September 25 the activities of Pirate Party supporters led to another spike in message volume. On that day a campaign reached its peak in which the Pirate Party aimed—without

5.4 Political Events and Their Shadows on Twitter

Table 5.4 Days identified by regression models and corresponding events political communication space

Date	Event	Estimated by model	Type
June 18, 2009 (Thursday)	Access Impediment Act	Underestimated	Independent event
June 19, 2009 (Friday)	Access Impediment Act (aftermath)	Underestimated	Follow-up activity
June 20, 2009 (Saturday)	Protests against Access Impediment Act	Underestimated	Campaign-initiated event
June 25, 2009 (Thursday)	Pirate party is included on popular aggregation platform for political tweets	Underestimated	Campaign-initiated event
August 30, 2009 (Sunday)	State elections	Underestimated	Media event
September 13, 2009 (Sunday)	Televised leaders' debate	Controlled for in model	Media event
September 18, 2009 (Friday)	Non event specific general increased political activity	Underestimated	n.a.
September 23, 2009 (Wednesday)	Non event specific general increased political activity	Underestimated	n.a.
September 24, 2009 (Thursday)	Non event specific general increased political activity	Underestimated	n.a.
September 25, 2009 (Friday)	Campaign by Pirate Party supporters to participate in TV-total election special reaches peak	Underestimated	Campaign-initiated event
September 27, 2009 (Sunday)	Election day	Controlled for in model	Media event
September 30, 2009 (Monday)	n.a.	Overestimated	Unrelated to campaign
October 1, 2009 (Thursday)	n.a.	Overestimated	Unrelated to campaign

avail—to be included in the election special of *TV-total*, a popular German comedy television program. The two biggest volume spikes are found on September 13, and September 27—the day of the televised candidate debate and election day, respectively. Both spikes were so strong, that they had to be controlled for in the model, so as not to confound the model by outliers.

When examining the event types leading to spikes in volume, we find media events—coverage of election nights and the televised leaders' debates—tended to lead to spikes in online comments. Twitter, therefore, seems to have become a channel through which audience members exchange their reactions to big political media events, reactions which, up until then, were confined to the audience's living rooms or water cooler conversations on the days following the events. The Pirate

Party was also successful in creating strong reactions to events initiated by their campaign. This was not true for any of the other parties. Beyond that, one event independent from any campaign led to a spike in Twitter activity—ratification of the Access Impediment Act, an event of strong interest to Pirate Party supporters and online users, if not the general public. It is interesting to note that nearly all events identified in the section of this chapter discussing key events during the campaign—including most media initiated events and controversies—did not lead to abnormal spikes in the volume of daily Twitter messages. These findings show that unusual shifts in the daily volume of messages explicitly contributing to the political communication space mirrored politically relevant events. Nevertheless, many important events during the campaign did not find visible shadows on Twitter while events of little significance for the campaign were clearly visible on Twitter.

When comparing the results of event detection based on differencing and regression models, we find that with the time series of all messages contributing to the political communication space, the regression model outperforms differencing. Although in this case the approach to event detection based on regression models performed somewhat better in identifying meaningful dates during the course of the campaign than the approach based on differencing, this does not necessarily follow for other cases.

5.4.3 Index of Political Relevance

After focusing on the analysis of time series documenting the daily volume of messages contributing to the political communication space, I will now move to those time series that offer a more focused and less aggregated view on references to specific political actors and events during the period under analysis. One possible way of identifying potentially politically relevant events is to determine a set of appropriate hashtags and determine for each day how many messages mentioned at least one of these hashtags and what share these messages had of the total number of messages posted that day. Yu-Ru Lin and colleagues have called this metric *event relevance ratio*. The higher the share that messages using hashtags listed on the index of political relevance have of all messages posted on that day, the higher is the political relevance of that day (Lin et al. 2014).

Of course, deciding which hashtags to list in the index of political relevance determines which political events and which political actors are considered in the measurement of political relevance. Focusing only on traditional political actors, on the one hand, might lead to an underestimation of events relevant to grass-roots movements or political activists. On the other hand, some of the events initiated by activists gathered high popularity online but remained of little consequence offline—for example the Yeaahh-flashmobs (Jungherr 2012). The inclusion of hashtags referring to these events might dwarf other events that were relevant to the campaign offline but found only moderate echo online. To account for this dynamic, I decided to calculate two indices of political relevance, one focusing only

5.4 Political Events and Their Shadows on Twitter

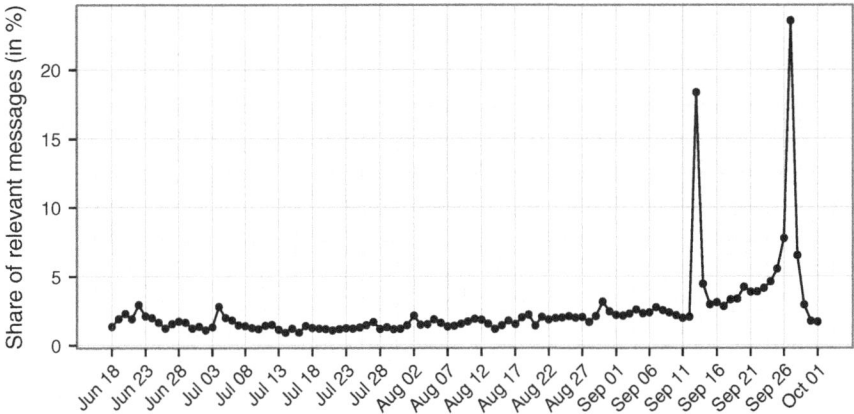

Fig. 5.11 Index of political relevance per day (traditional political actors)

on mentions of the campaign, the election, the televised leaders' debate, political parties, and the major candidates,[4] the other adding hashtags referring to two events during the campaign of high relevance to political activists.[5] The analysis of both these metrics does indeed offer a different picture of relevant events during the campaign.

The time series documenting the share of politically relevant messages on all messages posted by politically vocal users in Germany—Fig. 5.11—offers a similar picture of the campaign to the time series of all politically relevant hashtags. Two phases of political activity on Twitter emerge. From June 18 to September 12—the day preceding the televised debate between the two leading candidates—the share of politically relevant messages fluctuates mildly between 1 and 3 % of all daily messages. From September 13 to September 29, the share of politically relevant messages regularly fluctuates between 4 and 7 %, while being dominated by two

---

[4]Hashtags collected in this index were a subset of those hashtags contributing to the political communication space. The following concepts were accounted for by responding hashtags: Politics, the campaign, and the election: #btw09, #bundestagswahl, #politik, #wahlkampf, #wahlen, #sst; Televised debate: #tvduell; CDU/CSU: #cdu, #cducsu, #csu; SPD: #spd; FDP: #fdp; Bündnis 90/Die Grünen: #buendnis90, #bündnis, #bündnis90, #bündnis90diegrünen, #bündnis90grüne, #bündnisgrüne, #bündnisgrünen, #die_gruenen, #die_grünen, #diegrünen, #gruene, #grüne, #grünen; Die LINKE: #die_linke, #dielinke, #linke, #linkspartei; Piratenpartei: #piraten, #piratenpartei; Angela Merkel: #angie, #merkel, #angie_merkel, #angelamerkel, #angela_merkel; Frank-Walter Steinmeier: #steinmeier, #fws, #frank_walter_steinmeier, #steini, #frankwaltersteinmeier, #frank_steinmeier.

[5]In addition to the hashtags collected in the index of political relevance concentrating on traditional political actors, in this index four hashtags were included that referred to two campaigns by political activists during the run-up to election day. Protests against the Access Impediment Act: #petition, #zensursula; Yeaahh-flashmobs: #undallesoyeaahh, #yeaahh.

strong outliers on September 13—the day of the televised debate—and September 27—election day.

For this analysis, I decided on a simpler approach for detecting outliers than the one I had used in the preceding analyses. On the one hand, the time series contains less noise than the aggregated time series that provided the basis for the preceding analyses, thus less sophistication is needed to identify meaningful signals in the data. On the other hand, the analyses before have shown that advanced statistical methods do not necessarily offer a clearer picture of events underlying the dynamics of political Twitter use.

As the time series shown in Fig. 5.11 was clearly driven by two different variance regimes, I decided to split the time series on September 17. Following this, I used box-plots to identify outliers in both sections. In Table 5.5 I listed the days that were identified by outliers.

While Fig. 5.11 offered an intuitive picture of the dynamics dominating the course of the campaign, Table 5.5 offers only a very coarse view. Political Twitter messages reached unusually high shares in the overall Twitter conversation on days that were dominated by media events—namely, the state elections on August 30, the televised debate between Angela Merkel and Frank-Walter Steinmeier on September 13, and the federal election on September 27. The index of political relevance thus mirrors the most important events during the campaign, but is of no further help in determining significant yet less prominent events.

It is also interesting to note that even among the messages of politically vocal users the share of politically relevant messages mostly remains below 5 %. This changes somewhat once we look at days closer to the election, but even on days of high political relevance the share of politically relevant messages reaches only between 23 and 18 % of the total number. Politics seem only of minor importance in messages posted by politically interested Twitter users in Germany, even during a federal election campaign.

Broadly, the index of political relevance appears to be a very blunt instrument for identifying politically relevant events. One reason for this is the overall rising level of relevant Twitter messages during the last days of the campaign. This dynamic appears to be due to the general heightened level of interest in the campaign following the televised debate and not specifically campaign related events. Another reason might be that the share of politically relevant Twitter messages spiked in reaction to media events and not to campaign related events witnessed by Twitter users directly—such as party conventions. The view of the campaign offered by this construction of the political relevance index thus seems to mirror media attention

Table 5.5 Days identified by index of political relevance (traditional political actors)

Date	Event	Type
August 30, 2009 (Sunday)	State elections	Media event
September 13, 2009 (Sunday)	TV-debate between leading candidates	Media event
September 27, 2009 (Sunday)	Election day	Media event

5.4 Political Events and Their Shadows on Twitter

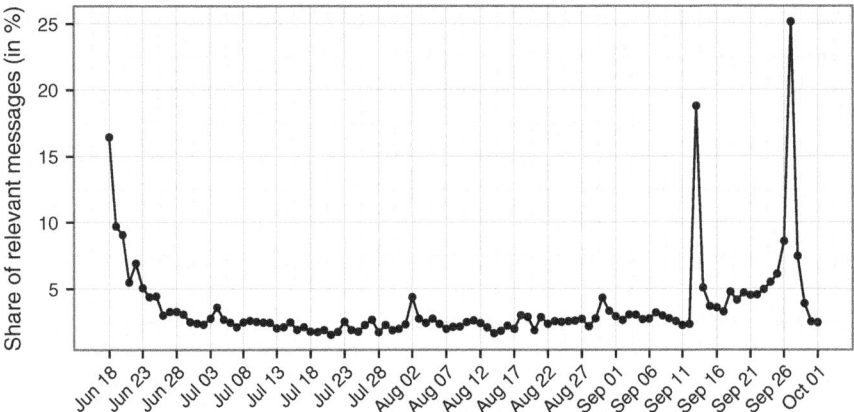

Fig. 5.12 Index of political relevance per day (traditional political actors and activists)

and not necessarily the campaign activities by political actors. By including hashtags of relevance to political activists and non-traditional actors in the index of political relevance this rather somber picture changes somewhat.

Figure 5.12 documents the daily share of messages using a selection of politically relevant hashtags and those referring to campaigns by political activists and non-traditional political actors. The time series is slightly more volatile than the one shown in Fig. 5.11. The one big difference between the time series is the considerable spike in message share on June 18—the day of the Access Impediment Act's ratification. Otherwise, the time series follows a similar pattern to that of the political relevance index.

Since the time series is dominated by spikes in the beginning and the end, I decided not to split the time series based on differing variance regimes but instead calculated outliers using box-plots over the whole series. The days identified by outliers are listed in Table 5.6.

The days identified by outliers in the index are mostly already known to us from previous analyses. We find the expected media events and also spikes on days of relevance to political activists—such as the day of the Access Impediment Act's ratification and mobilization for protests against it. On the whole, events organized or initiated by the Pirate Party leave a much more prominent shadow in the index of political relevance once we account for hashtags of relevance to political activists.

Both Tables 5.5 and 5.6 show two interesting patterns. First, the share of messages containing politically relevant messages rises steadily after the televised debate and in the run-up to the federal election. Second, spikes in volume are often connected to media or independent events. On the days following these spikes, the share of politically relevant messages remains somewhat above the baseline of typical days. Once an event raises interest in politics among Twitter users, they keep posting messages referring to politics more frequently than normal for a couple of days before moving on to other topics.

Table 5.6 Days identified by index of political relevance (traditional political actors and activists)

Date	Event	Type
June 18, 2009 (Thursday)	Access Impediment Act	Independent event
June 19, 2009 (Friday)	Access Impediment Act (aftermath)	Follow-up activity
June 20, 2009 (Saturday)	Protests against Access Impediment Act	Campaign-initiated event
June 22, 2009 (Monday)	Access Impediment Act (aftermath)	Follow-up activity
September 13, 2009 (Sunday)	Televised leaders' debate	Media event
September 25, 2009 (Friday)	Campaign by pirate party supporters to participate in TV-total election special reaches peak	Campaign-initiated event
September 26, 2009 (Saturday)	TV-total election special	Media initiated event
September 27, 2009 (Sunday)	Election day	Media event
September 28, 2009 (Monday)	Election (aftermath)	Follow-up activity

If we compare the index of political relevance with event detection based on regression or differencing we see that all three approaches make it possible to map the general dynamic of the campaign. Significantly, analyzing only a handful of political relevant hashtags—the index of political relevance—produced similar results to the analysis of the political communication space—a much more substantive collection of politically relevant hashtags. Nevertheless, the three approaches miss important stages of the campaign—be they important controversies or events initiated by the campaigns. One possible reason for this is that the preceding analyses were based on aggregated time series. It is possible that the aggregation of time series, documenting the mentions of political actors and referring to various campaign related phenomena, might introduce noise that hinders the identification of relevant events during the campaign. The following analyses will show whether or not the analysis of time series referring to single political parties, leading candidates or controversies will allow for a more reliable identification.

5.4.4 Parties

The previous sections showed that there was some potential for identifying politically relevant events by analyzing aggregated time series of messages using hashtags referring to politics. Still, this potential was somewhat diluted by the high count of false positives—days that were identified by spikes in the volume of Twitter

5.4 Political Events and Their Shadows on Twitter

Table 5.7 Descriptive metrics of messages referring to political parties

Party	Total number of messages	Max	Min	Mean	Median
CDU/CSU	33,343	1793	65	315	262
SPD	30,306	2268	49	285	197
FDP	20,822	1892	20	196	118
Bündnis 90/Die Grünen	15,474	1077	29	146	110
Die LINKE	8776	899	8	83	55
Piratenpartei	85,943	6471	230	811	578

messages but did not correspond with politically relevant events. In this and the following sections, I will examine whether or not time series referring to specific political actors or topics fair better in identifying relevant political events. In this section, I focus on the link between political events and mentions of political parties. My analysis includes mentions of parties that were already in Parliament CDU/CSU,[6] SPD,[7] FDP,[8] Bündnis 90/Die Grünen,[9] and Die LINKE.[10] I also included a new political player on Germany's political stage, the Pirate Party.[11]

The federal election campaign of 2009 marks the entry of the Pirate Party as a significant player in German politics. Early in 2009, well before the start of the campaign, public debate in Germany focused on a controversial piece of legislation—the Access Impediment Act. This issue was covered intensively by the media and brought Internet-related questions to the forefront of political media coverage. During the campaign's run, the fledgling Pirate Party managed to profit from this media attention to all things related to politics and the Internet. Naturally, the Pirate Party with its focus on questions related to Internet regulation and policy dominated the attention online. This becomes apparent once we examine the total number of Pirate Party hashtag mentions by politically vocal Twitter users during the course of the campaign in Table 5.7. The Pirate Party was by far the most-mentioned of all parties.

---

[6]The following hashtags were included referring to the CDU/CSU: #cdu, #cducsu, and #csu.

[7]The following hashtags were included referring to the SPD: #spd.

[8]The following hashtags were included referring to the FDP: #fdp.

[9]The following hashtags were included referring to Bündnis 90/Die Grünen: #buendnis90, #bündnis, #bündnis90, #bündnis90diegrünen, #bündnis90grüne, #bündnisgrüne, #bündnisgrünen, #die_gruenen, #die_grünen, #diegrünen, #gruene, #grüne, and #grünen.

[10]The following hashtags were included referring to Die LINKE: #die_linke, #dielinke, #linke, and #linkspartei.

[11]The following hashtags were included referring to die Piratenpartei: #piraten and #piratenpartei.

Table 5.7 shows the total number of hashtag mentions, the maxima, minima, median, and mean of mentions per day for the parties represented in the German Parliament and the Pirate Party. These very basic metrics already show a few characteristics of the time series. First, we see that the Pirate Party dominates by far the hashtag mentions of all parties. Thus, the communication sphere on Twitter during the campaign for the German federal election of 2009 was not normalized in that non-traditional political actors dominated the attention of Twitter users. This observation will be further discussed in Chap. 7, but for now let us focus on the other characteristics of the time series.

Examining the time series of parties' hashtag mentions in messages shown in Fig. 5.13, shows that they are dominated by similar patterns. Party mentions fluctuate relatively consistently around a low baseline through June and July. This baseline rises somewhat between August and September. From then on, the volume of messages mentioning political parties rises sharply only to drop off just as sharply after election day. For all parties, this pattern breaks on various days due to sudden increases in daily message volume. And while these increases do not necessarily lead to total peaks, they often result in volume peaks relative to the mention volume of days in their immediate vicinity.

Examining the link between volume peaks and political events produces mixed results. Table 5.8 shows that most peaks could be connected to big campaign-related media events (such as election night coverage on August 30 and September 27), campaign-initiated events (such as party conventions), and media-initiated events (such as the publication of interviews or digital objects, for example videos or caricatures). Still, most peaks in Twitter volume of party mentions did not rise directly in reaction to campaign related events. Instead, we see an increase in the volume of messages reacting to media coverage of the campaign and digital objects posted by campaigns, activists, or the media. There was also a considerable number of spikes that were not connected to specific events.

While these findings demonstrate which events tend to lead to peaks in the volume of Twitter messages mentioning political parties, we must also consider those that did not. Most events listed in Table 5.1 did not lead to spikes in the mention volume of parties. Thus, important campaign-related independent events, campaign-, or media-initiated events did not create shadows in digital trace data. This shows that Twitter users' attention to politics as manifested in their activity on the microblogging services provides only a very biased view of the campaign.

We also have to note that the messages contributing to peaks in message volume did not necessarily focus on one event, issue, or digital object. Instead, Twitter messages contributed to a multi-threaded conversation. This resulted in days on which a relatively high number of events or topics created reactions on Twitter which in combination resulted in relative volume peaks. Thus, these peaks happen on days when users did not focus their collective attention on one specific event of

5.4 Political Events and Their Shadows on Twitter

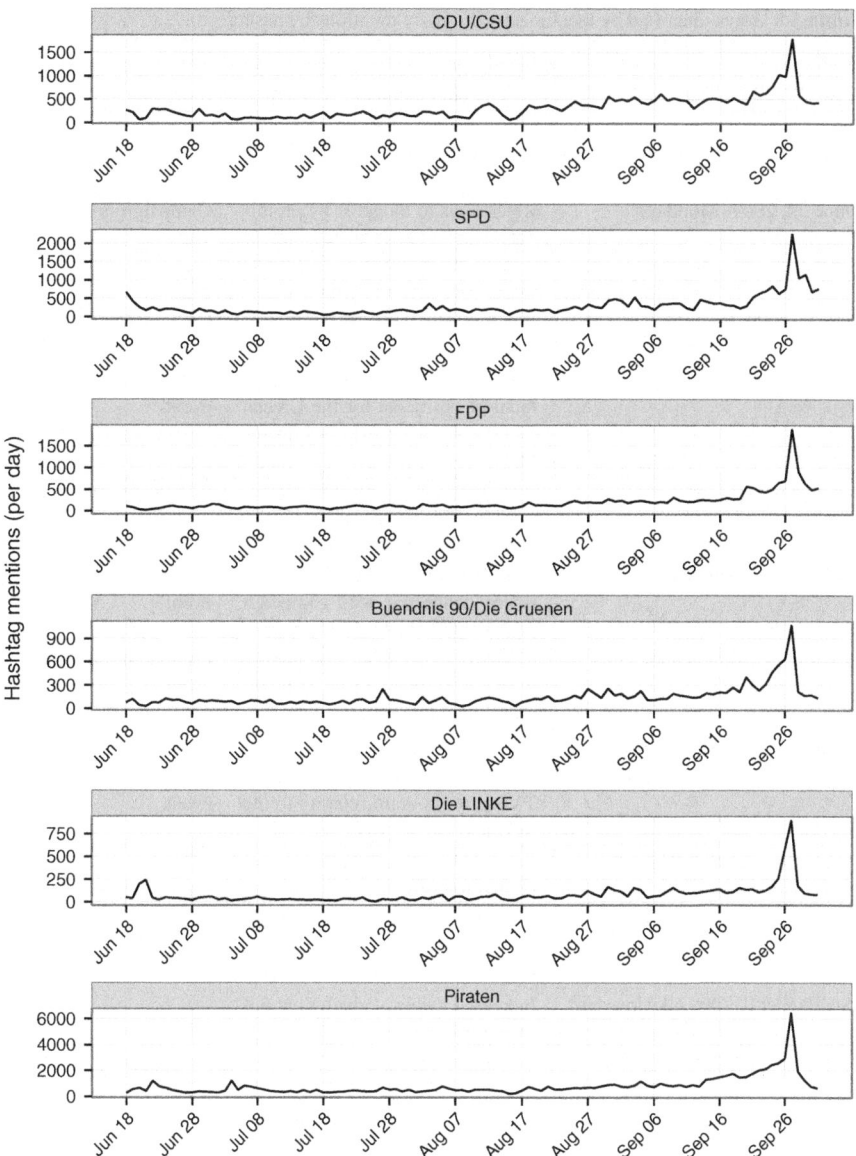

Fig. 5.13 Number of messages mentioning parties by hashtags

relevance to the campaign. This finding raises a serious issue for the identification of relevant events based on shifts in the mention volume of political topics in Twitter messages.

Table 5.8 Days identified by local maxima in party mentions by hashtag

Date	Event	Type
June 18, 2009 (Thursday)	Access Impediment Act, mentions focus on SPD	Independent event
June 20/21, 2009 (Saturday)	Party convention, Die LINKE	Campaign-initiated event
June 22, 2009 (Monday)	References to blogpost by prominent activist about his reasons for joining the Pirate Party and references to campaign video	Campaign-initiated event
July 4, 2009 (Saturday)	Pirate party convention	Campaign-initiated event
July 27, 2009 (Monday)	Reactions to controversial statement of politician for the Greens in support of the Access Impediment Act	Campaign-initiated event
August 3, 2009 (Monday)	Reactions to controversial statement by SPD politician in support of the Access Impediment Act	Campaign-initiated event
August 12, 2009 (Wednesday)	Conversation critiques various issues connected with campaign posters published by CDU/CSU	Campaign-initiated event
August 27, 2009 (Thursday)	Controversy about founding member of the Greens publicly switching to the pirates	Campaign-initiated event
August 30, 2009 (Sunday)	State elections	Media event
September 3, 2009 (Thursday)	Reactions to content posted by TV satire program relating to the SPD and Die LINKE	Media-initiated event
September 4, 2009 (Friday)	Increased levels of chatter but not related to events	–
September 7, 2009 (Monday)	Day of important TV appearance by Angela Merkel, still most chatter is not related to specific events	–
September 9, 2009 (Wednesday)	Increased levels of chatter but not related to events	–
September 20, 2009 (Sunday)	FDP party convention	Campaign-initiated event
September 21, 2009 (Monday)	Increased levels of chatter but not related to events	–
September 27, 2009 (Sunday)	Election day	Media event

5.4.5 Candidates

After analyzing messages referring to political parties, let us look at time series mentioning the two leading candidates of the two biggest parties—CDU/CSU and

5.4 Political Events and Their Shadows on Twitter

Table 5.9 Descriptive metrics of messages referring to leading candidates

Party	Total number of messages	Max	Min	Mean	Median
Angela Merkel	8323	1308	3	79	38
Frank-Walter Steinmeier	6454	1424	2	61	26

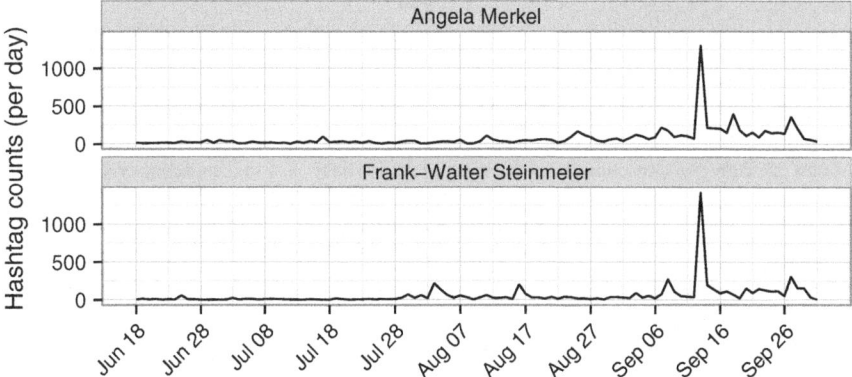

Fig. 5.14 Number of messages mentioning Angela Merkel and Frank-Walter Steinmeier by hashtags

SPD. In 2009 Angela Merkel entered the campaign as Germany's Chancellor and leading candidate for the CDU/CSU.[12] In contrast Frank-Walter Steinmeier entered as Germany's Foreign Minister and leading candidate for the Social Democrats (SPD).[13] Table 5.9 shows that both candidates were mentioned less often than political parties by political vocal Twitter users. Angela Merkel—the candidate who was mentioned most—was still mentioned less frequently than the party which was mentioned least often—Die LINKE. This observation already shows differences between the mentions of political parties and politicians by Twitter users in this data set.

Like the mentions of political parties, those of leading candidates followed similar patterns. Figure 5.14 shows both time series in direct comparison. We see that both time series demonstrate a much lighter upward trend than party mentions. It appears, therefore, that candidates are mentioned much more directly in connection with specific political events than political parties. Parties, in contrast, seem to bundle ever increasing levels of attention once the election day grows closer, somewhat more independently of specific events. Both time series are dominated by

---

[12]The following hashtags were included referring to Angela Merkel: #angie, #merkel, #angie_merkel, #angelamerkel, and #angela_merkel.

[13]The following hashtags were included referring to Frank-Walter Steinmeier: #steinmeier, #fws, #frank_walter_steinmeier, #steini, #frankwaltersteinmeier, and #frank_steinmeier.

Table 5.10 Days identified by local maxima in candidate mentions by hashtag

Date	Event	Type
July 17, 2009 (Friday)	Reactions to birthday of Angela Merkel	Independent event
August 3, 2009 (Monday)	Presentation of SPD campaign program	Campaign-initiated event
August 11, 2009 (Tuesday)	Reactions to interview and live chat with Angela Merkel organized by TV station RTL	Media-initiated event
August 16, 2009 (Sunday)	RTL Townhall: Frank-Walter Steinmeier	Media-initiate event
August 25, 2009 (Tuesday)	Reactions to controversy about birthday dinner for Josef Ackermann in chancellery	Independent event
September 7, 2009 (Monday)	Day of important TV appearance by Angela Merkel	Media-initiated event
September 8, 2009 (Tuesday)	Day of important TV appearance by Frank-Walter Steinmeier	Media-initiate event
September 13, 2009 (Sunday)	Televised leaders' debate	Media event
September 18, 2009 (Friday)	Yeaahh! flashmob at Merkel campaign event	Independent event
September 27, 2009 (Sunday)	Election day	Media event

outliers, the strongest of which falls on the day of the leaders' debate, not on election night—as was the case with party mentions.

Examining days on which volume spikes fell reveals that they more reliably identified politically relevant events than spikes in the volume of party mentions—compare Table 5.10. This is another indicator that candidate mentions have a closer connection with specific events than mentions of political parties. Still, even the events identified by peaks in the volume of political candidates do not offer us an unbiased or reasonably complete picture of the 2009 election run.

The strongest peak in both time series fell on the day of the televised candidate debate, September 13. On the day of the election—September 27—we also find a peak in the volume of messages mentioning Angela Merkel and Frank-Walter Steinmeier. Yet, this peak is much less prevalent than the corresponding spike in time series mentioning political parties. Other peaks in the mentions of Angela Merkel fall on July 17, Angela Merkel's birthday; August 11, an interview with Angela Merkel on the television station RTL and a subsequent live chat with her; August 25, a controversy about a birthday dinner for the then CEO of Deutsche Bank, Josef Ackermann, in the chancellery; September 7, Merkel appearing on the program *ARD Wahlarena*; and on September 18, posts concerning a flashmob organized by activists at a campaign stop by Merkel in Hamburg. Other dates identified by spikes in the volume of messages mentioning Frank-Walter Steinmeier were August 3, the official presentation of Steinmeier's campaign program *Deutschlandplan*;

5.4 Political Events and Their Shadows on Twitter 139

August 16, Steinmeier appears on a prominent television program *RTL Townhall*; and September 8, Steinmeier appears on the television program *ARD Wahlarena*.

5.4.6 Controversies

In this section I will examine whether or not big political controversies can be identified in messages posted by Twitter users. I will focus on the time series of hashtag mentions for five big controversies which arose during the course of the campaign: the ratification of the Access Impediment Act; the controversy about then Minister of Health, Ulla Schmidt (SPD) and her official car which was stolen during her holidays in Spain; the drafting of a key piece of legislation being outsourced by the then Minister of the Economy, Karl Theodor zu Guttenberg (CSU), to a legal firm; the controversy about a birthday dinner for then CEO of Deutsche Bank, Josef Ackermann, in the chancellery; and, finally, the controversy about an airstrike by the Bundeswehr on a stolen fuel truck in Kunduz, Afghanistan. These topics found heavy media coverage during the campaign and constituted key topics in public discourse. They all led to discernible reactions on Twitter, albeit with widely varying levels of intensity.

Table 5.11 shows that there were strong differences in the levels of interest that these controversies found with Twitter users. By far the strongest reactions were created by the ratification of the Access Impediment Act, followed by mentions of Karl-Theodor zu Guttenberg—although, it has to be said, that only a minority of his mentions focused on his role in the controversy about the outsourcing of legislation. Ulla Schmidt, Josef Ackermann, and the events in Kunduz received much fewer mentions. The low mention count of the controversial airstrike in Kunduz is especially interesting, since of all the controversies this was the one with the clearest connection to political key issues and resulted in the resignation of then Minister of Defense, Franz Josef Jung (CDU). Still, this issue received hardly any attention in the messages posted by politically vocal Twitter users. These findings suggest that Twitter messages cover specific parts of political campaigns— those connected with Internet policy and controversies about the personal conduct of politicians—but ignore others—abstract or complex political questions, such as

Table 5.11 Descriptive metrics of messages referring to various controversies during the campaign

Controversy	Total number of messages	Max	Min	Mean	Median
Access Impediment Act	65,456	9326	81	618	361
Ulla Schmidt	752	146	0	7	0
Karl-Theodor zu Guttenberg	1200	72	0	11	8
Josef Ackermann	515	224	0	5	0
Kunduz	97	15	0	1	0

foreign policy or defense. A closer examination of the dynamics for messages' time series referring to the controversies in question will offer another view at what phenomena drive the coverage of political controversies in Twitter messages.

Access Impediment Act

The Access Impediment Act (Zugangserschwerungsgesetz) was a piece of legislation introduced early in 2009 by the then Minister of Family Affairs, Ursula von der Leyen (CDU). It was ratified by Parliament on June 18. The law should have forced access providers to block access to a list of domains, IPs, and URLs of sites and sources under the suspicion of providing child pornography. The list was to have been maintained by the Federal Criminal Police Office (Bundeskriminalamt) and should have been kept secret from the public. Even at the early stages, the proposition and early drafts of the Access Impediment Act were met with strong protests by Internet and civil liberty activists who saw the law as superfluous in the fight against child pornography and also as a first step in the creation of an infrastructure that would potentially allow German law enforcement to censor content on the Internet without due process. The protest was channeled through the, up until then, most successful online petition to parliament with 134,014 signatures (Jungherr and Jürgens 2010). The protests also led to a significant increase in supporters of the Pirate Party, a party focusing on issues of Internet regulation and civil liberties. Both the online petition and the Pirate Party managed to attract significant media attention which introduced controversy about the Access Impediment Act to the general public. It comes as no surprise that the Access Impediment Act and its public face, Ursula von der Leyen, were a hot topic in Twitter messages posted during the campaign.

Figure 5.15 shows the time series of daily hashtag mentions for the controversy[14] and is dominated by a massive volume peak on June 18, the day of the Access Impediment Act's ratification in Parliament. In the following period the volume of messages from July onwards drops to reach a baseline of roughly 350 mentions on a typical day. This baseline is broken on a number of days when the volume of messages referring to the controversy spike somewhat. Still, these local peaks never reach the message volume shown before June 28.

Analyzing Table 5.12 events that happened on days identified by local maxima in the time series, it is shown that all peaks emerged in reaction to specific events connected with the controversy. June 18, the day of the strongest peak, was the day the Access Impediment Act was ratified. On July 23 users reacted with critique, humor, and satire to a press announcement of a proposal from Ursula von der Leyen for the development of behavioral guidelines on social networking sites for young users. On August 18 users were predominantly linking to news coverage referring

---

[14]The following hashtags were included referring to the controversy about the Access Impediment Act: #zensursula, #stoppschild, and #netzsperren.

5.4 Political Events and Their Shadows on Twitter

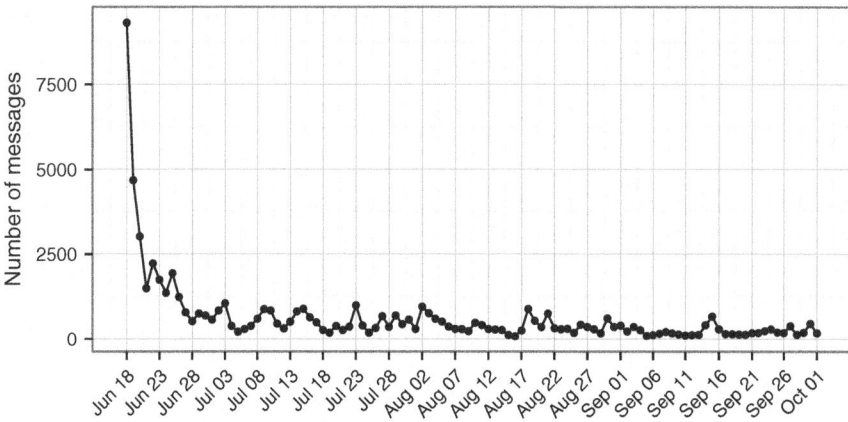

Fig. 5.15 Number of messages mentioning the controversy over the Access Impediment Act in hashtags

Table 5.12 Days identified by local maxima in the hashtag mentions of the Access Impediment Act

Date	Event	Type
June 18, 2009 (Thursday)	Access Impediment Act	Independent event
July 23, 2009 (Thursday)	Satirical reactions to proposal by Ursula von der Leyen for an official guideline for behavior on social networking sites for young people	Campaign-initiated event
August 18, 2009 (Tuesday)	References to case of Austrian journalist whose website was blocked by Austrian authorities	Independent event
September 15, 2009 (Tuesday)	Political talk show with Ursula von der Leyen	Media-initiated event

to an Austrian journalist, critical of the Austrian government, whose website had in turn been blocked by Austrian authorities. Twitter users cited this case as evidence of things to come were the Access Impediment Act to be implemented in Germany. Finally, on September 15 users commented heavily and predominantly critically on the television appearance of Ursula von der Leyen on a prominent political talk show—the *ZDF Wahlforum*—during which she defended the Access Impediment Act.

Events connected with the controversy about the Access Impediment Act led users to post more messages referring to the topic than on other days. However, the events identified by these peaks although connected offer no comprehensive map of the controversy. Instead, we see a rather idiosyncratic selection of topically related events. The events identified by local maxima led to largely critical and satirical reactions on Twitter, which contained links and concentrated on personal aspects of Ursula von der Leyen.

Ulla Schmidt

In late July a controversy arose about Ulla Schmidt's (SPD) potentially unjustified uses of her official car. The then Minister for Health had taken her official car and driver with her on holiday in Spain where the car was subsequently stolen. Between late July and August this incident led to a controversy about the minister's use of her official car and led Ulla Schmidt to postpone her campaign activities in support of Frank-Walter Steinmeier until the issue was settled. The controversy was widely covered by traditional media and kindled by statements from CDU/CSU and FDP politicians. While Twitter users reacted to this controversy and the connected media coverage, the volume of messages is dwarfed by that of messages commenting on the controversy about the Access Impediment Act.

The time series of relevant hashtag mentions[15] shown in Fig. 5.16 is dominated by a relatively high peak in volume around July 27, the day traditional media reported the story about the stolen car and started to cover the ensuing controversy. On no other day during the campaign was the controversy referred to as strongly on Twitter. After July 29 the volume of messages mentioning either Ulla Schmidt or her car drop drastically. On a typical day after the report no or only a handful of messages were referring to the controversy. Still, there are some days in which this baseline is broken and some 30 messages, or so, refer to her.

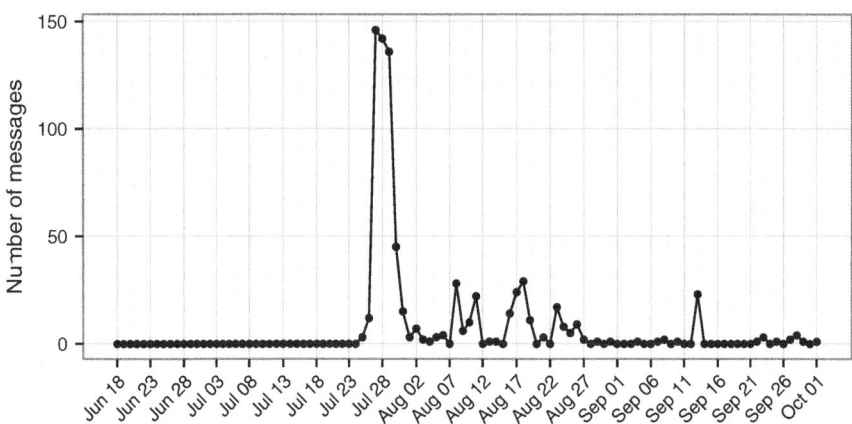

Fig. 5.16 Number of messages mentioning Ulla Schmidt in hashtags

---

[15]The following hashtags were included referring to Ulla Schmidt or her *Dienstwagen Controversy*. #urlaubsulla, #ullaschmidt, #sklasseulla, #ulla_schmidt, #limousinenulla, and #dienstwagenulla.

5.4 Political Events and Their Shadows on Twitter

Table 5.13 Days identified by local maxima in the hashtag mentions of Ulla Schmidt

Date	Event	Type
July 27, 2009 (Monday)	Messages post links to reports of Ulla Schmidt's stolen car and caricatures, also users are publicly negotiating the meaning of the event by either accusing or defending Ulla Schmidt	Independent event
August 8, 2009 (Saturday)	Frank-Walter Steinmeier announces Ulla Schmidt's participation in his shadow cabinet	Campaign-initiated event
August 11, 2009 (Tuesday)	Increased level of not event specific chatter	–
August 18, 2009 (Tuesday)	Links to new developments in the story	Media-initiated event
September 13, 2009 (Sunday)	Opponents of the SPD use the coverage of the televised debate between Angela Merkel and Frank-Walter Steinmeier to post comments about the controversy	Media event

Most of the days identified by local peaks—listed in Table 5.13—are indeed connected with the controversy and offer a view of key stages in the controversy. The volume peak around July 27 is produced by messages linking to early news reports about Ulla Schmidt's stolen car. Links to caricatures are also very prominent. Quite a few messages contributed to a public negotiation of meaning. Supporters of Ulla Schmidt were very vocal in defending her taking the official car to Spain, while critics tried to scandalize her behavior. On August 8 the volume of mentions spikes again, this time in reaction to the announcement by Frank-Walter Steinmeier that Ulla Schmidt was going to be a member of his shadow cabinet. The spike on August 18 reacts to new revelations by media reports in which it was shown that Ulla Schmidt had also taken her official car for holidays to Spain on other occasions. Finally, during the televised debate between Angela Merkel and Frank-Walter Steinmeier, supporters of Angela Merkel commented on Twitter about the controversy. This can be seen as an attempt at counter framing by political supporters to leverage the attention big media events receive in conversations online and to introduce topics in competition with the issues raised by journalists and traditional elites.

Analyzing messages referring to Ulla Schmidt and the controversy about her stolen car thus offers a comprehensive yet slanted map, one which focused on revelations damaging to her cause and largely omitted points in support of her position. Twitter messages thus seem to spike when driven by events or stimuli allowing users to post negative comments on the personal or professional conduct of politicians.

Karl-Theodor zu Guttenberg

On August 12 the story broke that the then Minister of the Economy, Karl-Theodor zu Guttenberg (CSU), had outsourced the drafting of a law for the regulation of finance markets to Linklaters, a British law firm. This story resulted in attacks on the minister by politicians from other parties who argued that he was spending taxpayers' money irresponsibly and displayed a lack of confidence in the abilities of the civil servants within his ministry. During the campaign, this controversy was covered heavily by traditional media and dutifully kindled by politicians from opposing parties. Yet, on Twitter this controversy makes only for a fraction of all mentions of Karl-Theodor zu Guttenberg.

Clearly, the time series documenting hashtag mentions of zu Guttenberg[16] shown in Fig. 5.17 is noisier than the time series of mentions to do with Ulla Schmidt. Karl Theodor zu Guttenberg is an almost daily topic in Twitter messages. There are several spikes in his daily mentions, but none so high as the spike Ulla Schmidt received, once the press started to cover the story of her stolen car. Obviously, zu Guttenberg was a more controversial politician who was a constant, if minor topic in the messages of politically vocal Twitter users. Table 5.14 lists the days of relative spikes in the volume of messages referring to zu Guttenberg and the events creating these spikes.

It is interesting to note that the press coverage of outsourcing legal drafts to the law firm Linklaters produced only a minor spike in zu Guttenberg's mentions. Instead, the mentions spiked in reaction to his alleged plans to curtail workers rights (August 17) and to support nuclear power plant owners (September 18). His

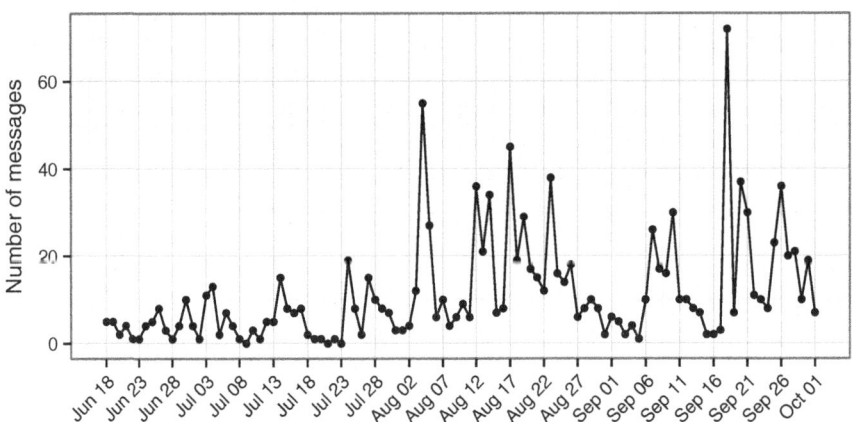

Fig. 5.17 Number of messages mentioning Karl-Theodor zu Guttenberg in hashtags

---

[16]The following hashtags were included referring to Karl-Theodor zu Guttenberg or the controversy: #guttenberg.

5.4 Political Events and Their Shadows on Twitter 145

Table 5.14 Days identified by local maxima in the hashtag mentions of Karl-Theodor zu Guttenberg

Date	Event	Type
August 4, 2009 (Tuesday)	Increased level of not event specific chatter	–
August 17, 2009 (Monday)	Critical reactions to reports about Guttenberg's alleged plans regarding workers's rights	Campaign-initiated event
August 23, 2009 (Sunday)	Appearance in political talk show *SAT1 Wahlarena*	Media-initiated event
September 18, 2009 (Friday)	Critical reactions to reports about Guttenberg's alleged plans regarding nuclear power plans	Campaign-initiated event

mentions also spiked somewhat in reaction to his television appearance on a popular political talk show (August 23). The interest of the media and fellow politicians in the outsourcing of legal drafts did not seem to be mirrored by the interest of Twitter users. Instead, they focused on his alleged statements with regard to social justice and the controversial issue of nuclear power, as well as his appearance on television. Again, Twitter attention appears to offer only a very selective view of a political controversy.

Josef Ackermann

On August 24 the story broke that in April 2008 Angela Merkel had invited the then CEO of Deutsche Bank, Josef Ackermann, and thirty guests chosen by him to the chancellery for a dinner in honor of his sixtieth birthday. The media and opposing politicians acted quickly on the story and a controversy arose as to whether or not it was appropriate for Angela Merkel to host a birthday party—as it was called by the media—for the head of one of the biggest German banks. Unsurprisingly, Twitter users reacted to the story in their messages. Figure 5.18 shows a time series for the mentions of Josef Ackermann and the controversy in hashtags used by politically vocal Twitter users.

The time series of relevant hashtag mentions[17] shown in Fig. 5.18 is dominated by a spike in Twitter mentions on August 24–27, the days following the breaking of the story. Following these days, the conversation about Josef Ackermann quietens down to return with only a small spike during the date of the televised debate between Angela Merkel and Frank-Walter Steinmeier. These days are listed in Table 5.15.

---

[17]The following hashtags were included referring to Josef Ackermann or the controversy: #ackermann, #ackermannsause, #ackermannbankett, #ackermannkanzlerinsause, #ackermannparty, #ackermanndinner, #ackermannessen, and #merkelackermannparty.

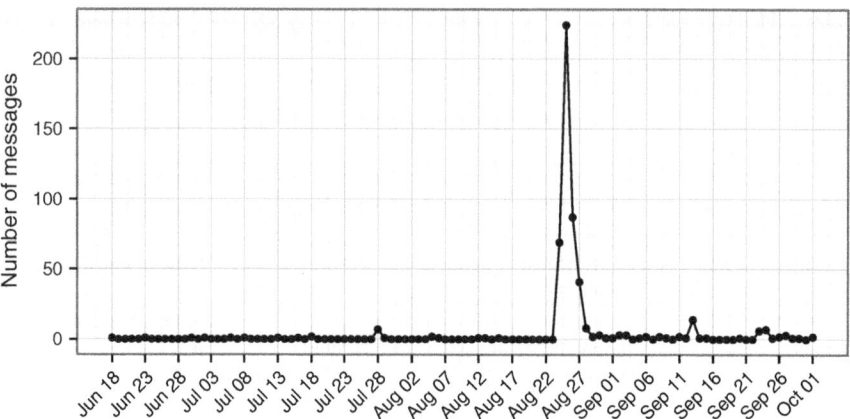

Fig. 5.18 Number of messages mentioning Josef Ackermann in hashtags

Table 5.15 Days identified by local maxima in the hashtag mentions of Josef Ackermann

Date	Event	Type
August 25, 2009 (Tuesday)	References to press coverage of birthday celebration for Ackermann in chancellery and satirical comments on the controversy	Independent event
September 13, 2009 (Sunday)	References to the Ackermann controversy in messages commenting on the televised debate between Angela Merkel and Frank-Walter Steinmeier	Media event

In this case, Twitter messages mirror the dramatic developments of the controversy: a big spike in attention once the story broke was followed by increased levels of attention over the following days. During the televised leaders' debate activists raised the topic again in online discussions accompanying the media event, thereby challenging the narratives of candidates and journalists.

Kunduz

On September 4 two fuel trucks were attacked near Kunduz, Afghanistan by US fighter planes in compliance with the request of a German officer. Following this attack, discrepancies arose in justification of the attack and the official account given by Germany's then Minister of Defense, Franz Josef Jung (CDU). The minister resigned in November following these events. The attack in Kunduz and its justification were important topics during the last weeks of the campaign, especially because the Afghanistan mission of Germany's Bundeswehr was a controversial issue for the German public. In contrast, the Kunduz controversy found virtually no echo in the messages of politically vocal Twitter users. Figure 5.19 shows all

5.4 Political Events and Their Shadows on Twitter

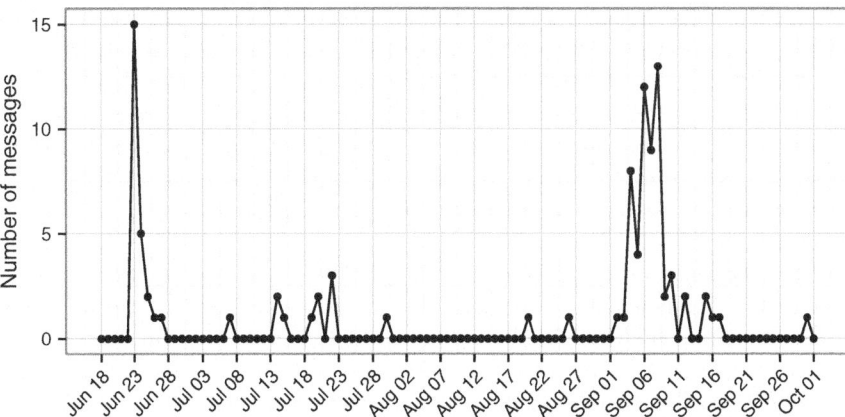

Fig. 5.19 Number of messages mentioning Kunduz in hashtags

Table 5.16 Days identified by local maxima in the hashtag mentions of Kunduz

Date	Event	Type
June 23, 2009 (Tuesday)	References to media reports of shots fired in Kunduz, Afghanistan	Independent event
September 4, 2009 (Friday)	References to air attack on stolen fuel tank	Independent event
September 6, 2009 (Sunday)	Official statement by government on the attack	Independent event
September 8, 2009 (Tuesday)	Parliament debate about the events in Kunduz, Afghanistan	Independent event

mentions of Kunduz and the air attack in messages posted during the course of the campaign.[18]

Of all the controversies analyzed in this section, the air attack in Kunduz, Afghanistan has probably the strongest claim to hard political relevance. The other controversies focused either on Internet regulation, a political topic of little interest to anyone but Internet activists, and the performance of politics generally. In contrast, the Kunduz controversy had the potential to revive a traditional cleavage in German politics, namely the question of whether or not the Bundeswehr should carry out missions in foreign countries. While the controversy was virtually nonexistent on Twitter, traditional media approached the issue in the context of its customarily high political volatility. The time series shows two spikes in volume—if we can call 15 messages a spike—one of which was connected to the air attack in Kunduz. Table 5.16 lists the days identified by local maxima and corresponding events.

---

[18]The following hashtags were included referring to the air attack in Kunduz, Afghanistan: #kunduz, #kundus, and #luftangriff_in_kundus.

The first spike, relative to the mentions on typical days, falls on June 23, referencing reports about shots fired in Kunduz. These shots were unrelated to the attack on the fuel trucks. Still, this peak shows that mentions of Kunduz react to media coverage of events connected with the town. On September 4 Twitter messages were referencing media reports of the attack, on September 6 Twitter users were referring to official government statements about the attack, while on September 8 messages referred to events connected with a special debate in Parliament on the topic.

While the peaks during this time series are clearly related to relevant stages of the controversy, the main point of note from this analysis is the topic's comparably low level of attention on Twitter. The politically vocal Twitter users in this data set were clearly not interested in the controversy. An issue of the highest political relevance was all but invisible on Twitter, an observation that spells caution for all looking to Twitter as a true mirror of political reality.

Common Patterns: Hashtag Mentions of Controversies

In this section I discussed Twitter messages which referred to one of five political controversies that arose during the campaign. These were different in type. Three focused on the personal behavior of politicians, one arose in reaction to a piece of legislation regarding the regulation of the Internet while the last one concerned Germany's military mission in Afghanistan. These controversies again varied strongly with regard to the levels of attention they found on Twitter. The debate about the Access Impediment Act created the biggest reaction. It was followed by— in descending order of relevance—various events connected with Karl-Theodor zu Guttenberg, the debate about Ulla Schmidt's stolen official car, and the dinner for Josef Ackermann's sixtieth birthday. Twitter users paid by far the least attention to events concerning the air attack in Kunduz, Afghanistan. Thus, Twitter users reacted very strongly—and negatively—to events concerning attempts at regulating the Internet and personalized political controversies, while topics of importance in the traditional political discussion—in this case foreign policy—seemed to garner little attention.

Twitter messages commenting on political controversies share temporal dynamics. Those commenting on a controversy tend to rise sharply in reaction to the initial media coverage. After 1 or 2 days, the volume of messages tends to reach an absolute peak only to fall off for a period of several days to reach a level slightly higher than the baseline of related hashtag mentions before the controversy. The subsequent pattern of Twitter messages depends on its further development. For cases in which no new facts arise after the initial coverage, mentions of the controversy basically flatline on Twitter—such a case was the controversy about the birthday dinner for Josef Ackermann. In other cases, the controversy keeps evolving, be it through the uncovering of new facts or new inputs by political actors. In these

5.4 Political Events and Their Shadows on Twitter

latter cases, Twitter coverage runs parallel to the time-line of information released by traditional media outlets on the issue, which happens in small peaks, albeit never reaching the message volume commenting on the controversy's initial coverage. Coverage of the Access Impediment Act, Ulla Schmidt, and the air attack in Kunduz followed this pattern, whereas the controversy about Karl-Theodor zu Guttenberg reveals yet another pattern. If a political actor polarizes opinion strongly, messages referring to him tend to peak regularly in reaction to events or statements, even if these statements or events are of minor importance. It seems as if Twitter users wait for any opportunity to post in critique or support controversial political figures. During the campaign for the federal election of 2009, Karl-Theodor zu Guttenberg was such a figure as evidenced by the high variance in the number of his hashtag mentions on Twitter.

Most messages posted in reaction to controversies contained links to reports by traditional media. In the case of the more popular controversies, many messages also linked to humorous and satirical content on the web, be it remixed images, or in some cases videos. Many messages were part of a collective negotiation of meaning. For example, the controversy about Ulla Schmidt's stolen car generated many such responses, as Twitter users posted messages giving reasons why they believed the story was of significance or, in contrast, why the whole affair was blown completely out of proportion. In these cases Twitter becomes a channel for the public exchange of different political viewpoints and sometimes even allows for the counter-framing of narratives established by traditional media or political elites. Still, to reach a larger audience, contributions to these negotiations have to be picked up by traditional media, thereby limiting Twitter's immediate influence on public discourse at large. We should also note that while some messages supported politicians embroiled in the respective controversies, most were heavily negative in tone.

These examples show that there is indeed information to be gained about political controversies by examining the temporal dynamics of messages referring to them on Twitter. Temporal patterns in Twitter messages can mirror the progression of controversies and sometimes even identify their different stages of development. But Twitter offers a far from unbiased view of political controversies. Topics of interest to heavy Internet users and topics allowing for personalization, scandalization, moral outrage, and visualization captured Twitter users' strongest attention during the campaign. Other topics were virtually ignored, thereby making Twitter an instrument unfit for determining such dynamics. These findings corroborate those from previous sections: Twitter offers a selective and sometimes fractured, even biased image of political reality distorted by the interests of users. This and other potential biases must be consciously addressed in attempts to use digital trace data collected on Twitter to analyze political and social events or other phenomena.

5.5 Twitter as a Sensor of Political Attention

In this chapter it could be shown that spikes in the volume of Twitter messages coincided most of the time with politically relevant events. This is a clear indicator that Twitter users indeed reacted to political stimuli—such as political events, political media coverage, or media appearances—by posting messages containing hashtags referring to politics. Twitter data might thus serve as valuable sources in mapping which elements of a campaign or media coverage received attention by politically vocal users as well as documenting the public negotiation of meaning between users commenting on events and controversies of high public attention.

At least as important is that during the campaign only a small selection of political events, media appearances by politicians, and controversies attracted enough collective attention by Twitter users to create measurable spikes in messages referring to politics. As a result, we should be cautious in expecting the dynamics of message volumes to offer a true, unbiased map of political events. Instead, we see a map mediated through the interests of Twitter users.

This mediation process explains the mixed levels of success in the detection of events relevant to the campaign in the analyses presented above. On the one hand, the general dynamics of time series documenting the daily message volume of Twitter messages referring to politics did indeed mirror the general stages of the campaign and did allow for the identification of high-profile events that were well covered by traditional media. On the other hand, the time series were much less helpful in identifying events that were important to the campaign but not as well covered. While big political media events met reliably with the attention of politically vocal Twitter users, most events during the campaign did not, leaving no visible traces, therefore, in the dynamics of Twitter messages referring to politics. The same was true for the analysis of political controversies, where personalized scandalization and issues related to Internet regulation left recognizable traces, while issues of objective political importance remained invisible. This makes it highly doubtful that the analysis of political events based on Twitter messages allows for a *true* mapping of the events in question; instead we will see an image of the events mediated through the interests of Twitter users.

In addition there remain three findings that pose serious technical challenges to the identification of important events during the course of the 2009 campaign. From mid September onwards, in most time series, there was a significant upward trend in the volume of messages mentioning politics. This upward trend, more likely than not, mirrored the gradual increase in public attention paid to politics during the final days of the campaign and is, therefore, probably the result of political activation through campaign activity and increased political media coverage. An increase in messages thus does not necessarily mirror reactions by Twitter users to specific events but might instead be a reflection of their temporally heightened political interest.

Messages using politically relevant hashtags in referring to general political concepts—such as abbreviations for the upcoming election, the names of political parties, or the names of the leading politicians—contributed to various conversations focusing on different aspects, events, or narratives connected with the general concept. Messages posted during 1 day using the hashtag #merkel might refer to a television appearance by Angela Merkel, her policy positions, or a statement made the day before. Calculating daily sums of all general concept mentions thus leads to an aggregate of these multi-threaded conversations. Two issues arise with this aggregation. On the one hand, peaks in messages referring to specific aspects, events, or narratives, all subsumed under one hashtag, might disappear in the daily aggregate. On the other hand, peaks in the daily use of politically relevant hashtags might not reflect increased attention to one aspect, event, or narrative but instead be the result of conversations about various topics in messages using the same hashtag. This multi-threaded nature of political conversations thus poses a general challenge to the identification and analysis of political events using Twitter data.

Most messages using politically relevant hashtags refer to media coverage of politics as opposed to political events experienced by Twitter users themselves. Messages linked either to content on websites of news agencies, newspapers, or television stations. Users also posted their reactions to the television appearances of political actors. While this opens up the possibility of using Twitter data to analyze public reactions to political media coverage and to examine which elements of political media coverage were picked up on Twitter and which were neglected, in the identification and examination of political events this presents a challenge, because Twitter might offer us a view on political events twice removed: the first filter is the decision of traditional media to cover campaign events; the second filter is the interest of Twitter users in politics. Forming an important exception to this are messages commenting on collective action or political niche topics, as for example seen in the reactions to the ratification of the Access Impediment Act. In these cases, Twitter might indeed offer an account of politically relevant events, which might be of interest to Twitter users but ignored by traditional media. Still, in the much more structured context of a political campaign, it is doubtful whether Twitter data allow a more direct identification and analysis of political events than is presented by the analysis of media coverage.

These observations show that Twitter indeed functions as a sensor for attention paid to political information by users of the microblogging service but much less reliably as a sensor for political events. Again, this speaks in support of Twitter data being read as offering a view of reality, mediated by the interests, intentions, and attention of Twitter users.

References

Aggarwal CC (2013) Outlier analysis. Springer, Berlin
Allan J (ed) (2002) Topic detection and tracking: event-based information organization. Kluwer Academic, Boston

Atefeh F, Khreich W (2013) A survey of techniques for event detection in Twitter. Comput Intell. doi:10.1111/coin.12017

Barnett V, Lewis T (1994) Outliers in statistical data, 3rd edn. Wiley, New York

Becker H, Naaman M, Gravano L (2011) Beyond trending topics: real-world event identification on Twitter. In: Nicolov N, Shanahan JG, Adamic L, Baeza-Yates R, Counts S (eds) ICWSM 2011: proceedings of the 5th international AAAI conference on weblogs and social media. Association for the Advancement of Artificial Intelligence (AAAI), Menlo Park, pp 438–441

Blei DM (2012) Probabilistic topic models. Commun ACM 55(4):77–84. doi:10.1145/2133806.2133826

Blei DM, Lafferty JD (2009) Topic models. In: Srivastava AN, Sahami M (eds) Text mining: classification, clustering, and applications. Chapman & Hall/CRC, Boca Raton

Boorstin DJ (1961) The image: a guide to pseudo events in America. Harper & Row, New York

Brandt PT, Freeman JR, Schrodt PA (2011) Real time, time series forecasting of inter- and intra-state political conflict. Conflict Manage Peace Sci 28(1):41–64. doi:10.1177/0738894210388125

Chakrabarti D, Punera K (2011) Event summarization using tweets. In: Nicolov N, Shanahan JG, Adamic L, Baeza-Yates R, Counts S (eds) ICWSM 2011: proceedings of the 5th international AAAI conference on weblogs and social media. Association for the Advancement of Artificial Intelligence (AAAI), Menlo Park, pp 66–73

Couldry N, Hepp A, Krotz F (eds) (2010) Media events in a global age. Routledge, Oxon

Dayan D, Katz E (1992) Media events: the live broadcasting of history. Harvard University Press, Cambridge

Golder SA, Macy MW (2011) Diurnal and seasonal mood vary with work, sleep, and daylength across diverse cultures. Science 333(6051):1878–1881

Hong L, Davison BD (2010) Empirical study of topic modeling in Twitter. In: Melville P, Leskovec J, Provost F (eds) SOMA 2010: proceedings of the first workshop on social media analytics. ACM, New York, pp 80–88. doi:10.1145/1964858.1964870

Hong L, Dom B, Gurumurthy S, Tsioutsiouliklis K (2011) A time-dependent topic model for multiple text streams. In: Apte C, Ghosh J, Smyth P (eds) KDD 2011: proceedings of the 17th ACM SIGKDD international conference on knowledge discovery and data mining. ACM, New York, pp 832–840. doi:10.1145/2020408.2020551

Jungherr A (2012) The German federal election of 2009: the challenge of participatory cultures in political campaigns. Transform Works Cult 10. doi:10.3983/twc.2012.0310

Jungherr A, Jürgens P (2010) The political click: political participation through e-petitions in Germany. Policy Internet 2(4):131–165. doi:10.2202/1944-2866.1084

Jungherr A, Jürgens P (2013) Forecasting the pulse: how deviations from regular patterns in online data can identify offline phenomena. Internet Res 23(5):589–607. doi:10.1108/IntR-06-2012-0115

Jungherr A, Jürgens P (2014a) Stuttgart's black Thursday on Twitter: mapping political protests with social media data. In: Gibson R, Cantijoch M, Ward S (eds) Analyzing social media data and web networks. Palgrave Macmillan, New York, pp 154–196

Jungherr A, Jürgens P (2014b) Through a glass, darkly: tactical support and symbolic association in Twitter messages commenting on Stuttgart 21. Soc Sci Comput Rev 32(1):74–89. doi:10.1177/0894439313500022

Keen KJ (2010) Graphics for statistics and data analysis with R. Chapman & Hall/CRC, Boca Raton

Kepplinger HM, Habermeier J (1995) The impact of key events on the presentation of reality. Eur J Commun 10(3):371–390. doi:10.1177/0267323195010003004

Kleinberg J (2003) Bursty and hierarchical structure in streams. Data Min Knowl Discov 7(4):373–397. doi:10.1023/A:1024940629314

Kleinberg J (2015) Temporal dynamics of on-line information streams. In: Garofalakis M, Gehrke J, Rastogi R (eds) Data stream management: processing high-speed data streams. Springer, Berlin

Krewel M, Schmitt-Beck R, Wolsing A (2011) The campaign and its dynamics at the 2009 German general election. Ger Polit 20(1):28–50. doi:10.1080/09644008.2011.554100

Landmann J, Zuell C (2008) Identifying events using computer-assisted text analysis. Soc Sci Comput Rev 26(2):483–497. doi:10.1177/0894439307313703

Lin YR, Keegan B, Margolin D, Lazer D (2014) Rising tides or rising stars? Dynamics of shared attention on Twitter during media events. PLoS One 9(5):e94093. doi:10.1371/journal.pone.0094093

Molotch H, Lester M (1974) News as purposive behavior: on the strategic use of routine events, accidents, and scandals. Am Sociol Rev 39(1):101–112

Petrović S, Osborne M, Lavrenko V (2010) Streaming first story detection with application to Twitter. In: HLT '10 human language technologies: proceedings of the 2010 annual conference of the North American chapter of the Association for Computational Linguistics. ACM, New York, pp 181–189

Ramage D, Dumais S, Liebling D (2010) Characterizing microblogs with topic models. In: Hearst M, Cohen W, Gosling S (eds) ICWSM 2010: proceedings of the 4th international AAAI conference on weblogs and social media. Association for the Advancement of Artificial Intelligence (AAAI), Menlo Park, pp 130–137

Ritter A, Mausam, Etzioni O, Clark S (2012) Open domain event extraction from Twitter. In: Yang Q, Agarwal D, Pei J (eds) KDD 2012: proceedings of the 18th ACM SIGKDD international conference on knowledge discovery and data mining. ACM, New York, pp 1104–1112. doi:10.1145/2339530.2339704

Romero DM, Tan C, Ugander J (2013) On the interplay between social and topical structure. In: Kiciman E, Ellison NB, Hogan B, Resnick P, Soboroff I (eds) ICWSM 2013: proceedings of the 7th international AAAI conference on weblogs and social media. Association for the Advancement of Artificial Intelligence (AAAI), Menlo Park, pp 516–525

Sakaki T, Okazaki M, Matsuo Y (2010) Earthquake shakes Twitter users: real-time event detection by social sensors. In: Rappa M, Jones P, Freire J, Chakrabarti S (eds) WWW 2010: proceedings of the 19th international conference on the world wide web. ACM, New York, pp 851–860. doi:10.1145/1772690.1772777

Schrodt PA (2010) Automated production of high-volume, real-time political event data. Paper presented at the annual meeting of the American Political Science Association, Washington, 2–5 September 2010

Schrodt PA, Yonamine J (2012) Automated coding of very large scale political event data. Paper presented at the new directions in text as data workshop, Harvard, October 2012

Schulz W (1976) Die Konstruktion von Realität in den Nachrichtenmedien: Analyse der aktuellen Berichterstattung. Alber, Freiburg

Shamma DA, Kennedy L, Churchill EF (2010) Conversational shadows: describing live media events using short messages. In: Hearst M, Cohen W, Gosling S (eds) ICWSM 2010: proceedings of the 4th international AAAI conference on weblogs and social media. Association for the Advancement of Artificial Intelligence (AAAI), Menlo Park, pp 331–334

Shoemaker PJ, Cohen AA (2006) News around the world: content practitioners and the public: content, practitioners and the public. Routledge, New York

Shumway RH, Stoffer DS (2011) Time series analysis and its applications: with R examples, 3rd edn. Springer, New York

Stone B (2009) The adventure continues. Twitter Blog. https://blog.twitter.com/2009/adventure-continues

Teevan J, Ramage D, Morris MR (2011) #twittersearch: a comparison of microblog search and web search. In: King I, Nejdl W, Li H (eds) WSDM 2011: Proceedings of the 4th ACM international conference on web search and data mining. ACM, New York, pp 35–44. doi:10.1145/1935826.1935842

Tukey J (1977) Exploratory data analysis. Addison-Wesley, Reading

Verma S, Vieweg S, Corvey WJ, Palen L, Martin JH, Palmer M, Schram A, Anderson KM (2011) Natural language processing to the rescue? Extracting "situational awareness" tweets during mass emergency. In: Nicolov N, Shanahan JG, Adamic L, Baeza-Yates R, Counts S (eds)

ICWSM 2011: proceedings of the 5th international AAAI conference on weblogs and social media. Association for the Advancement of Artificial Intelligence (AAAI), Menlo Park, CA, pp 386–392

Weng J, Lee BS (2011) Event detection in Twitter. In: Nicolov N, Shanahan JG, Adamic L, Baeza-Yates R, Counts S (eds) ICWSM 2011: proceedings of the 5th international AAAI conference on weblogs and social media. Association for the Advancement of Artificial Intelligence (AAAI), Menlo Park, CA, pp 401–408

Yao L, Mimno D, McCallum A (2009) Efficient methods for topic model inference on streaming document collections. In: Elder J, Fogelman FS, Flach P, Zaki M (eds) KDD 2009: proceedings of the 15th ACM SIGKDD international conference on knowledge discovery and data mining. ACM, New York, pp 937–946. doi:10.1145/1557019.1557121

Zhao WX, Jiang J, Weng J, He J, Lim EP, Yan H, Li X (2011) Comparing Twitter and traditional media using topic models. In: Clough P, Foley C, Gurrin C, Jones GJF, Kraaij W, Lee H, Mudoch V (eds) Advances in information retrieval: proceedings 33rd European conference on IR research, ECIR 2011, Dublin, Ireland, 18–21 April 2011. Springer, Berlin, pp 338–349. doi:10.1007/978-3-642-20161-5_34

Chapter 6
The Media Connection

6.1 The Connection Between Political Media Coverage and Twitter Activity

Political references on Twitter are highly interconnected with the coverage of politics in traditional media. In the previous chapters two findings illustrate this strong relationship. We have seen that messages contributing to political communication during the 2009 campaign contained more links to content on the Web than messages with no reference to politics. We have also seen that the volume of politically relevant Twitter messages spiked during three important mediated events over the course of the campaign—the televised leaders' debate together with election night coverage of state and federal elections. These findings illustrate the importance of this interconnection and also raise further questions regarding the nature of the relationship between the coverage of politics in traditional media.

In this chapter, I will focus on two questions. We have seen that dynamics in the volume of Twitter messages did not reliably mirror important events during the course of the campaign. Given the strong reaction of Twitter activity to a selection of important media events, it could be that Twitter was mirroring political media coverage more reliably. In other words, did temporal patterns in the volume of Twitter messages mentioning political actors mirror their coverage in traditional media?

Another obvious question is what do Twitter users post during the coverage of mediated events? Are their comments part of a deliberative discussion of the program, part of a public negotiation of meaning, contesting or affirmation of elite frames, or merely frivolous? In this chapter, I will analyze the content of the most often retweeted messages during the course of four prominent mediated events.

The results presented in this chapter will show that there are no easy or clearcut answers to these questions. For one, Twitter messages commenting on parties tended not to follow the temporal patterns of their coverage on television or in newspapers. In contrast, messages commenting on Frank-Walter Steinmeier followed patterns similar to his coverage in traditional media. Mentions of Angela Merkel followed the intensity of her coverage in newspapers, but deviated from her mentions on television. As such, Twitter appears to follow a hybrid (Chadwick 2013) between the coverage dynamics of traditional media and a channel specific coverage logic (Jungherr 2014a).

With regard to the content of Twitter messages commenting on mediated events, a similar picture emerges. Significant messages tended to offer context for the mediated events to which they were reacting. Prominently retweeted messages contained: commentary on ongoing events, be it factual or ironic; various elements of horse-race coverage; the indexing of politicians' statements; links to further information on the web; calls for mobilization. So again, we find a hybrid of various usage patterns.

In general, these findings illustrate the importance of political coverage by traditional media for Twitter activity related to politics. However, this relationship is not deterministic as only a selection of mediated events creates significant volume spikes on Twitter and the intensity of Twitter coverage of political actors follows different patterns from its coverage in traditional media. Prominent messages posted during mediated events also show that Twitter is used as a space for contextualizing and contesting the events presented by traditional media, thereby potentially opening up the political communication space to new actors.[1]

6.2 Data Set and Method

For the analyses presented in this chapter, I use three data sets: the *German Longitudinal Election Study (GLES) 2009 Campaign Media Content Analysis: Printmedia* (Rattinger et al. 2012a), the *GLES 2009 Campaign Media Content Analysis: TV* (Rattinger et al. 2012b), together with the Twitter data set that I already used in the preceding chapters. These three data sets allow for the direct comparison of daily mentions of political actors during 3 months directly preceding the election. Thus, the data offer a unique window into the dynamics that led to sudden increases of coverage in traditional media and on Twitter.

The *Campaign Media Content Analysis: Printmedia* (Rattinger et al. 2012a) documents the coverage of the campaign in six major German newspapers. The elements from the data set of interest in this analysis are: the date an article commenting on politics was published, the political actor (be it a politician or one of the five established parties) mentioned in it, as well as the title, and topic of the article. Using these data, I calculated daily sums for mentions of Angela Merkel, Frank-Walter Steinmeier, CDU/CSU, SPD, FDP, Bündnis 90/Die Grünen, and Die

---

[1] Some of the material presented in this chapter appeared previously in Andreas Jungherr (2014) "The Logic of Political Coverage on Twitter," *Journal of Communication* and has been reproduced here courtesy of *John Wiley and Sons*.

LINKE. In the totals of party mentions, I also included mentions of politicians associated with their respective parties. The data set includes all mentions of these actors in six major German newspapers (*BILD, Frankfurter Allgemeine Zeitung, Frankfurter Rundschau, Süddeutsche Zeitung, Tageszeitung*, and *Die Welt*) between June 29, and September 26. Since Sunday editions of the papers were not included in the original data set, this makes for 78 observations.

The *Campaign Media Content Analysis: TV* (Rattinger et al. 2012b) documents the coverage in the evening newscasts of four major television stations in Germany (*ARD, ZDF, RTL, SAT1*). Items used for this analysis are: the original broadcast date from a segment in a news program, the political actor mentioned (be it a politician or one of the five established parties), and the segment's topic. In preparing the data, I calculated daily totals of mentions for the two leading candidates and the five major parties, including the mentions of prominent politicians associated with their respective parties, except for Angela Merkel and Frank-Walter Steinmeier. The data set includes all mentions of these actors in segments from the evening newscasts of four major television stations between June 28, and September 26. This makes for 91 observations.[2]

Of the Twitter data set introduced in the preceding chapter, I use only an appropriate selection to allow for comparison with the GLES media data. In the following analysis, I focus exclusively on those messages from the data set in which a political actor was named explicitly in a hashtag (e.g. #cdu, #spd, #grüne, #piraten, #merkel, #steinmeier).[3]

The decision to collect only the messages of users who posted messages with politically relevant hashtags might again be criticized as potentially introducing a bias in data collection. The active use of hashtags presupposes a certain level of Twitter proficiency; users below this level are thus excluded from the analysis. This might exclude potentially relevant messages contributing to interactions on Twitter centered on politics. However, simply including all messages mentioning politically relevant keywords offers no obvious remedy. Using hashtags as a discriminatory device makes it possible to filter messages that users posted with the clear intention of contributing to the political discourse. Alternatively, including messages based on keywords would lead to the inclusion of significant noise in the analysis

---

[2]For more information on the data sets including descriptive metrics and the validity of the coding see Rattinger et al. (2012a,b).

[3]The following hashtags were collected in concepts: CDU/CSU: #cdu, #cducsu, #csu; SPD: #spd; FDP: #fdp; Bündnis 90/Die Grünen: #buendnis90, #bündnis, #bündnis90, #bündnis90diegrünen, #bündnis90grüne, #bündnisgrüne, #bündnisgrünen, #die_gruenen, #die_grünen, #diegrünen, #gruene, #grüne, #grünen; Die LINKE: #die_linke, #dielinke, #linke, #linkspartei; Piratenpartei: #piraten, #piratenpartei; Angela Merkel: #angie, #merkel, #angie_merkel, #angelamerkel, #angela_merkel; Frank-Walter Steinmeier: #steinmeier, #fws, #frank_walter_steinmeier, #steini, #frankwaltersteinmeier, #frank_steinmeier. This collection might still exclude some more exotic or more ambiguous spelling variations of the political actors in question. Still, this collection should account for the vast majority of the hashtags referring to the political actors in question and thus should offer a comprehensive view on the dynamics between them.

(i.e. false positives, spam, and automated links to political coverage on websites). So, while the focus on hashtags might potentially lead to an underestimation of the total volume of political coverage on Twitter, this approach is most likely to prevent data dilution by noise.

Since there was significant variation in the spelling of political actors, I collected the most prominent hashtag variations referring to each actor in encompassing concepts (e.g. #grüne, #gruene, #bündnis, #buendnis). These concepts sum up all appearances of relevant hashtags commenting on the respective political actors. For this analysis, I totalled hashtag occurrences collected in these concepts for each day between June 27, and October 1, 2009. Between June 27, and October 1, 2009, 18,832 users posted at least one message with one or more of the hashtags grouped in party concepts. During this time span, a total of 194,425 messages contained one or more of these hashtags. Table 6.1 shows descriptive metrics of political actors' mentions across different media types in direct comparison.

Table 6.1 Total mentions of political actors across different media types (June 28 to September 26)

	Total mentions	Max (daily mentions)	Min (daily mentions)	Median (daily mentions)
Newspaper mentions				
Merkel	1142	42	2	13
Steinmeier	533	21	0	6
CDU/CSU	2556	88	2	30
SPD	1586	53	1	20
FDP	745	45	2	8
Bündnis 90/Die Grünen	570	37	0	6
Die LINKE	505	56	0	4
TV mentions				
Merkel	433	16	0	4
Steinmeier	237	12	0	2
CDU/CSU	1002	68	0	8
SPD	739	45	0	7
FDP	389	42	0	3
Bündnis 90/Die Grünen	307	38	0	2
Die LINKE	301	52	0	2
Twitter mentions				
Merkel	8137	1308	3	43
Steinmeier	6319	1424	2	28
CDU/CSU	31,132	1793	65	292
SPD	27,525	2268	49	196
FDP	20,050	1892	34	128
Bündnis 90/Die Grünen	14,569	1077	29	113
Die LINKE	7975	899	8	99

6.3 Temporal Patterns in the Coverage of Politics on Twitter and Traditional Media

As stated before, the campaign for the German federal election of 2009 was fought rather reluctantly. The two biggest parties, CDU/CSU and SPD, governed Germany from 2005 to 2009 in a grand coalition. Both leading candidates, Angela Merkel and Frank-Walter Steinmeier, had to campaign against each other following the previous 4 years of political co-operation. This led to a campaign lacking drama, in which the main political actors did not polarize the electorate (Helms 2010; Krewel et al. 2011). Although the financial crisis was an ongoing topic, neither CDU/CSU nor SPD used the crisis to create division during the campaign. Traditional media covered ongoing efforts by the government to address the crisis. Angela Merkel managed to focus most of this coverage on her salvaging efforts, while it was tougher for Frank-Walter Steinmeier to display substantial contributions to the rescue efforts. Besides the financial crisis, the campaign was dominated by two events. First, on August 30, roughly a month before the federal election on September 27, state elections were held in the Saarland, Saxony, and Thuringia. The results of these elections were widely considered to be indicators for the upcoming federal election results. Second, on September 13 there was a widely promoted televised debate between the two leading candidates.

6.3.1 Temporal Dynamics

The first question to be addressed here is whether the dynamics of political actors' mentions in different media follow the same temporal patterns or whether different media react with different intensity to political events. To answer this question, I will perform a principle component analysis (PCA) on twenty-one time series documenting the mentions of political actors in newspapers, on TV, and on Twitter. This analysis allows groups of strongly correlated variables to be identified which thus might be influenced by the same underlying process. But let us start with a visual inspection of the time series. Figure 6.1 shows three time series documenting the aggregates of mentions for the political actors included in the analysis from newspapers, on TV, and on Twitter.

The figures document all mentions of the leading candidates from the CDU/CSU and SPD (Angela Merkel and Frank-Walter Steinmeier respectively) as well as the five major political parties (CDU/CSU, SPD, FDP, Bündnis 90/Die Grünen, and Die LINKE) in six major newspapers (BILD, FAZ, FR, SZ, TAZ, and Die Welt), in evening newscasts of Germany's four leading television stations (ARD, ZDF, RTL, and Sat1), and in hashtags on Twitter during the campaign for the federal election in 2009. All time series start on June 29. The time series for mentions in newspapers and on television end on September 26, the day before the federal election. Although the GLES data do not extend beyond this date, for Twitter more data are available.

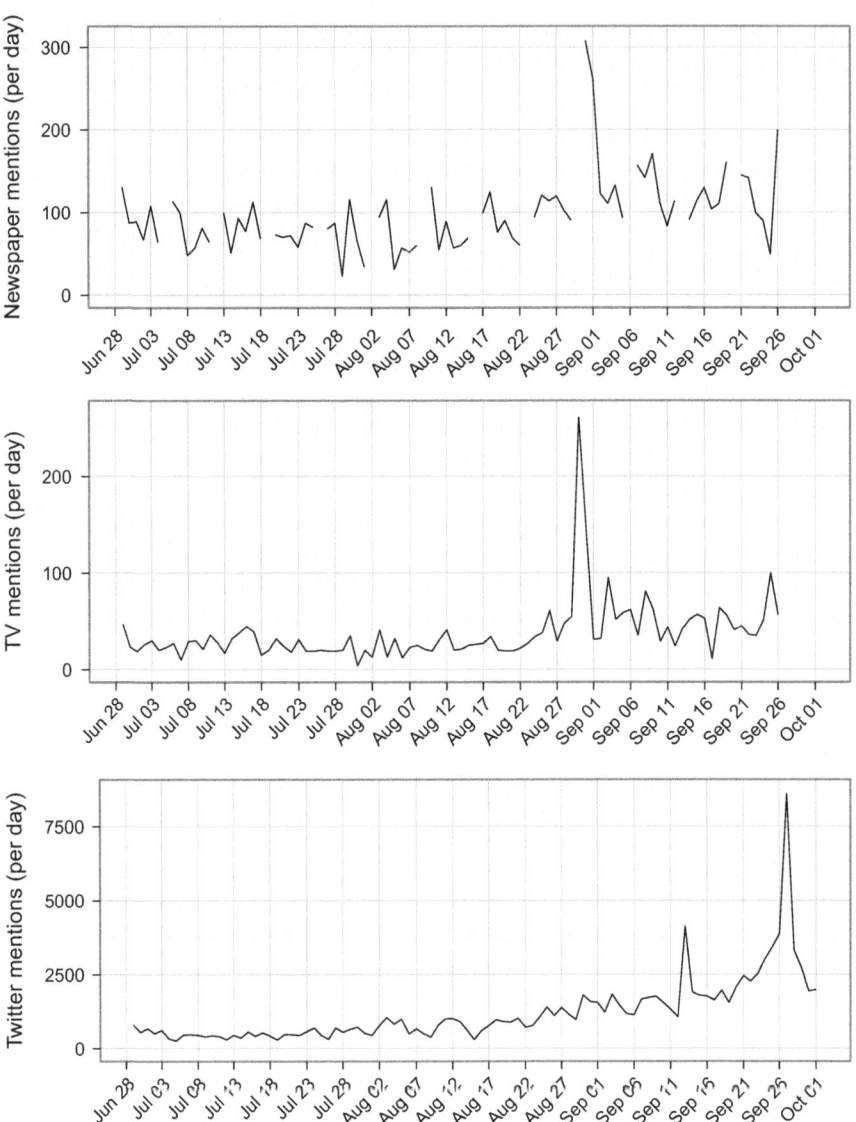

Fig. 6.1 Candidate and party mentions in newspapers, on TV, and on Twitter, aggregated for each media type

This time series ends on October 1, 4 days after the election. As the GLES analysis did not include Sunday editions of newspapers, the first of the three figures displays a missing value for each Sunday in the time period under examination.

A cursory glance at the plots in Fig. 6.1 shows that the mentions of political actors across all media types fluctuated strongly during the campaign. For all media types there seems to be a normal level of coverage, around which the daily mention counts of political actors swing. This baseline is repeatedly broken by outliers, i.e. days during which the mention count of a political actor rises well beyond the level of normal fluctuations in the respective medium. However, these fluctuations are not random; in fact, mentions of political actors across all media types appear to be highly sensitive to events. Newspaper and TV mentions of political actors rise in reaction to, for instance, the state elections on August 30. We also see the baseline of mentions rise as the time series approaches election day. This pattern manifests itself even more distinctly in the mentions of political actors in hashtags on Twitter which through much of July and August fluctuate in the low hundreds. This baseline rises steadily from the end of August onwards. Although these basic patterns are common for the mentions of political actors in all three media types, there are also marked differences. Once we compare the dates that brought spikes in the mentions of political actors, we see significant differences between traditional media and Twitter. Media coverage of political actors spikes in reaction to the state elections on August 30; in contrast, mentions of political actors on Twitter spike in reaction to the televised debate between Angela Merkel and Frank-Walter Steinmeier (September 13) as well as on the day of the federal election.

In total, Twitter activity did not consistently shadow the political coverage of traditional media. Instead, mentions spiked in reaction to media events that allowed for the public discussion and negotiation of meaning. The mentions of political actors on Twitter rose steadily following the televised debate between Angela Merkel and Frank-Walter Steinmeier. From that day the level of political discussion on Twitter rises irrespective of political events. Once politics has been established as a topic of public interest by a widely discussed media event, Twitter users comment much more heavily than before. This increase climaxes in the mention volume on election day, only to fall again rapidly after this. The differences between the aggregated time series are an early indicator that the mentions of political actors in different media types might follow different dynamics.

6.3.2 *Common Patterns in the Mentions of Political Actors Across Media Types*

A Principle Component Analysis (PCA) transforms correlated variables in a data set into a smaller set of new variables. These new variables are called principle components and are in turn often interpreted as processes driving the values of manifest variables. These processes in themselves are difficult to measure and thus called latent variables. In this analysis PCA helps us to identify latent variables (i.e. dynamics in political coverage following the same temporal patterns across various media or dynamics specific to different media channels) by grouping correlated manifest variables (i.e. the mentions of political actors in different media channels) in principle components. Based on the composition of these components, an interpretation of the underlying dominating coverage logic becomes possible.[4]

Consider our data set $X = (X_1, X_2, \ldots, X_n)$ where $X_1, X_2, \ldots, X_n$ are the vectors containing t observations of the time series documenting the mentions of political actors in newspapers, on TV, and on Twitter. Assume now that we are looking for m principle components. We can represent the jth principle component by a simple linear equation:

$$Y_i^j = b_1^j X_{1i} + b_2^j X_{2i} + \ldots + b_n^j X_{ni}, \text{ for } i = 1, \ldots, t, \text{ and } j = 1, \ldots, m \quad (6.1)$$

Here, Y^j is a time series representing a latent variable driving the realizations of X, i.e. the daily mentions of political actors across the different media types. The aim is to map the information contained in $X_1, X_2, \ldots, X_n$ onto the principle component scores $Y^1, Y^2, \ldots, Y^m$, such that these successively inherit the maximum possible variance from X. The factor loadings corresponding to the jth principle component are given by $b_1^j, b_2^j, \ldots, b_n^j$. These loadings measure how strongly the respective variables correlate with, or load onto, the jth principle component.

Consider now the first principle component, i.e. $j = 1$. The corresponding factor loadings $b^1 = (b_1^1, b_2^1, \ldots, b_n^1)$ are defined as:

$$b^1 = argmax_b \sum_{i=1}^{t} (b_1 * X_1 i + b_2 * X_2 i + \ldots + b_n * X_{ni})^2, \quad (6.2)$$

where b is constrained to be an n-dimensional unit vector.

The second principle component can be found by subtracting the first principle component from the data set X and then determining the loading vector which extracts the maximum variance from this new data matrix.

If all media were to cover political actors following the same logic, we should be able to identify seven principle components, one for each political actor (e.g. $Y^1 = Merkel_n, Y^2 = Steinmeier_n, Y^3 = CDU/CSU_n, Y^4 = SPD_n etc.$), onto which the mentions of political actors in different media would have to load. If media were to follow different dynamics in covering political actors, we would expect a different set of principle components, one for each media type (i.e. $Y^1 = Newspapers_n, Y^2 = TV_n, Y^3 = Twitter_n$).

To build a basis for this analysis, I disaggregated the time series shown in Fig. 6.1 into the daily mentions of seven political actors (i.e. Angela Merkel, Frank-Walter Steinmeier, CDU/CSU, SPD, FDP, Bündnis 90/Die Grünen, and Die LINKE) in each media type. The data set includes 90 observations for the mentions of political actors on TV and Twitter for every day between June 29 and September 26. Since the data set does not include Sunday editions of newspapers, newspaper mentions of

---

[4]To perform the PCA, I used the R package "psych" (Revelle 2009) and followed the instructions for performing and reporting PCA by Blunch (2008) and Field et al. (2012).

political actors are documented for only 78 observations (weekdays and Saturdays between June 29 and September 26). This makes for a total of 21 variables and 78 observations.

Before performing the PCA, I had to transform the time series documenting mentions of political actors on TV and Twitter. First, I had to eliminate the observations for mentions on Sundays, so as to make the data set compatible with the data on newspaper mentions. Second, I lagged the time series of TV and Twitter mentions by 1 day. The goal of this PCA is to show whether or not different media types are reacting to the same political events with comparable intensity. TV newscasts and Twitter mentions react to events during the same day; newspaper mentions react to the events from the preceding day. By lagging the observed time series it is possible to compare the reactions of newspapers, TV, and Twitter for the same event.[5] This data set of 21 variables and 78 observations is somewhat below the ideal observation count for a PCA. Still, two statistical tests, which check for the appropriateness of a given data set for PCA, indicate that we can proceed.[6]

One could argue that the time series show a trend component. This means that any given value is dependent on its preceding value. Performing a PCA whilst ignoring this trend component might result in skewed results. To check the robustness of the PCA performed above, therefore, I also calculated a PCA for the first differences in the time series. The analysis identified the same components onto which the same variables load. For the sake of clarity, I decided to present the results of the original time series.

As a next step, it is important to establish how many components can be reliably identified in the data. There are two criteria for this choice, both of which aim at assessing how much variance any given component adds to the analysis. Both are based on the *eigenvalue* which is associated with b^j as the eigenvector of the symmetric matrix $X^T X$. In this way, each principle component $j = 1, \ldots n$ corresponds to unique eigenvalues. Kaiser advocates the inclusion of all components with eigenvalues above one, thus contributing more variance to an analysis than the average component (Kaiser 1960). As an additional criterion, Cattel argues that one should plot the eigenvalues of each component against its component number.

---

[5]To check the validity of this assumption, I also performed a PCA with the original unlagged values. The results were statistically less satisfactory and produced factors that did not lend themselves to interpretation as successfully.

[6]The Bartlett's test checks whether or not the correlation matrix of the variables included in the PCA shows enough common variance to allow for a meaningful analysis. In this case, the Bartlett's test is highly significant $X^2(210) = 1958, p < 0.001$. This indicates that the correlations in the data set were sufficiently large for a PCA (Bartlett 1937). The Kaiser-Meyer-Olkin measure (KMO) verified the sampling adequacy for the analysis, KMO = 0.83. This value indicates that patterns in the correlation matrix of the variables is compact enough as to yield the identification of distinct and reliable components. Additionally, the KMO values of only five variables fell below 0.8 (Merkel, newspaper mentions = 0.79; Steinmeier, newspaper mentions = 0.65; Steinmeier, TV mentions lagged = 0.76; Merkel, Twitter mentions lagged = 0.59; Steinmeier, Twitter mentions lagged = 0.54), which means that all values lie above the acceptable level of 0.5 (Kaiser 1974). Thus, the results of both tests indicate that the data set offers an appropriate base for a PCA.

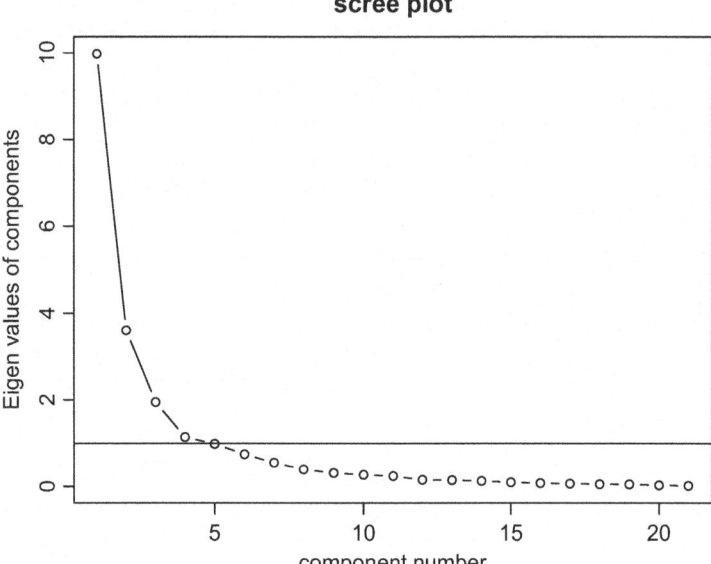

Fig. 6.2 Scree plot of PCA

According to this method, the analysis should include all components that lie before the inflexion point in the plot (Cattell 1966).

A first analysis showed that four components had eigenvalues over Kaiser's criterion of 1 and in combination explained 74 % of variance. Considering that one component showed an eigenvalue just above the Kaiser's criterion of 1 and after inspecting the scree plot—shown in Fig. 6.2—I decided to include only three components in the analysis. The consistency of components can be assessed by Cronbach's α (Cronbach 1951), a coefficient that shows how closely a set of items in a group are related. As shown in Table 6.2, Cronbach's α for components one and two indicates strong internal consistency while component three shows acceptable consistency.

The final step of the PCA is a rotation of the coordination system to facilitate the interpretation of identified components by increasing the component loadings of the variables. Following the assumption that components are correlated, it is possible to perform an oblique rotation. Since in our case this seems a reasonable assumption, I rotated the components obliquely using the "oblimin" method in the R package "psych" (Revelle 2009). Table 6.2 documents the results.

The variables loading onto the three components suggest the following interpretation of the latent variables driving their volume: Component 1 represents the mentions of political parties in traditional media (e.g. newspapers and TV). The driving force for this component seems to be a common logic of traditional media covering political parties. Component 2 represents mentions of political parties on Twitter. The driving force behind this component seems to be a special dynamic,

6.3 Temporal Patterns in the Coverage of Politics on Twitter and Traditional... 165

Table 6.2 Summary of principle component analysis results for mentions of political actors in newspapers, on TV, and on Twitter ($n = 78$)

	Rotated component loadings		
	Component 1: Np and TV (parties)	Component 2: Twitter (parties)	Component 3: Np, TV, and Twitter (S) + np and Twitter (M)
Merkel (np)	0.32	0.13	**0.42**
Steinmeier (np)	0.1	−0.1	**0.73**
CDU/CSU (np)	**0.81**	−0.15	0.12
SPD (np)	**0.76**	−0.23	−0.04
FDP (np)	**0.77**	0.16	−0.02
Bündnis 90/Die Grünen (np)	**0.87**	0.11	−0.1
Die LINKE (np)	**0.89**	0.05	0.02
Merkel (TV)—lagged	0.35	0.26	0.28
Steinmeier (TV)—lagged	0.15	0.01	**0.78**
CDU/CSU (TV)—lagged	**0.92**	−0.07	0.01
SPD (TV)—lagged	**0.83**	0.02	−0.02
FDP (TV)—lagged	**0.88**	0.13	−0.03
Bündnis 90/Die Grünen (TV)—lagged	**0.88**	0.08	0
Die LINKE (TV)—lagged	**0.93**	−0.02	0.02
Merkel (Twitter)—lagged	−0.1	0.13	**0.81**
Steinmeier (Twitter)—lagged	−0.13	0	**0.9**
CDU/CSU (Twitter)—lagged	0.08	**0.87**	0.08
SPD (Twitter)—lagged	0.01	**0.87**	0.13
FDP (Twitter)—lagged	−0.05	**0.98**	−0.02
Bündnis 90/Die Grünen (Twitter)—lagged	−0.03	**0.99**	−0.12
Die LINKE (Twitter)—lagged	0.18	**0.83**	0.09
Eigenvalues	7.84	4.64	3.05
% of variance	37	22	15
α	0.95	0.92	0.65

Note: Factor loadings over 0.4 appear in bold.

which determines the discussion of political parties on Twitter. Component 3 represents the TV mentions of Frank-Walter Steinmeier together with the newspaper and Twitter mentions of both leading candidates (i.e. Y^1 = Newspaper and TV mentions parties; Y^2 = Twitter mentions parties; Y^3 = Newspaper, TV, and Twitter mentions Steinmeier, and Newspaper and Twitter mentions Merkel). The mentions of Angela Merkel on TV do not load onto any component, which may indicate that her official role as Chancellor introduced a different dynamic into the coverage setting her apart from the coverage of her challenger. This appears not to be the case for her mentions on Twitter, though. The comparably weak factor loading of newspaper mentions for Angela Merkel indicates that her official role led to a different coverage dynamic also in this medium, although to a lesser degree than on TV. Besides this, Twitter mentions of the leading candidates seem to follow the same logic as their mentions in traditional media.

While one is well advised not to over-interpret the results of exploratory data analysis, the results of this PCA speak remarkably well to the question driving this analysis: does the political coverage across various media types follow similar dynamics or are there differences? The PCA shows two patterns: first, the mentions of political parties in traditional media (i.e. newspapers and TV) and on Twitter follow different dynamics. It seems fair to assess that both media types, traditional and new, follow different logics when it comes to the coverage of political events regarding parties. The second observation is not so clear-cut. We see that the coverage of Angela Merkel on TV follows a pattern independent of the mentions for political parties, her challenger Frank-Walter Steinmeier, and even her own mentions in newspapers as well as on Twitter. As discussed, this is probably due to the coverage she received in her official role as Chancellor, thereby creating news coverage independent of the campaign. Nevertheless, this part of her activities during the campaign did not seem to have influenced her mentions on Twitter much. We also see that the coverage of Frank-Walter Steinmeier on TV follows similar patterns to his and Angela Merkel's mentions in newspapers and on Twitter. The analysis shows that in the coverage of political parties Twitter messages follow different temporal dynamics—a different logic, if you like—than traditional media. With regard to the coverage of the two leading candidates, Twitter and traditional media thus display similar temporal patterns and, therefore, appear to follow the same logic.

A visual inspection of the mentions aggregated for each component enables us to assess what seems to be driving the differences in mention counts per component. Figure 6.3 shows the aggregated time series loading onto each component and the time series of the mentions for Angela Merkel in television news programs, as this time series did not load onto one of the components. The different patterns in Fig. 6.3 speak clearly to which political events drive the dynamics of political actors' mentions in different media types. The aggregated time series of Component 1 (newspaper and TV mentions of political parties) spikes in reaction to the state elections on August 30. Before that date, the mention counts of political parties in traditional media fluctuate steadily around a baseline of nearly 100 mentions per day. After August 30 this baseline rises somewhat. The mentions in Component 2 (Twitter mentions of political parties) follow a different pattern. Here we see a slow but steady increase in the daily mention count of political parties on Twitter, which culminates in a very dominating spike on election day, September 27. After this day, there is a sudden drop in the volume of messages mentioning political parties. Component 3 (Mentions of Angela Merkel and Frank-Walter Steinmeier in newspapers and on Twitter, plus mentions of Steinmeier on TV) shows another pattern. Here we find five spikes, the most prominent of which falls on September 13, the day of the televised debate between the two leading candidates. The second largest mention spike falls on September 27, election day. The three other mention

6.3 Temporal Patterns in the Coverage of Politics on Twitter and Traditional... 167

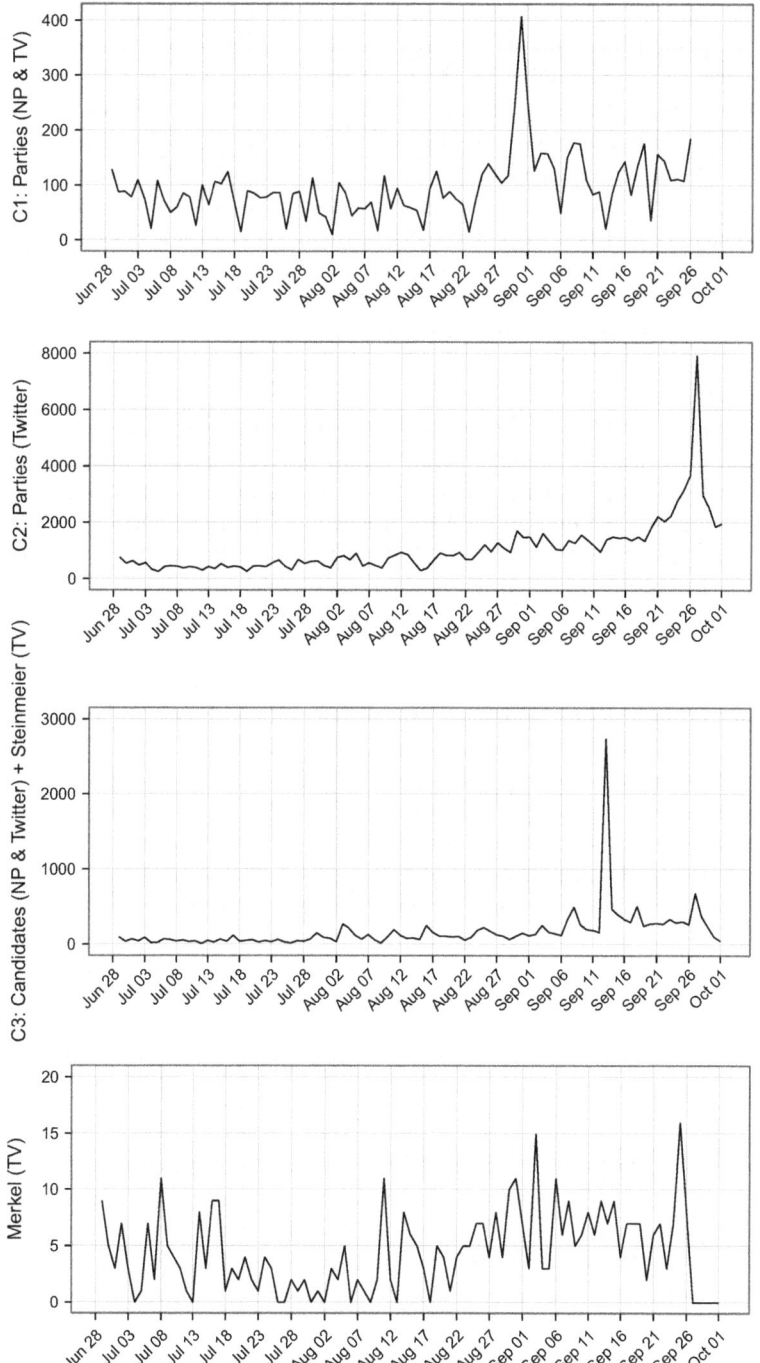

Fig. 6.3 Candidate and party mentions in newspapers, on TV, and on Twitter, aggregated for each component

spikes are much smaller, occurring on August 3, the launch of the SPD campaign program, September 8, the date of an important TV interview with Frank-Walter Steinmeier, and on September 18, the day of strong protests against Angela Merkel, which were organized online. Finally, the time series documenting the mentions of Angela Merkel in television news programs shows yet another pattern. This time series is fluctuating rather strongly. Nevertheless, there are six spikes that can be identified: July 8, coverage of Angela Merkel's participation at the G8 summit in L'Aquila, Italy and news about the employment of a former Stasi agent in her police protection detail, August 11, the day of an important TV interview with Angela Merkel, August 31, the day after the elections in several German states, September 3, reactions of Angela Merkel to the resignation of one CDU state governor, September 6, CDU party convention, and September 25, the G20 summit in Pittsburgh, USA.

There are three obvious lessons to be drawn from these patterns: the coverage of political parties in traditional media follow different queues; traditional media focus their coverage of parties on election days, be they at state or federal level, while Twitter reacted only to the federal election. The state elections, although a prominent topic in traditional media, did not lead to a significant echo on Twitter. It will be interesting to see if these differences in the reactions to so called first-order elections (federal election) and second order elections (state elections or EU elections) (Norris and Reif 1997; Reif and Schmitt 1980) remain stable or if specific electoral contexts allow for variation. Furthermore, with regard to the coverage of the leading candidates, Angela Merkel and Frank-Walter Steinmeier, traditional media and Twitter seem to follow roughly the same logic, as evidenced by coverage spikes connected with campaign and media events referring to the candidates. However, the mentions of Angela Merkel in newspapers loaded only very weakly onto the respective component while her TV mentions did not load onto any factor. As such, her official role as chancellor seems to have introduced a dynamic in her mention count within traditional media that it did not have on Twitter.

6.4 What Do Users Tweet About in Reaction to Mediated Events?

The previous section of this chapter showed that Twitter mentions of political actors did not necessarily follow patterns of political coverage in traditional media but still tended to react strongly to political events heavily covered by the media. In this section I will examine how Twitter was used during mediated events. To this end, I focus on Twitter messages posted during four mediated events which created high political interest and focused public attention.

Twitter coverage of mediated events features strongly in research on the political uses of Twitter (Jungherr 2014b). It has repeatedly been shown that the volume of

6.4 What Do Users Tweet About in Reaction to Mediated Events?

messages referring to politics rises significantly during mediated events (e.g. Bruns and Burgess 2011; Burgess and Bruns 2012; Hanna et al. 2013; Larsson and Moe 2012; Lin et al. 2014; Trilling 2014) and that users change their behavior—for instance by posting more messages containing comments on the shared experience and less containing interactions with other users (e.g. Jungherr 2014a; Lin et al. 2014; Trilling 2014). Politically interested users also frequently contest the frames used by candidates and journalists during the campaign—be it by posting contesting information or links to contesting content (e.g. Ampofo et al. 2011; Anstead and O'Loughlin 2014; Jungherr 2014a). Scholars have argued that public reactions to mediated events increasingly serve as the basis for journalists and politicians in assessing public opinion towards the events and the success or failure of the participants (e.g. Anstead and O'Loughlin 2014; Chadwick 2013; Hamby 2013; Kreiss 2014). Clearly, mediated political events are episodes during campaigns when the activity of Twitter users matters and when there is the increased possibility of Twitter users gaining recognition by journalists or political candidates assessing public reactions to these events. Twitter thus seems to become an integral element in the public negotiation of meaning for high profile media events (Dayan and Katz 1992). This makes the analysis of Twitter usage practices during mediated events an important topic if we want to examine Twitter's characteristics as a political communication space.

Figure 6.4 shows a time series for all messages that were posted between June 18 and October 1, 2009 by politically vocal Twitter users containing at least one of the 2629 politically relevant hashtags. We see that the volume of politically relevant messages remained largely stable during the period of examination. From the date of the state elections in the Saarland, Saxony, and Thuringia on August 30, 2009, to the date of the federal election on September 27, the volume of politically relevant messages keeps on rising, only to fall steeply after election day. The volume of

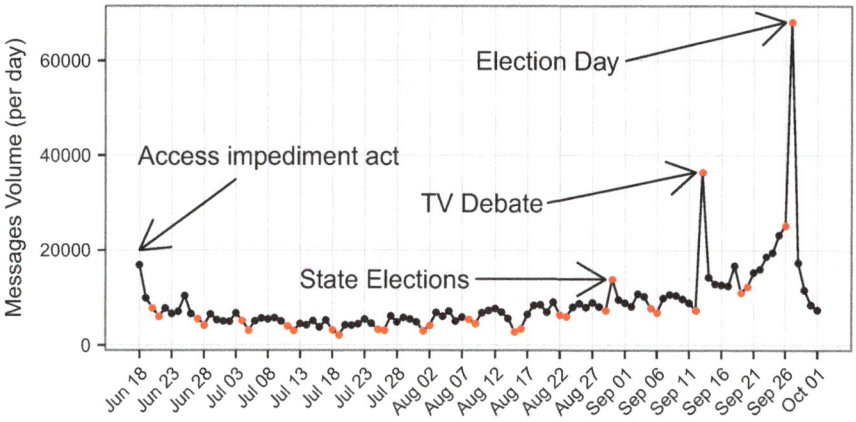

Fig. 6.4 Daily aggregates of messages using at least one of the 2629 politically relevant hashtags between June 18 and October 1, 2009

politically relevant messages spikes on days of four politically significant events. The first spike occurs on June 18, with the ratification of a law for the impediment of access to websites providing child-pornography, a law that was highly unpopular among political online activists, for various reasons. The second spike falls on August 30, the day of the state elections in the Saarland, Saxony, and Thuringia, whereas the third spike identifies the day of the televised debate between the two leading candidates of the CDU/CSU and SPD, Angela Merkel and Frank-Walter Steinmeier. The third and by far the biggest spike in the volume of messages referring to politics falls on September 27, election day.

The analysis of politically relevant messages posted during the campaign for the federal election of 2009 in Germany shows that days of televised campaign or media events—such as election day coverage or televised candidate debates—lead to users posting significantly more messages referring to politics than on other days, thus echoing patterns recorded in other countries. In the following sections I address shifts in the interactions between Twitter users over time and various characteristics of political Twitter messages posted during these episodes. In this discussion, I will focus on the temporal dynamics, active users, and content of the messages posted during the days in question.

6.4.1 Ratification of the Access Impediment Act: Temporal Dynamics and Content

The first mediated event that led to a spike in the volume of Twitter messages was the ratification of the Access Impediment Act by Parliament on June 18, 2009. This Act was a highly controversial piece of legislation aiming to hinder access to child pornographic material on the Internet. Critics argued that the law would introduce a technological and legal infrastructure allowing police and government to censor websites without due process. Advocates and critics of the law both argued highly moralistically; one side emphasizing the supposed protection of children through the proposed law, the other focusing on the suspected potential for government censorship of the Internet. These opposing views led to a highly controversial public debate about the proposed law in the run-up to its ratification. Opposition to the law focused the political attention of heavy Internet users. A highly successful online petition to Parliament led to increased media coverage of the topic (Jungherr and Jürgens 2010). After it became clear that the petition did little to influence the ratification of the Access Impediment Act, many of its supporters started to support Germany's Pirate Party. The Pirates became the object of high media attention and thus became a highly talked about, albeit finally unsuccessful, political actor during the campaign of 2009 (Bieber and Leggewie 2012). During this time the Access Impediment Act, and opposition to it, were important subjects of political online discussions (Albers 2009; Bieber and Schwöbel 2011).

On June 18 at 9:20 p.m., Parliament ratified the Act. The event was covered on television by *phoenix*, a channel dedicated to the coverage of political events. Internet users could access the coverage by live-stream on the *phoenix.de* website and through the official video live-feed covering Parliament sessions on *bundestag.de*. Links to both video-streams were widely disseminated on Twitter during the hours directly preceding the ratification.

Table 6.3 shows the number of messages posted during June 18, the number of users active on the day and the number of messages containing @messages, retweets, or URLs. To allow for a comparison with Twitter use by publics during other days, the table also shows the share that messages posted on June 18 had of all messages posted between June 18, and October 1, 2009; the share users who posted messages on June 18 had of all users who posted messages between June 28, and October 1, 2009; and the share of messages using @messages, retweets, URLs, and messages using no conventions had of all messages posted on June 18. The shares do not add up to 100 since various messages used more than one convention—such as @messages or retweets containing hyperlinks.

The messages posted on June 18, accounted for 0.6 % of all messages posted between June 18, and October 1, 2009. The share of messages contributing to the political communication space was somewhat higher at 2.9 %. This compares to the median day on which 0.04 % of all messages and 0.7 % of all messages contributing to the political communication space were posted. Roughly 30 % of all users who posted messages during the course of the analysis posted messages on June 18. This compares to only about 12 % of all users who contributed to the political communication space, which is double the share of all users contributing to the political communication space on the median day. We may thus infer that on June 18 more users posted more tweets referring to politics than usual.

Table 6.3 User behavior in all messages posted compared to political communication space on the day of the ratification of the Access Impediment Act, June 18, 2009

Usage convention	All messages	Pol. comm. space
Messages	64,991	26,747
Messages containing neither @messages, retweets, or URLs	32,160	11,077
@messages	13,635	4296
Retweets	6222	5973
Messages with URLs	20,557	11,942
Users	10,555	3846
% of all messages posted	0.6	2.9
% messages containing neither @messages, retweets, or URLs	49.5	41.4
% @messages	9.6	16.1
% retweets	9.6	22.3
% messages with URLs	31.6	44.6
% of all users active	32.2	12.1

The share of messages without @messages, retweets, or URLs of all messages on June 18, was roughly comparable to the share of these message throughout the analysis. For the political communication space, these messages had a significantly higher share on June 18, than between June 18, and October 1—41.4 % compared to 30.9 %. The share of @messages, retweets, and messages containing URLs for all messages on June 18 was clearly lower than the share of these conventions throughout the analysis. This corresponds with the observation that mediated events tend to lead to a decrease in interactions between users and references to content on Twitter or the web.

Figure 6.5 shows the temporal distribution of messages contributing to the political communication space, posted each hour on June 18, and June 19. The plot clearly shows that the volume of messages peaked violently on June 18 between 7 and 9 p.m., the hours of the parliamentary debate and ensuing ratification of the Access Impediment Act as well as their coverage on television and online video streams. After coverage ends, the hourly volume of messages drops but remains somewhat higher than in the hours directly preceding ratification. On the following day, the hourly volume of messages remains at roughly the same level as before the debate. This suggests that the volume spike on June 18 was indeed a reaction to the mediated coverage of the parliamentary debate and not due to an increase in general chatter on Twitter preceding the event.

Prior studies on the use of Twitter during mediated events showed common patterns: comments posted tended, on the one hand, to refer directly to the events. On the other hand, many messages tended to include links to information on the web, contextualizing the events on TV. People thus tend to use Twitter when contesting the frames of political elites or journalists and linking to potentially contradicting evidence on the Web (e.g. Ampofo et al. 2011; Anstead and O'Loughlin 2011; Jungherr 2014a). Daniel Kreiss and colleagues have called this practice *active*

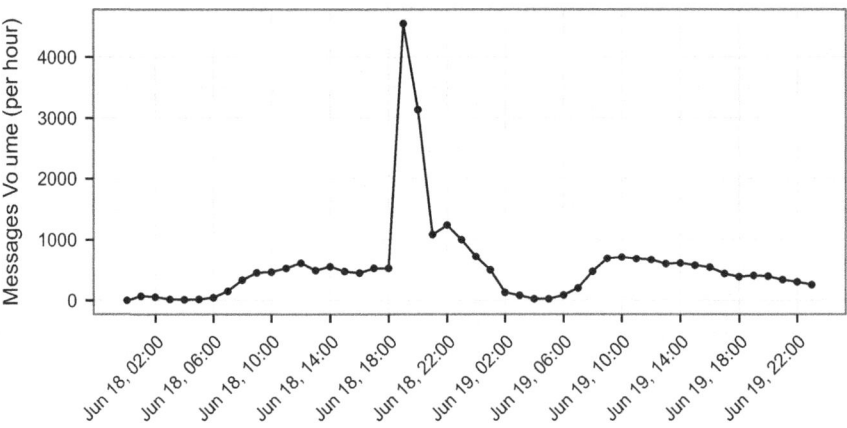

Fig. 6.5 Messages contributing to the political communication space posted between June 18, and June 19

6.4 What Do Users Tweet About in Reaction to Mediated Events? 173

spectatorship (Kreiss et al. 2014), entailing "alternately critical, embracing, raucous, or bawdy political communication among those witnessing live or mediated political events" (Kreiss 2014). How did users comment on the ratification of the Access Impediment Act on Twitter?

For this analysis, I focused on the most retweeted messages from June 18, 2009. The reasoning behind this decision is again based on the concept of collective curating that was discussed in Chap. 3. Calculating the total number of times each message was retweeted results in a list of messages ranked according to the attention they received from other Twitter users. Analyzing messages at the top of this list, therefore, allows us to assess which types of messages were retweeted the most and thus held the most meaning to politically vocal publics. On June 18 the most retweeted message was retweeted 187 times. The message ranked 100 was retweeted five times. I included all messages, therefore, with at least five retweets in the analysis. This resulted in a corpus of 137 messages. Table 6.4 shows the results.

Over 50% of the 137 most retweeted messages on June 18, 2009 contained commentary on the ratification of the Access Impediment Act, related political issues—such as censorship online—positions of parties, and related statements by politicians. Ten percent of all messages contained ironic commentary, mostly commenting on political issues connected with ratification of the Access Impediment Act. Most of the factual commentary focused on the ratification process itself. Other topics were referred to much less often. Five percent of all messages were advertising online polls, whilst another 5% of messages indexed the statements of

Table 6.4 Usage patterns in the 137 top RTs on the day of the Access Impediment Act's ratification, June 18, 2009

Use	Topic	%
Commentary (factual)		42
	Campaign	–
	Current events	–
	Election outcome	–
	Issues	5
	Journalists/media	2
	Parties	19
	Politicians	11
	Ratification of the AIA	63
Commentary (ironic)		10
	Campaign	–
	Current events	–
	Election outcome	–
	Issues	64
	Journalists/media	–
	Parties	7
	Politicians	–
	Ratification of the AIA	29

(continued)

Table 6.4 (continued)

Use	Topic	%
Hashtag hijacking		–
Horse-race coverage		5
	Online polls	100
	Projections	–
	Satire	–
	Traditional polls	–
Indexing		5
	Affirming	71
	Contesting	29
Information (links)		30
	Backchannel to event	–
	Main coverage of event	7
	Various sources	93
Mobilization		8
n.a.		–

politicians during the debate before the ratification. Yet another 30 % of messages contained links to sources on the Web, most of which pointed to content on the Web illustrating various aspects of the Access Impediment Act. A minority of links pointed to the main coverage of ratification for the Access Impediment Act on *phoenix.de* or *bundestag.de*. Eight percent of the most retweeted messages were mobilization attempts against the ratification of the Access Impediment Act. These usage patterns correspond well with those identified in the literature.

6.4.2 State Elections: Temporal Dynamics and Content

The second mediated event, leading to a considerable spike in the daily volume of Twitter messages contributing to the political communication space, fell on August 30, 2009, the day of elections in three German states—the Saarland, Sachsen, and Thüringen. The results of these elections, held so closely before the federal election, were widely seen as indicating the result of the upcoming federal election. Thus, they received a lot of media coverage and attention online.

Germany's public television stations, *ARD* and *ZDF*, provided election night coverage from 5:45 p.m. onwards. Also, local public stations, such as *SWR* and *mdr*, provided election night coverage. This coverage was accessible on television and through videostreams online.

Table 6.5 shows the number of messages posted on August 30, the number of users active on the day and the number of messages containing @messages, retweets, or URLs. To allow for a comparison, the table also shows the share messages posted on August 30 had on all messages posted between June 18 and

6.4 What Do Users Tweet About in Reaction to Mediated Events?

Table 6.5 User behavior in all messages posted compared to political communication space on the day of the state elections, August 30, 2009

Usage convention	All messages	Pol. comm. space
Messages	96,919	13,923
Messages containing neither @messages, retweets, or URLs	51,609	6891
@messages	14,262	1636
Retweets	5282	2440
Messages containing URLs	34,397	4825
Users	13,528	3327
% of all messages posted	1	1.5
% messages containing neither @messages, retweets, or URLs	53.2	49.5
% @messages	14.7	11.8
% retweets	5.4	17.5
% messages with URLs	35.5	34.7
% of all users active	41.3	10.5

October 1, 2009; the share users who posted messages on August 30 had on all users who posted messages between June 18 and October 1, 2009; and the share of messages using @messages, retweets, URLs, and messages using no conventions had within all messages posted on August 30. The shares do not add up to 100 because various messages used more than one convention—such as @messages or retweets containing hyperlinks.

The messages posted on August 30 were equivalent to 1 % of all messages posted between June 18, and October 1, 2009. The share of messages contributing to the political communication space was somewhat higher at 1.5. This compares to the median day on which 0.04 % of all messages were posted, and 0.7 % of all messages contributed to the political communication space. Roughly 41 % of all users who posted messages during the course of the analysis posted messages on August 30. This compares to only about 10 % of all users who contributed to the political communication space. This is nearly double the share of all users contributing to the political communication space on the median day. This demonstrates that on August 30 more users than usual posted a greater number of tweets referring to politics.

The share of messages without @messages, retweets, or URLs of all messages on August 30 was roughly comparable to the share of these messages during the course of the analysis. For the political communication space, these messages had a significantly higher share on August 30, than between June 18, and October 1—49.5 % compared to 30.9 %. The share of @messages, retweets, and messages containing URLs from all messages on August 30 was clearly lower than the share of these conventions during the course of the analysis. This corresponds with patterns identified on June 18, and the general observation that mediated events tend to lead

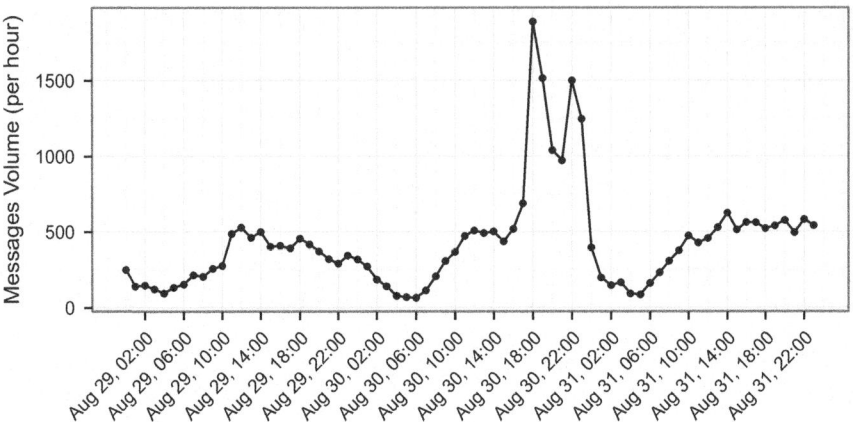

Fig. 6.6 Messages contributing to the political communication space posted between August 29, and August 31

to a decrease in interactions between users and references to content on Twitter or the web.

Figure 6.6 shows the temporal distribution of messages contributing to the political communication space posted each hour from August 29 through to August 31. The plot shows clearly that the volume of messages peaked on August 30, between 6 and 10 p.m., the hours of the main election night coverage by the media. In comparison to the peak on June 18, the peak on August 30 is flatter yet covers more hours. After reaching its peak between 6 and 7 p.m.—the time span during which the first official projections are published—the volume of Twitter messages drops somewhat, only to rise again at 10 p.m.—coinciding with one of Germany's top news programs, *ZDF heute journal*. After 11 p.m., the hourly volume of messages drops but remains somewhat higher than in the hours directly preceding election night coverage. The following day, the hourly volume of messages remains at roughly the same level it had before, demonstrating that the volume spike on August 30 was indeed a reaction to the mediated coverage on election night and not due to an increase in general chatter on Twitter preceding the event.

To analyze the content of tweets posted on this day, I focused on the most retweeted messages on June 30, 2009. On that day, the most retweeted message was retweeted 139 times. In contrast, the message ranking 100 was retweeted seven times. I included all messages, therefore, with at least seven retweets in the analysis which resulted in a corpus of 121 messages. Table 6.6 shows the result.

Thirty-two percent of the 121 most retweeted messages on August 30, 2009 contained commentary on the state elections. Only 3% of all messages contained ironic commentary. The share of commentary—either factual or ironic—was thus much lower than during the broadcast of the Access Impediment Act's ratification. Most of the factual commentary focused on the outcome of the election or the campaign, whereas 21% of the most retweeted messages on August 30 focused

6.4 What Do Users Tweet About in Reaction to Mediated Events?

Table 6.6 Usage patterns in the 121 top RTs on the day of the state elections, August 30, 2009

Use	Topic	%
Commentary (factual)		29
	Campaign	31
	Current events	–
	Election outcome	40
	Issues	9
	Journalists/media	3
	Parties	3
	Politicians	14
Commentary (ironic)		3
	Campaign	25
	Current events	–
	Election outcome	25
	Issues	25
	Journalists/media	–
	Parties	–
	Politicians	25
Hashtag hijacking		–
Horse-race coverage		21
	Online polls	92
	Projections	8
	Satire	–
	Traditional polls	–
Indexing		8
	Affirming	50
	Contesting	50
Information (links)		20
	Backchannel to event	4
	Main coverage of event	–
	Various sources	96
Mobilization		18
n.a.		–

on horse-race coverage. Most of these messages linked or referred to online polls or official projections of the election results. Furthermore, 20 % of the most retweeted messages provided links to further information, most of those published by various sources—be they media or blogs. A minority of tweets also contained links to digital backchannels of the election night—such as blogs or websites that were commenting on the media coverage. Eighteen percent of the most retweeted messages contained attempts at mobilizing Twitter users to vote or to participate in the campaign for the federal election. In 8 % of the most retweeted messages Twitter users indexed statements made by politicians. Messages affirming or contesting the statements of politicians roughly balanced out.

In comparison with the most retweeted messages during ratification of the Access Impediment Act, messages retweeted during state election night coverage tended to contain more horse-race coverage, mobilization, and indexing. In contrast, the most retweeted messages on August 30 tended to contain less commentary or links to further information on the Web. The differences in these usage patterns mirror the differences between the events to which they were referring. Ratification of the Access Impediment Act was a political event with little opportunity for mobilization or horse-race coverage, both practices lending themselves more readily to Twitter coverage of election results. Thus, changes in usage patterns on Twitter seem to mirror the nature of events to which they are reacting.

6.4.3 Televised Leaders' Debate: Temporal Dynamics and Content

The third mediated event, leading to one of the biggest spikes in the daily volume of Twitter messages contributing to the political communication space, occurred on September 13, 2009, the day of the televised leaders' debate between Angela Merkel and Frank Walter Steinmeier. Televised debates have been a regular part of election campaigns in Germany since 2002. To date they have not yet reached the level of importance they hold in the US; still, since 2002 they have become an important and well covered element of German campaigns. They are probably best considered as activating events, leading to increased political involvement by the public running up to election night (e.g. Maier and Faas 2011; Maier et al. 2013).

The debate was covered live on ARD, ZDF, RTL, Sat 1, and Phoenix. Following the debate, various stations ran post-debate coverage that assessed the respective performances of the candidates as well as the strategic relevance of the debate for the coming election. The debate coverage was accessible on television and through videostreams online.

Table 6.7 shows the number of messages posted on September 13, the number of users active on the day and the number of messages containing @messages, retweets, or URLs. To allow for a comparison with Twitter use by publics during other days, the table also shows the share that messages posted on September 13 had within all messages posted between June 18, and October 1, 2009; the share users who posted messages on August 30 had on all users who posted messages between June 18, and October 1, 2009; and the share of messages using @messages, retweets, URLs, and messages using no conventions had within all messages posted on September 13. The shares do not add up to 100 because various messages used more than one convention—such as @messages or retweets containing hyperlinks.

The messages posted on September 13 accounted for 1.4 % of all messages posted between June 18, and October 1, 2009. The share of messages contributing to the political communication space was clearly higher, at 3.9 %. This compares to the median day on which 0.04 % of all messages were posted, and 0.7 % of

6.4 What Do Users Tweet About in Reaction to Mediated Events? 179

Table 6.7 User behavior in all messages posted compared to political communication space on the day of the televised debate, September 13, 2009

Usage convention	All messages	Pol. comm. space
Messages	136,626	36,500
Messages containing neither @messages, retweets, or URLs	77,597	23,980
@messages	18,774	3140
Retweets	11,496	6163
Messages containing URLs	41,219	6423
Users	15,501	5480
% of all messages posted	1.4	3.9
% messages containing neither @messages, retweets, or URLs	56.8	65.7
% @messages	13.7	8.6
% retweets	8.4	16.9
% messages with URLs	30.2	17.6
% of all users active	47.4	17.3

all messages contributing to the political communication space. Roughly 47 % of all users who posted messages during the course of the analysis posted messages on August 30. This compares to just above 17 % of all users who contributed to the political communication space. This is somewhat more than double the share of all users contributing to the political communication space on the median day, demonstrating that on September 13 more users posted more tweets referring to politics than usual.

The share of messages without @messages, retweets, or URLs from all messages on September 13 was somewhat higher than the share of these messages during the course of the analysis. For the political communication space, these messages had a significantly higher share on September 13 than between June 18, and October 1— 65.7 % compared with 30.9 %. The share of @messages, retweets, and messages containing URLs within all messages on August was clearly lower than the share of these conventions during the course of the analysis. This corresponds with patterns identified on June 18 and August 30 and the general observation that mediated events tend to lead to produce a decrease in interactions between users and references to content on Twitter or the web.

Figure 6.7 shows the temporal distribution of messages contributing to the political communication space, posted each hour from September 12, through to September 14. The plot clearly shows that the volume of messages peaked on September 13 between 8 and 11 p.m., the hours of the televised debate and accompanying post-debate coverage. After 10 p.m., the hourly volume of messages drops but remains somewhat higher than in the hours directly preceding election night coverage. The following day, the hourly volume of messages remains at roughly the same level it had before the debate. The spike on September 13 was

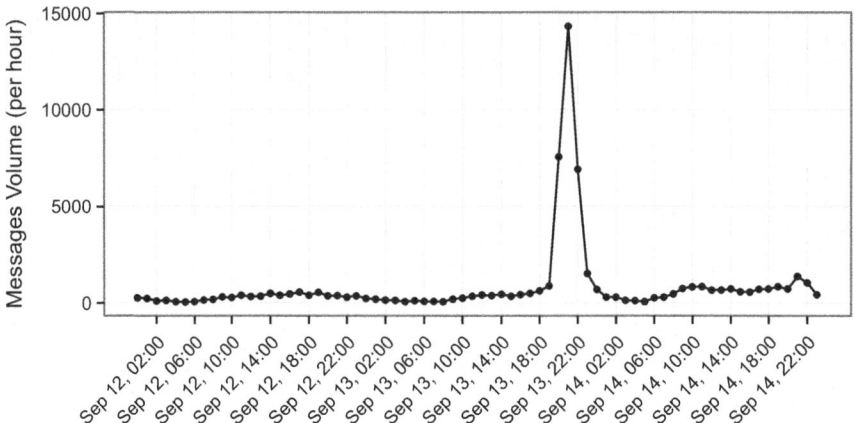

Fig. 6.7 Messages contributing to the political communication space posted between September 12, and September 14

thus indeed a reaction to the mediated coverage of the election night and not due to an increase in general chatter on Twitter preceding the event.

For this analysis I focused on the most retweeted messages on September 13, 2009. On that day the most retweeted message was retweeted 78 times. The message ranked 100 was retweeted eight times. I included all messages, therefore, with at least eight retweets in the analysis, resulting in a corpus of 116 messages. Table 6.8 shows the result.

Forty-one percent of the 116 most retweeted messages on September 13, 2009 contained commentary on the debate. Sixteen percent of these retweets contained ironic commentary. Most of the factual commentary focused on the performances of Angela Merkel and Frank-Walter Steinmeier during the debate, closely followed by comments on the overall format of the televised debate itself and political issues raised or neglected. Nearly half of all ironic commentary focused on the televised debate itself, one third focused on the performance of the candidates while one sixth focused on political parties. Fourteen percent of the most retweeted messages contained horse-race coverage. Most of these messages linked or referred to online polls, while a smaller portion referenced (by linking or referencing) traditional polls. Twelve percent of the most retweeted messages provided links to further information and half of them linked to various sources providing further or contesting information on issues raised during the debate or on the debate itself—be they published by traditional media or blogs. Beyond that, links to digital backchannels for the event—such as blogs or websites that were covering the debate—as well as links to the main coverage of the event on the websites of the respective television stations were rather prominent amongst that number. Eleven percent of the most retweeted messages contained attempts at mobilizing Twitter users to participate in online polls or in the campaign for the federal election. In 11 % of the most retweeted messages Twitter users also indexed statements made by

6.4 What Do Users Tweet About in Reaction to Mediated Events? 181

Table 6.8 Usage patterns in the 116 top RTs on the day of the televised debate, September 13, 2009

Use	Topic	%
Commentary (factual)		25
	Campaign	7
	Current events	3
	Election outcome	3
	Issues	24
	Journalists/media	3
	Parties	–
	Politicians	31
	TV-debate	28
Commentary (ironic)		16
	Campaign	–
	Current events	–
	Election outcome	–
	Issues	–
	Journalists/media	5
	Parties	16
	Politicians	32
	TV-debate	47
Hashtag hijacking		6
Horse-race coverage		14
	Online polls	86
	Projections	–
	Satire	–
	Traditional polls	14
Indexing		11
	Affirming	38
	Contesting	62
Information (links)		12
	Backchannel to event	36
	Main coverage of event	14
	Various sources	50
Mobilization		11
n.a.		6

politicians, with messages contesting candidates' statements slightly outweighing statements affirming candidates' arguments. Meanwhile, 6 % of the most retweeted messages present evidence of hashtag hijacking—a practice with which fringe groups and marketers use the attention attracted by politically relevant hashtags to distribute their own messages. Finally, 6 % of the most retweeted messages could not be categorized as contributing to either of these usage practices.

Compared with the most retweeted messages during the night of the state elections on August 30, messages retweeted during the televised debate tended to contain more commentary, hashtag hijacking, and messages not conforming with these usage functions. Indexing was largely stable across these two events. In contrast, the most retweeted messages on September 13 tended to contain somewhat less horse-race coverage, links to further information on the Web, and mobilization. Again, differences in these usage patterns mirror the differences between the events to which they were referring. The televised debate allowed users more room to comment on the event itself than coverage of the election results. Attention on the event also clearly attracted a more diversely motivated set of users to comment on Twitter than previous events. This is shown by the large share of messages containing ironic commentary, attempts at hashtag hijacking, and messages not really conforming with any of the usage functions discussed above.

6.4.4 Election Day: Temporal Dynamics and Content

The last mediated event, leading to a considerable spike in the daily volume of Twitter messages contributing to the political communication space, occurred on September 27, 2009, the day of the federal election. Germany's public television stations, ARD and ZDF, provided election night coverage from 5:45 p.m. onwards. This coverage was accessible on television and through videostreams online.

Table 6.9 shows the number of messages posted on September 27, the number of users active on the day and the number of messages containing @messages, retweets, or URLs. To allow for a comparison, the table also shows the share that messages posted on September 27 had within all messages posted between June 18 and October 1, 2009; the share that users who posted messages on September 27

Table 6.9 User behavior in all messages posted compared to political communication space on election day, September 27, 2009

Usage convention	All messages	Pol. comm. space
Messages	175,019	68,160
Messages containing neither @messages, retweets, or URLs	96,747	38,509
@messages	28,611	6384
Retweets	17,607	13,960
Messages containing URLs	48,075	18,522
Users	19,821	12,152
% of all messages posted	1.7	7.3
% messages containing neither @messages, retweets, or URLs	55.3	56.5
% @messages	16.3	9.4
% retweets	10.1	20.5
% messages with URLs	27.5	27.2
% of all users active	60.6	38.3

6.4 What Do Users Tweet About in Reaction to Mediated Events? 183

had from all users who posted messages between June 18 and October 1, 2009; and the share of messages using @messages, retweets, URLs, and messages using no conventions had within all messages posted on September 27. The shares do not add up to 100 because various messages used more than one convention—such as @messages or retweets containing hyperlinks.

The messages posted on September 27 accounted for 1.7 % of all messages posted between June 18, and October 1, 2009. The share of messages contributing to the political communication space was clearly higher at 7.3 %. This compares with the median day on which 0.04 % of all messages were posted, and 0.7 % of all messages contributing to the political communication space. Roughly 60 % of all users who posted messages during the course of the analysis posted messages on September 27. This compares with only about 38 % of all users who contributed to the political communication space. This is more than three times the share of all users contributing to the political communication space on the median day. This demonstrates that—somewhat expectedly—on September 27 more users posted more tweets referring to politics than usual.

The share of messages without @messages, retweets, or URLs within all messages on September 27 was much higher than the share of these message during the whole run of the analysis. Especially for the political communication space these messages had a significantly higher share on September 27, than between June 18, and October 1—56.5 % compared with 30.9 %. The share of @messages, retweets, and messages containing URLs from all messages on August was clearly lower than the share of these conventions during the course of the analysis. This corresponds with patterns identified before and the general observation that mediated events lead to a decrease in interactions between users and references to content on Twitter or the web.

Figure 6.8 shows the temporal distribution of messages contributing to the political communication space posted each hour from September 26, through to September 28. The plot clearly shows that the volume of messages peaked on September 27, between 5 and 10 p.m., the hours of the main election night coverage by the media. After 11 p.m. the hourly volume of messages declines but still remains somewhat higher than during hours directly preceding election night coverage. On the following day the hourly volume of messages remains at roughly the same level it had before election day. The relative spike on September 26, between 8 and 10 p.m. was a reaction to a political talk-show targeted at young and first-time voters. Both these observations show that the volume spike on September 27 was indeed a reaction to the mediated coverage of election night and not an increase in general chatter on Twitter preceding the event.

For this analysis, I focused on the most retweeted messages from September 27, 2009. On that day, the most retweeted message was retweeted 114 times. The message ranked 100 was retweeted eighteen times. I included all messages, therefore, with at least eighteen retweets in the analysis. This resulted in a corpus of 137 messages. Table 6.10 shows the result.

Fifty-four percent of the 137 most retweeted messages on September 13, 2009 contained voter mobilization efforts. Twenty-two percent of the most retweeted

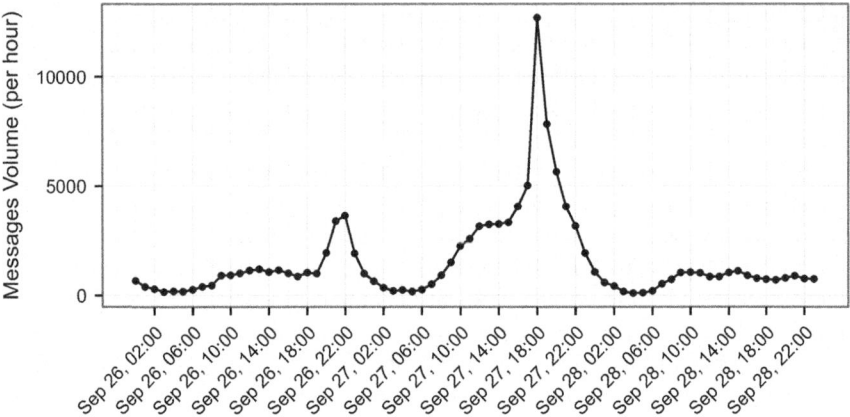

Fig. 6.8 Messages contributing to the political communication space posted between September 26 and September 28

Table 6.10 Usage patterns in the 137 top RTs on election day, September 27, 2009

Use	Topic	%
Commentary (factual)		4
	Campaign	20
	Current events	–
	Election outcome	40
	Issues	–
	Journalists/media	–
	Parties	20
	Politicians	20
Commentary (ironic)		9
	Campaign	8
	Current events	–
	Election outcome	75
	Issues	8
	Journalists/media	–
	Parties	8
	Politicians	–
Hashtag hijacking		–
Horse-race coverage		22
	Online polls	40
	Projections	47
	Satire	10
	Traditional polls	3

(continued)

Table 6.10 (continued)

Use	Topic	%
Indexing		—
	Affirming	—
	Contesting	—
Information (links)		12
	Backchannel to event	25
	Main coverage of event	—
	Various sources	75
Mobilization		54
n.a.		—

messages contributed to horse-race coverage. Most of these messages linked or referred to official projections or online polls, with few parodying horse-race coverage by posting obviously satirical poll results. Thirteen percent of the most retweeted messages contained commentary on the election result, mostly with ironic content. Twelve percent of the most retweeted messages provided links to further information, most of those published by various sources—be they media or blogs. A minority of these tweets contained links to digital backchannels of the election night—such as blogs or websites that were commenting on the media coverage of election night.

Compared with the most retweeted messages during other events, the messages posted on the day of the federal election in 2009 contained significantly more messages containing attempts to mobilize voters and somewhat more horse-race coverage. In contrast, the most retweeted messages on September 13 tended to contain less commentary or links to further information on the Web without any evidence of indexing statements made by politicians. These patterns mirror the nature of the event to which the messages were referring. The prominence of mobilizing messages especially is clearly connected with the election, as is the volume of messages offering horse-race coverage.

6.5 Twitter and Political Coverage by Traditional Media

In this chapter I focused on the interconnection between political coverage in traditional media and Twitter messages referring to politics. In general, the analyses point to hybrid relationships between the two channels. Twitter messages referring to politics followed cues similar to traditional media in some cases but also diverged from these patterns in specific cases. Here Twitter seems to combine coverage logics from traditional media with those specific to Twitter (Jungherr 2014a). Similar findings emerged from analyzing the content of popular messages posted during mediated events.

The analyses of four mediated events, which led to spikes in the daily volume of Twitter messages, have largely confirmed patterns found in other studies on the coverage of mediated events on Twitter. In general terms, the volume of Twitter messages spiked in reaction to mediated events. Thus media coverage of socially relevant events seems to focus the collective attention of Twitter users and provides them with a series of stimuli to which they react by posting messages commenting on elements of the coverage they are watching.

During the course of a given event's media coverage, users tended to interact less frequently amongst one another and posted less messages referring to content on the Web and posted less retweets than during other times. This goes to show that most Twitter users seem to focus on the media coverage of an event and phrase their responses accordingly; this observation suggests that traditional media coverage rather than Twitter's online setting frames and shapes these immediate responses. Interaction with other users about the event seems to become of importance only after the coverage of the event has ended.

Finally, the Twitter messages which rose to prominence during various mediated events during the campaign for the 2009 federal election tended to offer context for the mediated events to which they were reacting. Prominently retweeted messages: contained commentary on ongoing events, be it factual or ironic; included various elements of horse-race coverage; contributed to the indexing of politicians' statements; possessed links to further information on the web and calls for mobilization. In this, prominent messages opened up political discourse to the opinions of Twitter users offering commentary and links to further, potentially contesting, information on the Web which allowed for the contextualization of statements and episodes in the mediated coverage of political events.

References

Albers H (2009) Onlinewahlkampf 2009. Aus Politik und Zeitgeschichte 59(51):33–38

Ampofo L, Anstead N, O'Loughlin B (2011) Trust, confidence, and credibility: citizen responses on Twitter to opinion polls during the 2010 UK General Election. Inf Commun Soc 14(6):850–871. doi:10.1080/1369118X.2011.587882

Anstead N, O'Loughlin B (2011) The emerging Viewertariat and BBC Question Time: television debate and real-time commenting online. Int J Press Polit 16(4):440–462. doi:10.1177/1940161211415519

Anstead N, O'Loughlin B (2014) Social media analysis and public opinion: the 2010 UK General Election. J Comput Mediat Commun. doi:10.1111/jcc4.12102

Bartlett MS (1937) Properties of sufficiency and statistical tests. Proc R Stat Soc Ser A Math Phys Sci 160(901):268–282. doi:10.1098/rspa.1937.0109

Bieber C, Leggewie C (eds) (2012) Unter Piraten: Erkundungen in einer neuen politischen Arena. transcript, Bielefeld, DE

Bieber C, Schwöbel C (2011) Politische Online-Kommunikation im Spannungsfeld zwischen Europa- und Bundestagswahl. In: Tenscher J (ed) Superwahljahr 2009: Vergleichende Analysen aus Anlass der Wahlen zum Deutschen Bundestag und zum Europäischen Parlament. VS Verlag für Sozialwissenschaft, Wiesbaden

Blunch NJ (2008) Introduction to structural equation modelling using SPSS and AMOS. SAGE, London

Bruns A, Burgess J (2011) #ausvotes: How Twitter covered the 2010 Australian federal election. Commun Polit Cult 44(2):37–56

Burgess J, Bruns A (2012) (not) the Twitter election: the dynamics of the #ausvotes conversation in relation to the Australian media ecology. Journal Pract 6(3):384–402. doi:10.1080/17512786.2012.663610

Cattell RB (1966) The scree test for the number of factors. Multivar Behav Res 1(2):245–276. doi:10.1207/s15327906mbr0102_10

Chadwick A (2013) The hybrid media system: politics and power. Oxford University Press, Oxford

Cronbach LJ (1951) Coefficient alpha and the internal structure of tests. Psychometrika 16(3):297–334. doi:10.1007/BF02310555

Dayan D, Katz E (1992) Media events: the live broadcasting of history. Harvard University Press, Cambridge

Field A, Miles J, Field Z (2012) Discovering statistics using R. SAGE, London

Hamby P (2013) Did Twitter kill the boys on the bus? Searching for a better way to cover a campaign. Discussion Paper Series #D-80, Joan Shorenstein Center on the Press, Politics and Public Policy, Boston. http://shorensteincenter.org/wp-content/uploads/2013/08/d80_hamby.pdf

Hanna A, Wells C, Maurer P, Shah DV, Friedland L, Matthews J (2013) Partisan alignments and political polarization online: a computational approach to understanding the French and US presidential elections. In: Weber I, Popescu AM, Pennacchiotti M (eds) PLEAD 2013: proceedings of the 2nd workshop politics, elections and data. ACM, New York, pp 15–21. doi:10.1145/2508436.2508438

Helms L (2010) The German federal election, September 2009. Elect Stud 29(2):289–292. doi:dx.doi.org/10.1016/j.electstud.2010.02.005

Jungherr A (2014a) The logic of political coverage on Twitter: temporal dynamics and content. J Commun 64(2):239–259. doi:10.1111/jcom.12087

Jungherr A (2014b) Twitter in politics: a comprehensive literature review. Soc Sci Res Netw. http://papers.ssrn.com/sol3/papers.cfm?abstract_id=2402443

Jungherr A, Jürgens P (2010) The political click: political participation through e-petitions in Germany. Policy Internet 2(4):131–165. doi:10.2202/1944-2866.1084

Kaiser HF (1960) The application of electronic computers to factor analysis. Educ Psychol Meas 20(1):141–151. doi:10.1177/001316446002000116

Kaiser HF (1974) An index of factorial simplicity. Psychometrika 39(1):31–36. doi:10.1007/BF02291575

Kreiss D (2014) Seizing the moment: the presidential campaigns' use of Twitter during the 2012 electoral cycle. N Media Soc. doi:10.1177/1461444814562445

Kreiss D, Meadows L, Remensperger J (2014) Political performance, boundary spaces, and active spectatorship: media production at the 2012 Democratic National Convention. Journalism. doi:10.1177/1464884914525562

Krewel M, Schmitt-Beck R, Wolsing A (2011) The campaign and its dynamics at the 2009 German General Election. Ger Polit 20(1):28–50. doi:10.1080/09644008.2011.554100

Larsson AO, Moe H (2012) Studying political microblogging: Twitter users in the 2010 Swedish election campaign. N Media Soc 14(5):729–747

Lin YR, Keegan B, Margolin D, Lazer D (2014) Rising tides or rising stars? Dynamics of shared attention on Twitter during media events. PLoS One 9(5):e94093. doi:10.1371/journal.pone.0094093

Maier J, Faas T (2011) 'Miniature Campaigns' in comparison: the German televised debates, 2002–09. Ger Polit 20(1):75–91. doi:10.1080/09644008.2011.554102

Maier J, Faas T, Maier M (2013) Mobilisierung durch Fernsehdebatten: Zum Einfluss des TV-Duells 2009 auf die politische Involvierung und die Partizipationsbereitschaft. In: Weßels B, Schoen H, Gabriel OW (eds) Wahlen und Wähler: Analysen aus Anlass der Bundestagswahl 2009. Springer, Wiesbaden, pp 79–96. doi:10.1007/978-3-658-01328-8_4

Norris P, Reif K (1997) Second-order elections. Eur J Polit Res 31(1):109–124. doi:10.1111/1475-6765.00308

Rattinger H, Roßteutscher S, Schmitt-Beck R, Weßels B (2012a) Campaign media content analysis, print media (gles 2009): Za5307 data file version 1.0.0. GESIS data archive, Cologne. doi:10.4232/1.11387

Rattinger H, Roßteutscher S, Schmitt-Beck R, Weßels B (2012b) Campaign media content analysis, TV (gles 2009): Za5306 data file version 1.1.0. GESIS data archive, Cologne. doi:10.4232/1.11401

Reif K, Schmitt H (1980) Nine second-order national elections: a conceptual framework for the analysis of European election results. Eur J Polit Res 8(1):3–44. doi:10.1111/j.1475-6765.1980.tb00737.x

Revelle W (2009) psych: procedures for personality and psychological research (version 1.3.2). Northwestern University, Evanston. http://CRAN.R-project.org/package=psych

Trilling D (2014) Two different debates? Investigating the relationship between a political debate on TV and simultaneous comments on Twitter. Soc Sci Comput Rev. doi:10.1177/0894439314537886

Chapter 7
Predictor of Electoral Success and Public Opinion at Large

7.1 The Connection Between Attention on Twitter and Electoral Fortunes

The previous chapters have shown that Twitter data allow researchers to analyze objects of attention by politically vocal Twitter users. Still, the slightly more ambitious target of reliably identifying events during the campaign connected with parties, candidates, or controversies through data collected on Twitter proved to be harder. Nevertheless, researchers have recently used Twitter data in attempts to reach even more ambitious research goals. Among political scientists, interest has focused on the ways in which digital trace data collected on Twitter might reflect public opinion on parties or political candidates and might even be used to predict election outcomes. On the face of it, this connection appears to be highly dubious. After all, Twitter users tend not to be a representative sample of society at large (Smith and Brenner 2012) and Twitter is a communication environment easily manipulated by campaigns, consultants, or activists (Mustafaraj et al. 2011). Still, a number of papers with high visibility among scholars and in media reports have repeatedly claimed ability to infer public opinion, political support, or even election results based on messages posted on Twitter (e.g. Bermingham and Smeaton 2011; Chen et al. 2012; DiGrazia et al. 2013; Fink et al. 2013; Gaurav et al. 2013; Skoric et al. 2012; Soler et al. 2012; Tjong et al. 2012; Tumasjan et al. 2010).

Unfortunately, the authors of these studies are usually content with reporting correlations between some metrics of politically relevant activity on Twitter and some metrics of political support. They neglect any systematic discussion about their theoretical conception of public opinion and their implicitly assumed mechanism by which specific metrics of Twitter data should be connected with specific metrics of public opinion. The surprising correlations reported in these studies, thereby, remain unexplained. This makes it very hard to assess whether one is really seeing a systematic reflection of public opinion in Twitter data or merely falling victim to spurious correlations between some random—or cleverly selected—variables.

Accordingly, these studies have been heavily contested on the soundness of their approach as well as the validity of their results (e.g. Chung and Mustafaraj 2011; Diaz et al. 2014; Gayo-Avello 2011; Gayo-Avello et al. 2011; Huberty 2013; Jungherr 2013; Jungherr et al. 2012; Metaxas et al. 2011).

In this chapter, I will test two models implicitly underlying the arguments of proponents who believe that Twitter data hold information on public opinion at large or on the subsequent electoral fortunes of political actors. The first sees mentions of a political actor in a Twitter message as indicating the support or voting intention of this actor by the user posting the message. The second takes the mention of a political actor in a Twitter message as indicating general relevance during the campaign, independent of the support or voting intention of the user mentioning the political actor. I will test these models on three metrics documenting mentions of political actors on Twitter during the campaign for the federal election of 2009 in Germany. These tests will show that Twitter data allowed for no systematic inferences on public opinion at large or on the subsequent fortunes of political actors. While Twitter data indeed hold information on shifts and objects of political attention by politically vocal Twitter users, the data allow for no inferences on public opinion at large or the electoral chances of political actors. Thus, Twitter data hold information on political attention, not political support.

7.2 Predicting Election Results Using Twitter Data: The Evidence

Over the last years, predicting election results with digital trace data has become a popular research topic. Tweets mentioning candidates or parties are seen as indicators for either voting intentions on election day or for current political support.

Studies trying to identify political dynamics through digital trace data fall into two groups: studies in the first group try to establish correlations between measures of general public opinion, such as surveys, and the dynamics in the volume of Twitter messages commenting on politics (e.g. O'Connor et al. 2010). Studies in the second seek correlations between the volume of Twitter messages commenting on parties or candidates and their subsequent electoral fortunes. These studies often claim to predict election results using Twitter data (e.g. Tumasjan et al. 2010). Both approaches seek to supplement or even replace traditional methods of opinion polling by way of digital trace data.

The second group of studies especially has met with strong criticism focusing on the methodological validity of the approach (e.g. Metaxas et al. 2011). An even greater challenge is posed by studies replicating and sometimes even falsifying the results of studies claiming to predict election results using Twitter data accurately (e.g. Huberty 2013; Jungherr et al. 2012). This opposition has led to lively debates between proponents and their critics. Table 7.1 shows a list of studies presenting supporting evidence for the possibility of predicting elections using data collected

7.2 Predicting Election Results Using Twitter Data: The Evidence

Table 7.1 Predicting elections results with Twitter data

	Supporting evidence	Critique
AT	Lampos et al. (2013)	
EC	Gaurav et al. (2013)	
ES	Soler et al. (2012)	
FR	Ceron et al. (2014)	
GE	Tumasjan et al. (2010, 2011, 2012)	Jungherr et al. (2012) and Jungherr (2013)
IE	Bermingham and Smeaton (2011)	
IT	Ceron et al. (2014)	
NG	Fink et al. (2013)	
NL	Tjong et al. (2012) and Sanders and van den Bosch (2013)	
PY	Gaurav et al. (2013)	
SG	Skoric et al. (2012)	
UK	Franch (2013), Thapen and Ghanem (2013), Lampos (2012), and Lampos et al. (2013)	
USA	O'Connor et al. (2010), Chen et al. (2012), DiGrazia et al. (2013), Jensen and Anstead (2013), Beauchamp (2013), Contractor and Faruquie (2013), Shi et al. (2012), and Marchetti-Bowick and Chambers (2012)	Chung and Mustafaraj (2011), Gayo-Avello (2011), Gayo-Avello et al. (2011), Metaxas et al. (2011), Huberty (2013), and Diaz et al. (2014)
VE	Gaurav et al. (2013)	

on Twitter and studies in opposition. The studies are grouped in accordance with the country on which their cases are based.

The studies can also be grouped on the basis of Twitter metrics used to predict poll dynamics or election results. One group of studies used mention counts or mention shares of political parties or candidates. Another used the share of positive mentions for parties or candidates in their analyses (Table 7.2).

Looking at the available evidence provides a rather muddled picture. Even within studies claiming a systematic link between Twitter data and opinion polls or election results, there appears to be considerable disagreement about where the expected statistical relationship is to be found. This disagreement concerns the conception of both independent and dependent variables.

Suggestions for potentially independent or in other words predictive metrics appear in a wide variety of forms: the mention share that a party received within all party mentions during a given time-span (e.g. Bermingham and Smeaton 2011; Sanders and van den Bosch 2013; Skoric et al. 2012; Soler et al. 2012; Tjong et al. 2012; Tumasjan et al. 2010), the mention share of political candidates (e.g. Chen et al. 2012; DiGrazia et al. 2013; Fink et al. 2013; Gaurav et al. 2013; Skoric et al. 2012), the share of positive mentions a party received (e.g. Bermingham and Smeaton 2011; Thapen and Ghanem 2013), the positive mention share of candidates (e.g. Fink et al. 2013; O'Connor et al. 2010; Shi et al. 2012), the share

Table 7.2 Predictive metrics of election or poll results

	Supporting evidence	Critique
Mention share	Bermingham and Smeaton (2011), Gaurav et al. (2013), Tumasjan et al. (2010, 2011), Tjong et al. (2012), Chen et al. (2012), DiGrazia et al. (2013), Fink et al. (2013), Skoric et al. (2012), Thapen and Ghanem (2013), Jensen and Anstead (2013), Soler et al. (2012), Shi et al. (2012), and Sanders and van den Bosch (2013)	Chung and Mustafaraj (2011), Jungherr et al. (2012), Gayo-Avello (2011), Gayo-Avello et al. (2011), Metaxas et al. (2011), Huberty (2013), and Diaz et al. (2014)
Share of positive mentions	Bermingham and Smeaton (2011), Franch (2013), O'Connor et al. (2010), Thapen and Ghanem (2013), Lampos (2012), and Shi et al. (2012)	Fink et al. (2013), Chung and Mustafaraj (2011), Gayo-Avello (2011), Gayo-Avello et al. (2011), Metaxas et al. (2011), and Huberty (2013)
Various potentially relevant words	Beauchamp (2013), Contractor and Faruquie (2013), Lampos et al. (2013), and Marchetti-Bowick and Chambers (2012)	
Not specified	Ceron et al. (2014)	

of users commenting on a candidate or party (e.g. Tjong et al. 2012), the share of mentions for a candidate followed by a word indicative of electoral success or failure (e.g. Jensen and Anstead 2013), the relative increase of positive mentions of a candidate (e.g. Franch 2013) or simply a collection of various potentially politically relevant words identified by their statistical relationship with polls or political actors in the past (e.g. Beauchamp 2013; Contractor and Faruquie 2013; Lampos et al. 2013; Marchetti-Bowick and Chambers 2012).

Suggestions for the dependent variable, metrics of political success, show a similar variety. They include the vote share that a party received on election day (e.g. Bermingham and Smeaton 2011; Franch 2013; Sanders and van den Bosch 2013; Skoric et al. 2012; Soler et al. 2012), the vote share of a party adjusted to include votes only for parties included in the analysis (e.g. Tumasjan et al. 2010), the vote share of candidates on election day (e.g. DiGrazia et al. 2013; Fink et al. 2013; Gaurav et al. 2013; Jensen and Anstead 2013; Skoric et al. 2012), campaign tracking polls (e.g. Beauchamp 2013; Contractor and Faruquie 2013; Fink et al. 2013; Lampos 2012; Lampos et al. 2013; O'Connor et al. 2010; Shi et al. 2012; Thapen and Ghanem 2013), politicians' job approval ratings (e.g. Marchetti-Bowick and Chambers 2012; O'Connor et al. 2010), and the number of seats in parliament that a party received after the election (e.g. Tjong et al. 2012).

Some of these metrics appear on occasions to be statistically related. But the high variation in the operationalization of independent and dependent variables indicates that this relationship is far from stable given different temporal or electoral contexts. This conjecture is supported by studies testing various metrics of Twitter data in their relationship to various metrics of electoral success (e.g. Diaz et al. 2014; Gayo-Avello 2011; Huberty 2013; Jungherr et al. 2012). This has led various researchers to emphasize that case studies seemingly successful in finding a statistical relationship between some metrics in Twitter data and some metrics of electoral success should not be taken as indicators for the generalizability of their findings (e.g. Gayo-Avello 2012, 2013; Metaxas et al. 2011). This point is important as researchers have shown that skewness in the demographic variables of Twitter users to the general population varies over time and political Twitter use is highly dependent on political events. Hence, this makes the development of statistical models accounting for this skewness increasingly difficult (Diaz et al. 2014).

This problem is exacerbated by the fact that nearly all studies addressing this question have been conducted after the day of the election they tried to predict. Thus, instead of predictions they offer assessments of statistical relationships between various metrics. Some authors are quite open about this limitation (e.g. Fink et al. 2013; O'Connor et al. 2010), others less so (e.g. DiGrazia et al. 2013; Rojas 2013; Tumasjan et al. 2010). Most studies do not spend much effort on justifying their choice of metrics—be it Twitter data or electoral success—which makes it hard to assess if the statistical relationships identified offer more than accounts of spurious correlations, which are bound to appear between variables given large enough data sets.

Critics have approached this problem in two ways: the first aims to improve the procedure and transparency of how predictions are performed, while the second aims to propose and examine possible mechanisms leading to the statistical relationship between some metrics of Twitter data and some metrics of electoral success in some contexts: in other words, they seek to construct a theoretical basis of the discussion.

The first approach seeks to improve the procedure and transparency in predicting election results with digital trace data. In this, it resembles an effort to optimize a research algorithm. To be deemed meaningful, predictions have to be transparently documented and performed before the day of the event due to be predicted. Researchers have to justify their decisions with regard to their choice of independent and dependent variables, their approach to data collection, data preparation (e.g. time spans over which data are aggregated, the inclusion or exclusion of specific messages or actors, attempts to account for demographic biases inherent in Twitter data), and data analysis (e.g. various approaches to sentiment analysis). Beyond that, researchers should document how stable the results of their predictions were across various operationalizations (e.g. Gayo-Avello 2011, 2012, 2013; Metaxas et al. 2011).

The second approach to advance the discussion on the relationship between Twitter data and measures of political success seeks to develop a theoretical footing. In political science, election forecasts are not primarily used to predict future events; instead, they are used as measures to evaluate theories trying to explain political phenomena and behavior. As such, the quality of scientific forecasts depends not necessarily on their ability to predict election results, but instead on the transparency of their approaches. In other words, studies have to document carefully how theoretically justified mechanisms should lead us to expect a specific election outcome. If election outcomes should diverge from a forecast, these findings can be used either to examine how this specific election diverged from those before or how our understanding of elections is flawed. Either way, scientific predictions allow for improvement in our understanding of political phenomena. In contrast, competition with the results and methods of professional pollsters is of little interest to social scientists (Gelman and King 1993).

This stands in striking contrast to most studies using Twitter data to predict elections. Most authors explicitly state their interest in supplementing, improving or even replacing the results of survey based polling by new metrics (e.g. Bermingham and Smeaton 2011; Ceron et al. 2014; Franch 2013; O'Connor et al. 2010; Rojas 2013; Thapen and Ghanem 2013; Tjong et al. 2012). This is somewhat ironic, as in practically all cases the metric by which authors evaluated the success of their predictions—the mean absolute error (MAE)—was higher than the MAE usually found in survey-based approaches.

Instead of focusing on efforts to tweak the results of predictions based on Twitter data to compete with industry polls, it seems more sensible to propose and examine mechanisms that might lead metrics of political support on Twitter to follow or diverge from metrics of electoral success or public opinion, as measured by traditional surveys. To do this, we need to discuss which Twitter metrics can be seen as measures of political support or rather as metrics for public attention of Twitter users to politics and how these might relate to public opinion at large or voting intentions (e.g. Diaz et al. 2014; Gayo-Avello 2011, 2012, 2013; Jungherr 2013; Metaxas et al. 2011).

7.3 Mechanisms Linking Twitter Messages with Opinion Polls and Election Results

Common to the studies discussed above is their authors' apparent lack of interest in potential mechanisms leading to emergence of the reported correlations. Still, the reasoning presented in these studies allows us to reconstruct the underlying models. A series of studies has shown a close relationship between the raw counts of mentions a political actor received on Twitter and the subsequent vote share or share in opinion polls (e.g. Bermingham and Smeaton 2011; Chen et al. 2012; DiGrazia et al. 2013; Fink et al. 2013; Gaurav et al. 2013; Skoric et al. 2012; Soler et al. 2012; Tjong et al. 2012; Tumasjan et al. 2010). Following the reasoning of their authors, one could simply count Twitter messages mentioning political actors, calculate the share of their mentions of all mentions of political actors and thus reliably predict their respective vote shares. To quote two proponents of this approach:

7.3 Mechanisms Linking Twitter Messages with Opinion Polls and Election... 195

> [...] the mere number of tweets mentioning a political party can be considered a plausible reflection of the vote share and its predictive power even comes close to traditional election polls. (Tumasjan et al. 2010)

and

> [...] data extracted from social media platforms yield accurate measurements of public opinion. It turns out that what people say on Twitter or Facebook is a very good indicator of how they will vote. [...] In the future, you will not need a polling organization to understand how your elected representative will fare at the ballot box. Instead, all you will need is an app on your phone. (Rojas 2013)

Although the authors of these studies tend to explicate neither the nature nor the mechanism of this surprising relationship, they seem to share an underlying set of assumptions regarding the nature of the relationship between tweets and votes. The act of posting a tweet mentioning a political actor can obviously be read as a reaction by the user to a received stimulus connected with the actor in question. We can easily imagine a series of possible stimuli leading a user to mention a political actor in a tweet. A user might have come in contact with a political actor—be it directly or through media coverage—and post her reactions to this meeting on Twitter; she might have been exposed to general coverage of the campaign in the media and parties' campaign activity and have in general, therefore, a higher level of political mobilization or involvement, leading her simply to post her political convictions about a political actor without specific incidents prompting her to do so; the user might be a political activist and post messages referring to political actors regardless of specific incidents or campaign related media coverage or party activities; or, the user might react to her perception of political opinions and the voting intentions of other people by posting messages mentioning political actors.

Already this short selection of possible motivations should indicate that behind aggregates of mention counts of political actors, there stand a myriad of micro-level decisions following a variety of potential motives. Following the proponents of the *more tweets, more votes* model, these different motivations to post messages mentioning political candidates should have no effect on the relationship stability between aggregated tweet share and vote share. It would not matter if messages mentioning a political candidate were posted referencing a media appearance, commenting on her performance during a stump speech, criticizing her platform, ridiculing her campaign materials, declaring outrage at her role in a developing political controversy, expressing heartfelt support for her person, or critiquing others for their political attitudes; in aggregate all her mentions would be signals for her potential success at the polls:

> We believe that Twitter and other social media reflect the underlying trend in a political race that goes beyond a district's fundamental geographic and demographic composition. If people must talk about you, even in negative ways, it is a signal that a candidate is on the verge of victory. The attention given to winners creates a situation in which all publicity is good publicity. (Rojas 2013)

Following this reasoning, the act of posting Twitter messages mentioning political actors could be read as proxy for at least four variables:

- evidence of the author's political support for a given party or candidate;
- evidence of the author's voting intention for a given party or candidate on election day;
- reaction by the author on her (valid) perception of political support for a given party or candidate by others;
- reaction by the author on her (valid) perception of voting intentions for a given party or candidate on election day by others.

Based on these interpretations, aggregates of Twitter mentions should be related either to:

- results of opinion polls, if Twitter mentions of political candidates would offer evidence of the author's political support for a given party or candidate or document her reactions to her (valid) perception of political support for a given party or candidate by others; or
- election results, if Twitter mentions of political candidates would offer evidence of the author's voting intention for a given party or candidate on election day or document her reactions to her (valid) perception of voting intentions for a given party or candidate on election day by others.

Another Twitter metric potentially holding information on the electoral chances of political actors might be their share of users commenting on political parties overall (e.g. Tjong et al. 2012). The reasoning behind this type of operationalization is more closely connected to the logic of surveys and voting. By counting only users mentioning parties we move one step closer to the one-person-one-vote logic of elections and opinion polls. Instead of potentially skewing one's results by including mentions by highly active Twitter users, this approach would appear to be more robust given the highly uneven nature of content production on Twitter where a small minority of people posts a large number of messages, thereby potentially skewing the results of analyses looking for Twitter messages reflecting public opinion (e.g. Metaxas and Mustafaraj 2012; Mustafaraj and Metaxas 2010; Mustafaraj et al. 2011).

Based on these observations, we can formulate two models implicitly underlying the available literature: (1) Mentions of political actors in a Twitter message are indicators of the support or voting intention for this actor by the user posting the message; (2) Mentions of political actors in Twitter messages might be seen as indicators of a political actor's general relevance during the campaign independent of the support or voting intention of the user mentioning the political actor. These two models propose a direct relationship between Twitter mentions of political actors and political opinions or voting intentions of Twitter users. Figure 7.1 shows a schematic of these models putting them into the context of our previous discussion about the analysis of macro-phenomena based on aggregates of data documenting micro-behavior.

These models are clearly very ambitious with regard to the political phenomena they attempt to discern based on Twitter messages. Fortunately, their validity can be tested rather easily. In a first step, I will test whether or not aggregates of four

7.4 Method

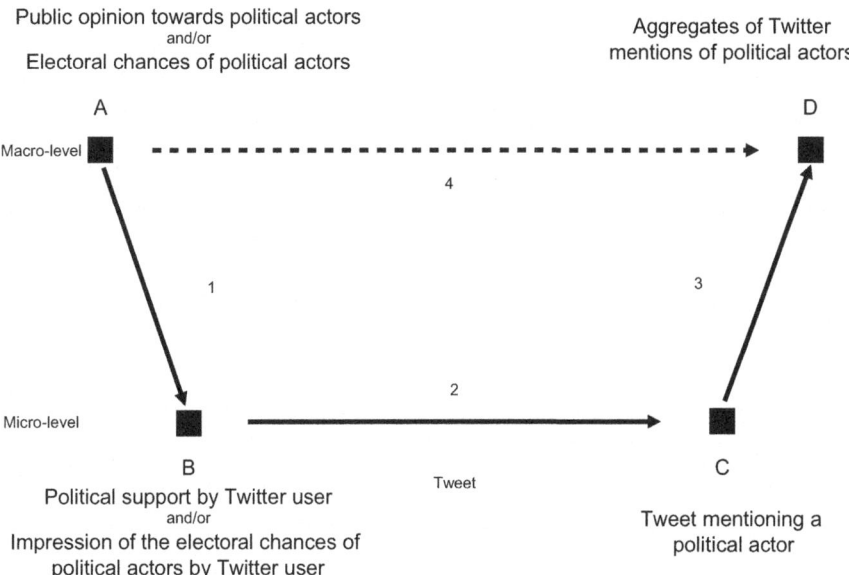

Fig. 7.1 Potential mechanism allowing the detection of public opinion and/or electoral chances of political actors through Twitter data

different Twitter metrics—share of users mentioning a political party, mention share, share of explicitly positive mentions, and share of explicitly negative mentions—documenting the mentions of political actors between June 18, and October 1, were systematically related to their election results. Second, I will test whether or not the mentions of Twitter users over time follow the same trend as their poll results. Both analyses will provide negative results, thereby raising doubts about our expectation for aggregates of political actors' Twitter mentions to reflect public opinion or their electoral chances.

7.4 Method

As shown above, papers examining the relationship between politically relevant Twitter messages and subsequent electoral results usually focus on the number of messages a political actor, be it a party or a candidate, was mentioned in and the subsequent number of votes or vote share—this actor actually received. Thus, these metrics offer a promising point at which to start examining the relationship between Twitter messages and election results for the federal election of 2009 in Germany. I focus exclusively on those cases where a political actor was named explicitly in a hashtag (e.g. #cdu, #spd, #grüne, #piraten, #merkel, #steinmeier et al.). All potential mentions of political actors in the text of Twitter messages without hashtags are thus excluded from the analysis. As discussed above, this selection might lead to an underestimation of the total number of messages commenting on parties or candidates, but should not impact the identification of relative dynamics between mentions of different political actors. Since there was significant variation in the spelling of political actors, I collected the most prominent hashtag variations referring to each actor in encompassing concepts (e.g. #grüne, gruene, bündnis, buendnis et al.). These concepts sum up all appearances of relevant hashtags commenting on the respective political actor.[1] For this analysis, the occurrence of all hashtags collected in these concepts were summed up for each day between June 18, and October 1, 2009.

7.5 Twitter Metrics and Their Relationship to the Electoral Fortunes of Parties

7.5.1 Aggregates, Twitter Metrics: Users, Mentions and Sentiment

Based on the available literature, I decided to examine the relationship between aggregates of four Twitter metrics of political parties' mentions with their respective vote share: shares of users mentioning a party, shares of mentions, shares of positive mentions, and shares of negative mentions. I calculated the vote share of each of the six parties included in the analysis[2] as the share that their number of votes on election day had on the sum of all votes that the six parties received.[3] The vote shares reported in Table 7.3 might, therefore, diverge somewhat from the shares reported in the official election results. In accordance with the literature, I then calculated

---

[1]The following hashtags were collected in concepts: CDU/CSU: #cdu, #cducsu, #csu; SPD: #spd; FDP: #fdp; Bündnis 90/Die Grünen: #buendnis90, #bündnis, #bündnis90, #bündnis90diegrünen, #bündnis90grüne, #bündnisgrüne, #bündnisgrünen, #die_gruenen, #die_grünen, #diegrünen, #gruene, #grüne, #grünen; Die LINKE: #die_linke, #dielinke, #linke, #linkspartei; Piratenpartei: #piraten, #piratenpartei; Angela Merkel: #angie, #merkel, #angie_merkel, #angelamerkel, #angela_merkel; Frank-Walter Steinmeier: #steinmeier, #fws, #frank_walter_steinmeier, #steini, #frankwaltersteinmeier, #frank_steinmeier. This collection might still exclude some more exotic or more ambiguous spelling variations of the political actors in question. Still, this collection should account for the vast majority of the hashtags referring to the political actors question and thus should offer a comprehensive view on the dynamics between them.

[2]The parties selected for this comparison are five that managed to gather enough votes to enter the German Parliament (i.e. CDU/CSU, SPD, FDP, Bündnis 90/Die Grünen, and Die LINKE) and the Piratenpartei. The Pirate Party was included in the analysis despite its subsequent failure to enter Parliament since it dominated the political online-sphere and received extensive media coverage in the run-up to the election.

[3]The amount of votes used in this analysis is based on the official vote-count reported by the *Bundeswahlleiter* (Der Bundeswahlleiter 2009).

7.5 Twitter Metrics and Their Relationship to the Electoral Fortunes of Parties

Table 7.3 Twitter metrics shares between June 18, and October 1, 2009 compared to vote share

Party	Vote share	User share	Mention share	Sentiment (+) share	Sentiment (−) share
CDU/CSU	35.23	34.68	17.13	5.06	24.79
SPD	24.01	37.15	15.57	6.75	14.43
FDP	15.18	34.76	10.7	8.39	8.83
Bündnis 90/Die Grünen	11.16	19.85	7.95	3.02	4.28
Die LINKE	12.39	13.05	4.5	9.77	2.81
Piratenpartei	2.04	61	44.15	67.01	44.87
MAE	-	16.93	14.04	21.66	14.28

the mean absolute error (MAE) for the relationship of each metric with the vote share of political parties to assess its stability. The MAE calculates the average of the absolute errors from the forecasts for each variable (in this case the difference between the actual vote share and shares in various Twitter metrics) (Hyndman and Koehler 2006). Table 7.3 documents the results.

Let us focus first on the relationship between the electoral success of political actors and their share of all users commenting on political parties. The reasoning behind this type of operationalization is connected with the logic of surveys and voting. By counting only users mentioning parties we approximate the one-person-one-vote reality of elections and opinion polls. In total 19,258 users from the data set used one of the neutral hashtags, listed in the previous section, in at least one of their messages. The MAE reported in Table 7.3 shows that the share of users mentioning political parties is a very unreliable indicator of their respective vote share. We find the Pirate Party dominating the communication space with 11,747 users commenting on it. The second strongest party is the SPD with 7155 users directly followed by the FDP (6694 users) and the CDU/CSU (6679).[4] This order is not even close to the order of parties according to their actual vote share. Based on this metric, the vote share of the Pirate Party, the FDP, the SPD would have been overestimated by between 9 % and 60 % points.

Table 7.3 also shows the relationship between neutral mentions shares of political parties and their respective vote shares. Again, we can clearly see that the Pirate Party by far dominated the mention shares of political parties. If the simple argument that more tweets equals more votes would be true, from 2009 to 2013 the Pirate Party would have been the leading partner in German government. Still, one could argue that maybe the Pirate Party should be treated as an outlier. We also see that a prognosis based on Twitter messages would calculate the order of parties wrongly. CDU/CSU, SPD, and FDP were the parties with the most mentions on

---

[4]Because some users referred to more than one party in their messages, the user-counts of the parties do not add up to the total number of users. Since users could and obviously did mention more than one party during the run of the campaign, this can be read as an indicator that this metric also does not correspond with the one-person-one-vote logic of elections.

Twitter (apart from the Pirate Party) and the three parties that gathered the most votes, but for Bündnis 90/Die Grünen and Die LINKE this relationship is not stable. Bündnis 90/Die Grünen received more mentions on Twitter than Die LINKE but less votes on election day. So even if we exclude the Pirate Party from our analysis, the relationship based on more tweets equals more votes is not stable. Calculating vote shares based on mention share thus would obviously overestimate the vote share of the Pirate Party by roughly 40 % points and underestimate the vote share of CDU/CSU, SPD, Die LINKE, and FDP in a range of between 5 % and 18 % points.

In light of these findings, the absolute dominance by the Pirate Party on the Internet while at the same time remaining an insignificant actor on election day, the unstable relationship between the ranking of parties based on their hashtag mentions and votes together with the finally clear under- and overestimation of vote share resulting from prognoses based on Twitter mentions, show that the total amount of mentions on Twitter had—if at all—a very weak connection with the election results of political parties.

Recently, some studies were successful in showing that for elections in some countries there appeared to be correlations between the number of votes and the number of hashtag mentions a party or candidate received on Twitter (e.g. Ceron et al. 2014; DiGrazia et al. 2013; Franch 2013). This offers another interesting approach for checking the relationship between tweets and votes in the federal election of 2009 in Germany. For this analysis, I decided to include all parties that stood for election in 2009. This leads to 27 observations. For robust regression results this number of observations is too small. Still, for an illustrative comparison to the results of previous research, this should suffice.

The previously reported results are reinforced once we look not only at the parties being successful enough to enter Parliament but also the Pirate Party. In Fig. 7.2 we see the relationship between number of votes and the number of hashtags used for all political parties running in the 2009 federal election.[5] To illustrate the poor

---

[5]In addition to the party concepts mentioned before, for this analysis a number of party concepts was included in the analysis that were excluded before: Nationaldemokratische Partei Deutschlands (NPD): #npd; Mensch Umwelt Tierschutz (Die Tierschutzpartei): #tierschutzpartei; DIE REPUBLIKANER (REP): #republikaner, #rep; Ökologisch-Demokratische Partei (ödp): #ödp; Familien-Partei Deutschlands (FAMILIE): #familienpartei; Rentnerinnen und Rentner Partei (RRP): #rrp; Rentner-Partei-Deutschland (RENTNER): #rentnerpartei; Bayernpartei (BP): #bayernpartei; DEUTSCHE VOLKSUNION (DVU): #dvu; Partei Bibeltreuer Christen (PBC): #pbc, #bibeltreuechristen; Bürgerrechtsbewegung Solidarität (BüSo): #büso; Die Violetten; für spirituelle Politik (DIE VIOLETTEN): #violetten, #dievioletten, #die_violetten; Marxistisch-Leninistische Partei Deutschlands (MLPD): #mlpd; Ab jetzt... Bündnis für Deutschland, für Demokratie durch Volksabstimmung (Volksabstimmung): #volksabstimmung, #abjetztbündnisfürdeutschlandfürdemokratiedurchvolksabstimmung; Freie Wähler Deutschland (FWD): #fwd, #freie_wähler, #freiewähler; CHRISTLICHE MITTE—Für ein Deutschland nach GOTTES Geboten(CM): #christlichemitte; Deutsche Zentrumspartei—Älteste Partei Deutschlands gegründet 1870 (ZENTRUM): #zentrum, #zentrumspartei; Partei für Soziale Gleichheit, Sektion der Vierten Internationale (PSG): #psg; Allianz der Mitte (ADM): #adm; Deutsche Kommunistische Partei (DKP): #dkp. As before, this selection of hashtags might underestimate the number of party mentions somewhat.

7.5 Twitter Metrics and Their Relationship to the Electoral Fortunes of Parties

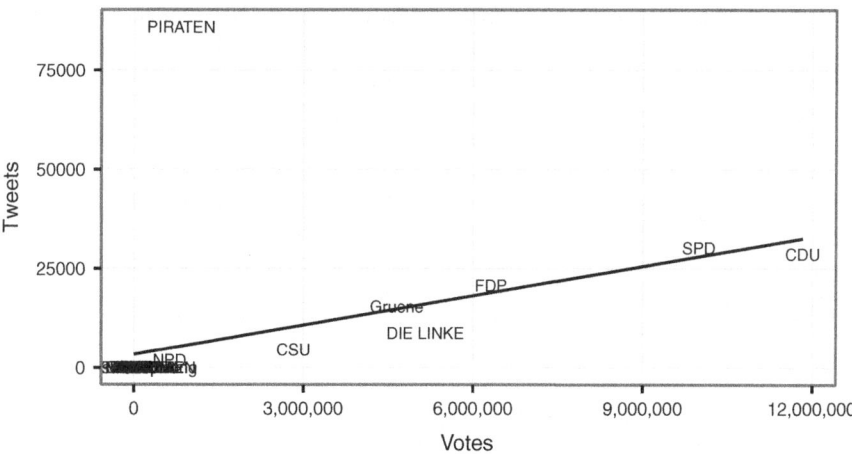

Fig. 7.2 Votes and tweets per party (all parties)

relationship, I included a regression line. The r squared value of 0.193 is a reminder of the poor fit of the simple regression model of tweets versus votes. We see a cluster of parties with a low number of votes and few hashtag mentions. We also see the Pirate Party being a massive outlier with a minimal number of votes but by far the most Twitter mentions. We also see that a prognosis of parties' vote shares based on their mentions in hashtags would perform poorly. It is evident that the vote share of the CSU, DIE LINKE, and CDU would have been underestimated and the vote share of FDP and SPD would have been overestimated. The bad fit of this model is additional evidence that the relationship between votes and tweets was weak for the campaign of 2009.

This conclusion is further supported by a more detailed analysis of the relationship between votes and hashtag mentions for parties that could attract only less than 250,000 votes on election day. Figure 7.3 shows this relationship that remained obscured in the previous figure. In this graph we see an even less stable relationship between votes and tweets than before. Again, a regression line illustrates this observation. If we calculate a simple regression model of votes versus tweets including only parties achieving 250,000 votes or less we see an even lower r squared (0.0548) than when including all parties in the model. Considering these various approaches in determining the relationship between votes and tweets for political parties during the campaign, we find no evidence for a strong or deterministic relationship between the two variables.

Up until now, this analysis focused only on neutral hashtags mentioning political parties. Without any further knowledge about the content of the messages containing one of these neutral hashtags, one could assume that positive and negative mentions of parties would be roughly equally distributed. Given this assumption, one could assume that high hashtag counts of parties would also speak for high support. A feature special to the political communication space on Twitter in Germany allows

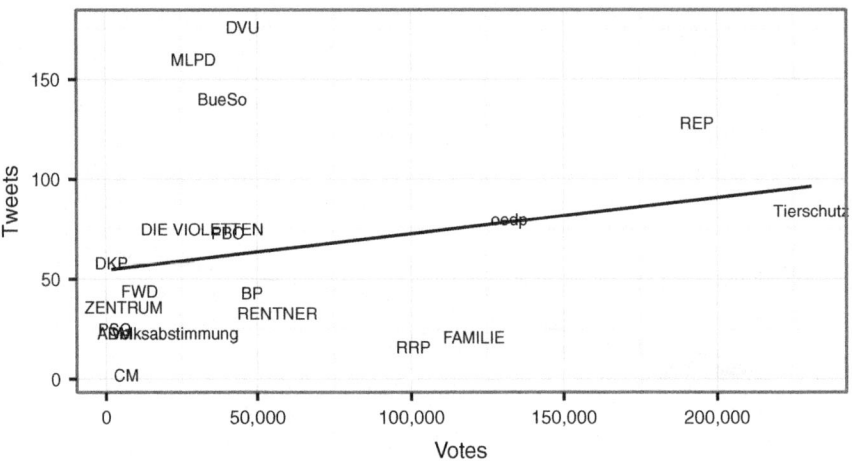

Fig. 7.3 Votes and tweets per party (only parties with less than 250,000 votes)

us to test this assumption. As mentioned above, during the campaign of 2009 users started to mark their messages explicitly in support of or in opposition to one of the parties in the race. These hashtags were a combination of a party's name followed by a + or a − sign (e.g. #cdu+ or #fdp-). This convention helps us to understand the relationship between positive and negative mentions on Twitter. In line with the summation of hashtags referring to the same party, I constructed party-concepts for explicitly positive or negative mentions.

The MAE reported in Table 7.3 for the relationship between the share of explicitly positive or explicitly negative hashtag mentions of political parties show that these metrics also failed to provide an accurate forecast of the respective parties' vote share. Based on positive hashtag mentions, the vote share of the Pirate Party would have been overestimated by roughly 65 % points while the vote shares of the CDU/CSU, SPD, and Greens would have been underestimated by between 8 % and 30 % points. Prognoses based on shares of explicitly negative hashtag mentions fared equally badly.

Most party-mentions using these conventions also marked tweets critiquing a party. For each party, negative mentions heavily outnumbered positive mentions. This pattern is especially visible on the day of the election. Thus, parties are clearly mentioned on Twitter mostly negatively. Given this pattern, using counts of party mentions—even by neutral hashtags—will be including significant amounts of messages posted in opposition to a party. Critique of a party voiced in Twitter messages would thus become an indicator for its success on election day. This paradox should be addressed by advocates of predicting elections by means of Twitter mentions.

Table 7.3 shows that aggregates of counts from users mentioning political parties in hashtags, aggregates of neutral hashtag mentions and of explicitly positive as well as negative hashtag mentions did not allow for precise prognoses of their respective vote shares. Although it is implicitly assumed in the literature that these aggregates would allow researchers to infer the chances of parties mentioned on Twitter, given these results, this relationship seems dubious at best and non-existent at worst.

7.5.2 Dynamics of Hashtag Mentions Compared to Shifts in Opinion Polls

Another possible connection between Twitter metrics and metrics of political support might be found in the daily volume of messages mentioning a political party and their poll results. Various studies have looked at aspects of this potential relationship with varying degrees of success (e.g. Bermingham and Smeaton 2011; Fink et al. 2013; O'Connor et al. 2010; Thapen and Ghanem 2013). Twitter messages commenting on parties during the run-up to the federal election of 2009 in Germany offer another perspective on this possible relationship.

Figure 7.4 shows poll results from various polling firms for five traditional parties in Germany published between June 26, and September 27, 2009. The data were collected from the website *Wahlen, Wahlrecht und Wahlsysteme*[6] that documents polling results for various elections in Germany. The diagram includes polls published by six different institutes: *Institut für Demoskopie Allensbach*,[7] *TNS Emnid*,[8] *Forsa*,[9] *Forschungsgruppe Wahlen*,[10] *GMS*,[11] and *infratest dimap*.[12] Combining these polling firms' results reveals the dynamics of political support for each party during the course of the campaign. The straight lines show the trend from all polling results' time series for each party based on a simple linear regression model. The light grey areas around the regression lines document the .99 confidence intervals, which are included in the diagram to indicate the variance across the results. By way of comparison, Fig. 7.5 documents the daily volume of the parties' hashtag mentions between June 26, and September 27, 2009. Again, regression lines show the trend in each respective time series while the light grey areas show the 0.99 confidence interval.

Poll results are rather steady over the course of the campaign which largely reinforces the assessment of the campaign as being uneventful. In contrast, the daily hashtag shares for parties are fluctuating strongly, as already indicated by results from prior sections. The daily mention shares for the CDU/CSU and SPD especially

---

[6] http://www.wahlrecht.de.

[7] http://www.ifd-allensbach.de.

[8] https://www.tns-emnid.com.

[9] http://www.forsa.de.

[10] http://www.forschungsgruppe.de/Startseite/.

[11] http://www.gms-gmbh.com/index.php/en/.

[12] http://www.infratest-dimap.de.

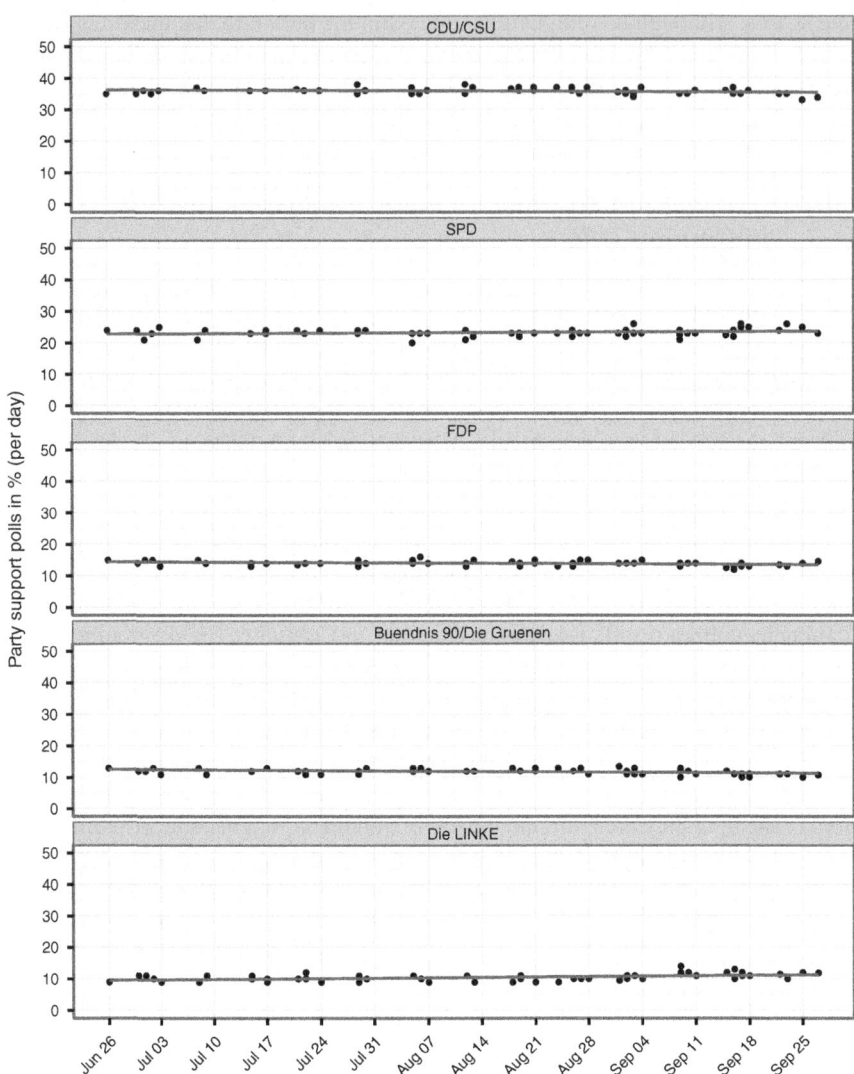

Fig. 7.4 Party support polls with trend

are fluctuating heavily. The daily hashtag share for Die Grünen is also fluctuating, albeit less strongly. The hashtag shares for the FDP and Die LINKE appear rather stable. As discussed in previous chapters, the spikes in the time series are connected to events during the campaign, i.e. connected with the parties or their candidates.

7.5 Twitter Metrics and Their Relationship to the Electoral Fortunes of Parties

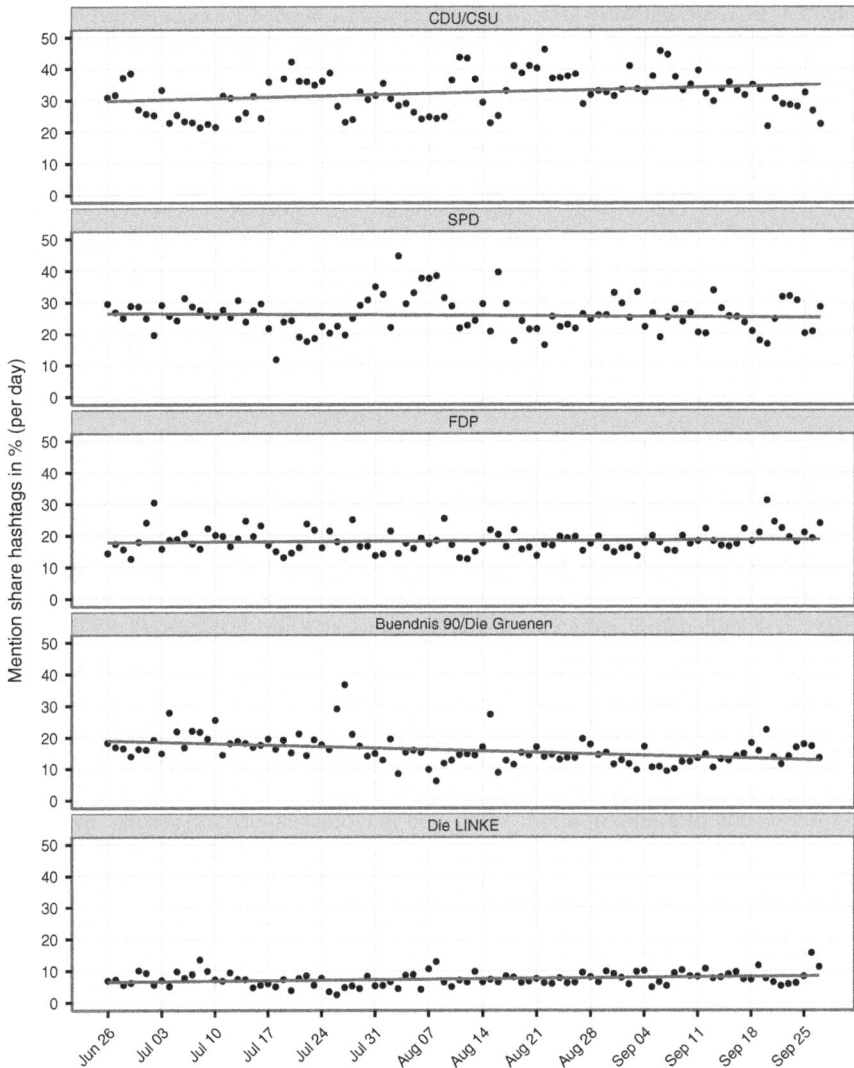

Fig. 7.5 Mention share hashtags per party with trend

There are two ways to read Table 7.4 regarding the potential of Twitter metrics to forecast election results. First, we could focus on the intercept values of the different linear regression models. If values of the intercepts between opinion polls and either of the Twitter based metrics would be reliably related for all parties, we could interpret that as a sign that shares of this metric's raw counts would potentially be valid indicators for forecasting future values in public opinion polls and—given that opinion polls correspond with election results—perhaps even of election results. The table shows that this is not the case, reinforcing the findings of previous sections.

Table 7.4 Intercepts and slopes in models of poll and hashtag mention dynamics per party through the course of the campaign

Party	Metrics	Intercepts	Slopes
CDU/CSU	Poll results	36.31	−0.01
	Hashtag mentions	30.24	0.05
SPD	Poll results	22.78	0.01
	Hashtag mentions	26.48	−0.014
FDP	Poll results	14.46	−0.01
	Hashtag mentions	17.8	0.01
Bündnis 90/Die Grünen	Poll results	12.60	−0.015
	Hashtag mentions	19.01	−0.066
Die LINKE	Poll results	9.51	0.019
	Hashtag mentions	6.45	0.02

Second, we could focus on the slopes of the different linear regression models. Even if the intercepts of Twitter metrics do not correspond with the intercepts of results from opinion polls or the election results, it might be possible to account for this difference by applying statistical weights. If the trends of various time series were correlated, future values of a Twitter metrics' time series might be used to predict unobserved future values for time series of opinion polls or even to forecast election results—given of course that correlations from the past would also hold in the future. For this, it is interesting to compare the slopes of polls' time series with the time series of various Twitter metrics. If slopes were to show similar directions and values, we could assume this precondition to be met and use Twitter metrics to infer results of public opinion polls—and maybe even election results. Still, the values show little if any systematic relationship between the direction and dynamics of regression models' slopes fit to opinion polls and various Twitter metrics. It has accordingly to be doubted that Twitter metrics allow for systematic forecasts of opinion polls or election results.

Table 7.4 shows the intercepts and slopes of the regression models for poll results and hashtag mentions per party in direct comparison. The poll results of the CDU/CSU, SPD, and FDP remain largely stable during the course of the campaign with very little variation in the results. Results for Bündnis 90/Die Grünen show a slightly declining trend through the course of the campaign while poll results for Die LINKE show a slightly increasing trend. However, the differences between the dynamics are very small. The trends in the time series documenting the hashtag mention counts show a slightly different pattern. Mentions of the CDU/CSU show a slight increase, mentions of Bündnis 90/Die Grünen show a slight decrease while mentions of the SPD, FDP, and die Die LINKE remain largely stable.

The examination of time series documenting opinion poll results and various Twitter metrics showed that Twitter metrics did not systematically share the dynamics and trends of poll results, thereby rendering futile election forecasts with weighted Twitter mentions based on past correspondence with opinion polls.

The reason for these different dynamics lie in the high reactiveness of Twitter mentions to political events, media coverage, and political controversies. Thus, Twitter metrics seem to be a truer mirror of political interests and attention than of the political attitudes or voting intentions of users posting Twitter messages mentioning political actors. Twitter data might thus be more productively used in analyzing political controversies and objects of political attention than as a forecast medium for political behavior in elections.

Thus, poll results and daily mention shares of political parties follow different patterns: (1) time series of hashtag mentions show significantly more variance than poll results; (2) the intercepts of linear regression models of poll results and hashtag mention counts show very different intercepts, and (3) trends pointing in different directions.

7.6 No Indicator of Political Support or Public Opinion at Large

These analyses support the framework for the use of Twitter data in the analysis of social phenomena presented in Chap. 3. Various Twitter metrics did not provide us with adequate predictions of election results or results of public opinion polls. While this is no indicator that the political attitudes and beliefs of Twitter users did not find expression in their tweets, this is a clear indicator that Twitter based metrics did not allow for inferences of public opinion at large or the electoral chances of political parties mentioned on Twitter. More generally, there was no sign of a link between the macro-phenomenon of political opinion and aggregates of political parties' Twitter mentions.

The results presented above raise a number of issues that should be addressed in further research into the relationship between Twitter messages and election results. First, we saw that for the federal election of 2009 in Germany, none of the tested Twitter metrics—users mentioning parties by hashtags, hashtags counts, counts of explicitly positive or negative mentions—was a valid indicator of the votes parties received on election day. The strongest deviation between Twitter mentions and votes occurred in the case of the Pirate Party, a party that dominated the political discourse on Twitter but was all but insignificant on election day. The strength of a party offline was not mirrored by its strength online, which contradicts the expectations of the normalization thesis which expects that over time strong political actors would grow to dominate online discourse (Margolis and Resnick 2000). This observation indicates that the potential for predicting election results by counting Twitter messages depends heavily on a successful normalization process for the political online sphere. This potential precondition should be examined further.

We also saw that the share of hashtag mentions that parties received was fluctuating from day to day. Any attempt at connecting Twitter messages posted during a given time span to election results thus has to include a discussion on why the respective time span was chosen. Potential patterns within these fluctuations may offer potentially insightful research opportunities.

Another point raised during the analysis was that once one focuses on explicitly positive and negative comments on political parties, the negative mentions heavily outnumber the positive mentions. Thus, Twitter seems to be a medium most intensively used to voice political opposition and not support. This raises an interesting paradox for researchers trying to construct systematic connections between Twitter messages and votes. Why should high counts of messages predominantly published in opposition to a party be indicative of its subsequent success on election day? This question shows that research in this field has to address explicitly possible theoretical links between the volume of Twitter messages—be they supportive or critical—mentioning a political party and its subsequent vote share. At present, this discussion is largely absent from the literature.

These observations show that in considering Twitter's function as a sensor, it neither indicates public opinion at large nor allows inferences on the electoral chances of parties mentioned in tweets. In the following concluding chapter, I will discuss the meaning of the results presented here and in the previous chapter for the analysis of social phenomena based on Twitter data.

References

Beauchamp N (2013) Predicting and interpolating state-level polling using Twitter textual data. Paper presented at the annual meeting of the American Political Science Association, Chicago, IL, 29 Aug–1 Sept 2013

Bermingham A, Smeaton AF (2011) On using Twitter to monitor political sentiment and predict election results. In: Bandyopadhyay S, Okumura M (eds) SAAIP: proceedings of the workshop sentiment analysis where AI meets psychology at the international joint conference for natural language processing (IJCNLP), Chiang Mai, TH, pp 2–10

Ceron A, Curini L, Iacus SM (2014) Every tweet counts? How sentiment analysis of social media can improve our knowledge of citizens' political preferences with an application to Italy and France. New Media Soc 16(2):340–358. doi:10.1177/1461444813480466

Chen L, Wang W, Sheth AP (2012) Are Twitter users equal in predicting elections? A study of user groups in predicting 2012 U.S. Republican Presidential Primaries. In: Aberer K, Flache A, Jager W, Liu L, Tang J, Guéret C (eds) Social informatics: proceedings of the 4th international conference (SocInfo 2012). Springer, Heidelberg, DE, pp 379–392. doi:10.1007/978-3-642-35386-4_28

Chung J, Mustafaraj E (2011) Can collective sentiment expressed on Twitter predict political elections? In: Fox D, Burgard W, Roth D, Shapiro D, Fromherz M (eds) AAAI 2011: proceedings of the 25th AAAI conference on artificial intelligence. Association for the Advancement of Artificial Intelligence (AAAI), Menlo Park, CA, pp 1170–1771

Contractor D, Faruquie TA (2013) Understanding election candidate approval ratings using social media data. In: Schwabe D, Almeida V, Glaser H, Baeza-Yates R, Moon S (eds) WWW 2013: proceedings of the 22nd international conference on world wide web, international world wide web conferences steering committee, Geneva, CH, pp 189–190

Der Bundeswahlleiter (2009) Bundestagswahl 2009: Ergebnisse der Wahl zum 17. Deutschen Bundestag. http://www.bundeswahlleiter.de/de/bundestagswahlen/BTW_BUND_09/E2_BTW_2009_Ergebnisse_IVU_ueberarbeitet.pdf

Diaz F, Gamon M, Hofman J, Kıcıman E, Rothschild D (2014) Online and social media data as a flawed continuous panel survey. Microsoft Research. http://research.microsoft.com/en-us/projects/flawedsurvey/

DiGrazia J, McKelvey K, Bollen J, Rojas F (2013) More tweets, more votes: social media as a quantitative indicator of political behavior. PLoS One 8(11):e79449. doi:10.1371/journal.pone.0079449

Fink C, Bos N, Perrone A, Liu E, Kopecky J (2013) Twitter, public opinion, and the 2011 Nigerian Presidential election. In: Bilof R (ed) SocialCom 2013: the 5th IEEE international conference on social computing. IEEE, Washington, DC, pp 311–320. doi:10.1109/SocialCom.2013.50

Franch F (2013) (wisdom of the crowds)2: 2010 UK election prediction with social media. J Inf Technol Polit 10(1):57–71. doi:10.1080/19331681.2012.705080

Gaurav M, Srivastava A, Kumar A, Miller S (2013) Leveraging candidate popularity on Twitter to predict election outcome. In: Grossman RL, Uthurusamy R (eds) SNAKDD 2013: proceedings of the 7th workshop on social network mining and analysis, vol 7. ACM, New York, NY. doi:10.1145/2501025.2501038

Gayo-Avello D (2011) Don't turn social media into another 'literary digest' poll. Commun ACM 54(10):121–128. doi:10.1145/2001269.2001297

Gayo-Avello D (2012) No, you cannot predict elections with Twitter. IEEE Internet Comput 16(6):91–94. doi:10.1109/MIC.2012.137

Gayo-Avello D (2013) A meta-analysis of state-of-the-art electoral prediction from Twitter data. Soc Sci Comput Rev 31(6):649–679. doi:10.1177/0894439313493979

Gayo-Avello D, Metaxas PT, Mustafaraj E (2011) Limits of electoral predictions using twitter. In: Nicolov N, Shanahan JG, Adamic L, Baeza-Yates R, Counts S (eds) ICWSM 2011: proceedings of the 5th international AAAI conference on weblogs and social media. Association for the Advancement of Artificial Intelligence (AAAI), Menlo Park, CA, pp 490–493

Gelman A, King G (1993) Why are American Presidential election campaign polls so variable when votes are so predictable? Br J Polit Sci 23(4):409–451. doi:10.1017/S0007123400006682

Huberty ME (2013) Multi-cycle forecasting of congressional elections with social media. In: Weber I, Popescu AM, Pennacchiotti M (eds) PLEAD 2013: proceedings of the 2nd workshop politics, elections and data. ACM, New York, NY, pp 23–30. doi:10.1145/2508436.2508439

Hyndman RJ, Koehler AB (2006) Another look at measures of forecast accuracy. Int J Forecast 22(4):679–688. doi:10.1016/j.ijforecast.2006.03.001

Jensen MJ, Anstead N (2013) Psephological investigations: tweets, votes, and unknown unknowns in the republican nomination process. Policy Internet 5(2):161–182. doi:10.1002/1944-2866.POI329

Jungherr A (2013) Tweets and votes, a special relationship: the 2009 federal election in Germany. In: Weber I, Popescu AM, Pennacchiotti M (eds) PLEAD 2013: proceedings of the 2nd workshop politics, elections and data. ACM, New York, NY, pp 5–14. doi:10.1145/2508436.2508437

Jungherr A, Jürgens P, Schoen H (2012) Why the pirate party won the German election of 2009 or the trouble with predictions: a response to Tumasjan, A., Sprenger, T.O., Sander, P.G. and Welpe, I.M. "Predicting elections with Twitter: what 140 characters reveal about political sentiment". Soc Sci Comput Rev 30(2):229–234. doi:10.1177/0894439311404119

Lampos V (2012) On voting intentions inference from Twitter content: a case study on UK 2010 general election. arXiv. http://www.arxiv.org/abs/1204.0423

Lampos V, Preotiuc-Pietro D, Cohn T (2013) A user-centric model of voting intention from social media. In: Schuetze H, Fung P, Poesio M (eds) ACL 2013: proceedings of the 51st annual meeting of the association for computational linguistics. The Association for Computer Linguistics, Stroudsburg, PA, pp 993–1003

Marchetti-Bowick M, Chambers N (2012) Learning for microblogs with distant supervision: political forecasting with Twitter. In: Daelemans W (ed) EACL '12: proceedings of the 13th conference of the European chapter of the Association for Computational Linguistics. Association for Computational Linguistics, Stroudsburg, PA, pp 603–612

Margolis M, Resnick D (2000) Politics as usual: the cyberspace "Revolution". SAGE Publications, Thousand Oaks, CA

Metaxas PT, Mustafaraj E (2012) Social media and the elections. Science 338(6106):472–473. doi:10.1126/science.1230456

Metaxas PT, Mustafaraj E, Gayo-Avello D (2011) How (not) to predict elections. In: SocialCom 2011: the 3rd IEEE International conference on social computing. IEEE, Washington, DC, pp 165–171. doi:10.1109/PASSAT/SocialCom.2011.98

Mustafaraj E, Metaxas PT (2010) From obscurity to prominence in minutes: political speech and real-time search. In: WebSci 2010: proceedings of the WebSci10 - extending the Frontiers of society on-line

Mustafaraj E, Finn S, Whitlock C, Metaxas PT (2011) Vocal minority versus silent majority: discovering the opinions of the long tail. In: SocialCom 2011: the 3rd IEEE international conference on social computing. IEEE, Washington, DC

O'Connor B, Balasubramanyan R, Routledge BR, Smith NA (2010) From tweets to polls: linking text sentiment to public opinion time series. In: Hearst M, Cohen W, Gosling S (eds) ICWSM 2010: proceedings of the 4th international AAAI conference on weblogs and social media. Association for the Advancement of Artificial Intelligence (AAAI), Menlo Park, CA, pp 122–129

Rojas F (2013) How Twitter can help predict an election. Washington Post. http://articles.washingtonpost.com/2013-08-11/opinions/41299678_1_tweets-social-media-data-congressional-district

Sanders E, van den Bosch A (2013) Relating political party mentions on Twitter with polls and election results. In: DIR-2013: proceedings of the 13th Dutch-Belgian information retrieval workshop, pp 68–71

Shi L, Agarwal N, Agrawal A, Garg R, Spoelstra J (2012) Predicting US Primary elections with Twitter. Paper presented at the workshop social network and social media analysis: methods, models and applications (NIPS)

Skoric M, Poor N, Achananuparp P, Lim EP, Jiang J (2012) Tweets and votes: a study of the 2011 Singapore general election. In: Jr RHS (ed) HICSS 2012: proceedings of the 45th Hawaii international conference on system science. IEEE Computer Society, Washington, DC, pp 2583–2591. doi:10.1109/HICSS.2012.607

Smith A, Brenner J (2012) Twitter use 2012. Pew Research Center's Internet & American Life Project. http://www.pewinternet.org/Reports/2012/Twitter-Use-2012.aspx

Soler JM, Cuartero F, Roblizo M (2012) Twitter as a tool for predicting elections results. In: ASONAM 2012: IEEE/ACM international conference on advances in social networks analysis and mining. IEEE Press, Los Alamitos, CA, pp 1194–1200. doi:10.1109/ASONAM.2012.206

Thapen NA, Ghanem MM (2013) Towards passive political opinion polling using Twitter. In: Cocea M, Gaber M, Wiratunga N, Göker A (eds) Proceedings of the BCS SGAI workshop on social media analysis 2013. School of Computing Science and Digital Media, Robert Gordon University, Aberdeen, UK, pp 19–34

Tjong E, Sang K, Bos J (2012) Predicting the 2011 Dutch Senate election results with Twitter. In: Proceedings of the workshop on semantic analysis in social media. Association for Computational Linguistics, Stroudsburg, PA, pp 53–60

Tumasjan A, Sprenger TO, Sandner PG, Welpe IM (2010) Predicting elections with Twitter: what 140 characters reveal about political sentiment. In: Hearst M, Cohen W, Gosling S (eds) ICWSM 2010: proceedings of the 4th international AAAI conference on weblogs and social media. Association for the Advancement of Artificial Intelligence (AAAI), Menlo Park, CA, pp 178–185

Tumasjan A, Sprenger TO, Sandner PG, Welpe IM (2011) Election forecasts with Twitter: how 140 characters reflect the political landscape. Soc Sci Comput Rev 29(4):402–418. doi:10.1177/0894439310386557

Tumasjan A, Sprenger TO, Sandner PG, Welpe IM (2012) Where there is a sea there are Pirates: response to Jungherr, Jürgens, and Schoen. Soc Sci Comput Rev 30(2):235–239. doi:10.1177/089443931140412

Chapter 8
Conclusion: Twitter and the Analysis of Social Phenomena

8.1 Early Days

We are still in the early days of digital tools' widespread use in political communication. Many of the tools featured prominently in political campaigns today did not exist only a few years ago. This makes their use by politicians and the public highly experimental. Shifts in the behavior of users or the use of tools from campaign cycle to campaign cycle are highly likely, thus creating a moving target for researchers interested in the effects of digital tools on political communication and organization (Karpf 2012).

The same holds for the use of digital trace data in the social sciences. At present, the field is slowly moving towards accepting that these data sources might indeed hold significant research potential. Still, there is far from a consensus on how this potential might be realized. Even very basic practices—such as data acquisition, data publication, together with the use and the interpretation of various metrics—are only seldom discussed systematically, rendering the interpretation and comparison of findings unnecessarily difficult (Jungherr 2014). It might well be that research done at this early stage of adopting digital tools and digital trace data might age rather badly (Parks 2014). Still, progress in the future requires tinkering in the present.

In this book, I advocate approaching digital trace data with two objectives. First, I believe it is essential for researchers to analyze closely and take seriously the dynamics of a particular communication space—in this case Twitter. It might well be that in the larger scheme of things political communication on Twitter merits only a footnote. Still, if we want to use digital trace data to draw meaningful conclusions about larger political phenomena, we must first understand the varying data-generating processes and dynamics of digital services providing the data.

Secondly, supported by the findings presented in this book, I strongly believe that digital trace data hold potential for social scientists well beyond merely analyzing user behavior and communication patterns on a specific digital service. Users document parts of their direct and mediated experiences in their personal usage patterns of digital tools, and—since they chronicle and provide access to digital artefacts produced by this behavior—, digital trace data potentially allow researchers to access the publicly documented experiences, voiced opinions, and points of interest from large subsets of the population that otherwise would remain hidden. Still, for this research potential to be realized, scientists have to examine much more systematically which parts of the experiences from which subsets of the population tend to leave imprints in digital trace data. Only a more systematic understanding of this mediation process makes it possible to evaluate which parts of social reality are covered on digital services and can thus in turn be analyzed through digital trace data. As shown earlier, this debate unfortunately is still largely missing from a field that, at present, seems more interested in documenting single-shot correlations between some metrics in digital trace data and some metrics of social reality.

8.2 Characteristics of Twitter as a Political Communication Space

The analyses presented in this book identified many characteristics of Twitter as a political communication space. They focused on the type of influential actors, communication practices by normal users and politicians together with the interconnection between the coverage of politics on Twitter and in traditional media. These findings are important steps towards understanding the dynamics governing Twitter as a political communication space and thereby also offer insights on how data collected on Twitter can be used in the analysis of social phenomena.

One of the key issues connected with the effects of digital tools on political communication is whether they open up the political communication space to new political actors or predominantly enable traditional political actors to dominate the political communication space online. This discussion has become known as the normalization vs transformation debate. Proponents of the normalization thesis expect traditional political actors to dominate political communication with digital tools, while proponents of the transformation thesis expect new political actors to rise in prominence, thanks to their use of digital tools (e.g. Chaffee and Metzger 2001; Margolis and Resnick 2000; Schweitzer 2011). While these expectations are probably best understood as ideal types, a recent addition to the discussion of digital tools' effects on political communication expects them to create a hybrid model of communication. In this view, traditional political actors and practices still dominate the political communication space at large, but new political actors have the opportunity to gain visibility based on their successful use of digital tools. Digital tools, therefore, will not transform the political communication sphere completely, but instead open it up somewhat to new voices (Chadwick 2013). The results of the analyses presented in the previous chapters speak to this debate.

8.2 Characteristics of Twitter as a Political Communication Space

During the campaign for the federal election of 2009, new political actors—such as normal Twitter users, communication consultants, or programmers—routinely managed to attract more attention on Twitter than traditional political actors—such as politicians, parties, or journalists. In this, Twitter can indeed be seen as opening up the political discourse to new voices, albeit not replacing traditional actors completely.

With regard to communication practices, the results also speak in favor of a hybrid pattern. On the one hand, many of the messages retweeted most often during mediated events tended to contain content or links to content that was directly challenging statements and positions of traditional political actors. Again, this can be seen as an opening up of the political discourse through Twitter by directly mirroring the interests of its users as manifested in their behavior. On the other hand, many of the messages retweeted most often also contained elements of political communication's traditional logic—such as links to polls, and polling results or content indexing the statements of political actors. As such, the content of the most prominently retweeted messages did contain elements of political coverage's new and old logics.

The use of Twitter by politicians indicates that most of them transported their offline communication patterns online. This finding corresponds with the expectations of those advocating digital practices' normalization. During the 2009 campaign, politicians tended predominantly to post messages containing information on the campaign while interacting with other Twitter users only sporadically. This shows that Twitter was used much more strongly as a medium for broadcasting rather than public dialogue. There was only little evidence of messages in which politicians actively tried to mobilize their followers to vote or volunteer in their campaign.

Generally speaking, the volume of Twitter messages tended to react to political events during the campaign of 2009. In this sense, Twitter can indeed be seen as a sensor of social phenomena, as discussed above. However, it is important to note that messages predominantly tended to react to media coverage of events and not to the events themselves. Thus, Twitter messages tended to mirror the media coverage of the campaign more than the campaign. It is possible that this finding is more true for election campaigns than for political events less routinely covered by media—such as collective action or protests. Additionally while media coverage of a political event might function as a stimulus for users to comment on the event, this relationship is not deterministic. Only a minority of events covered by the media during the course of the campaign led to significant spikes in the volume of messages. This indicates that the relationship between media coverage and online attention has to be analyzed in greater detail.

In general, digital trace data collected on Twitter did not offer an objective view of the campaign. Only a selection of political events that were covered by the media led to spikes in the volume of Twitter messages, while most political events, topics, and actors were ignored by users. Twitter thus did not mirror agendas during the campaign—be it the public agenda, the agenda of political elites, or the media agenda. Instead, as discussed above, we find a view of the campaign mediated by the interests of politically vocal Twitter users. As shown in Chap. 6, objects of attentions by users were related to media coverage of politics but did not follow it deterministically.

It is important to keep in mind that the findings presented in this study are limited by the scope and the time frame of the analyses. First, the analyses presented are restricted to data collected on Twitter. These findings about the prominence of new political actors can, therefore, speak only to their role in the political communication space on Twitter. As has been discussed above, the political communication space online consists of many interconnected services—such as Twitter, Facebook, and blogs. These platforms appear to be highly reactive to political media coverage and might in turn influence media coverage of specific issues or actors, leading to a highly complicated set of interconnections. If we want to measure the influence or prominence of a political actor in the political communication space as a whole, it is, therefore, not enough simply to measure her prominence on one of these services. Instead, it is important to gain an understanding of how prominence and influence on one of these platforms might spill over onto others. Whilst a topic beyond the scope of this book, it is one fundamental area of future research in political communication which will be able to advance our understanding of the interconnections between various spheres of political communication on- and offline. This will make possible an assessment of what the influence for specific political actors in one sphere of political communication means for their influence on the political communication sphere as a whole.

Secondly, the analyses presented in this book focused on the use of Twitter during an election campaign at a very early stage of the service's adoption in Germany. Some of the findings—such as the prominence of non-traditional actors on Twitter or the predominant use of Twitter by politicians as extension of their communication routine—might indeed reflect this early phase of Twitter adoption. Since in 2009 Twitter was still a new tool for political communication, it might be that traditional political actors—such as politicians, parties, journalists, and media—were at that time largely ignoring it or expending very little effort in maintaining their presences there. Given these factors, the prominence of non-traditional actors might in fact not be a feature of Twitter, but may simply result from the limited efforts by traditional actors to gain prominence on the service. Furthermore, the largely unimaginative uses of Twitter by politicians might be due to their inexperience with the service. While these possibilities appear rather unlikely, given the accordance of the findings presented above with other findings in the literature, it will be interesting to see if and how political Twitter use in Germany will change over time.

8.3 A Framework for the Use of Twitter in the Analysis of Social Phenomena

Increasingly researchers turn to digital trace data in the analysis of social phenomena. We can group these approaches into two categories. In one, Twitter is treated as a sensor in documenting the reactions of users to their direct or mediated experiences through data traces produced by interactions of users with the service (e.g. Chakrabarti and Punera 2011; Jungherr and Jürgens 2014; Sakaki et al. 2010; Shamma et al. 2011). In the second category of studies, researchers go even as far as to draw inferences on attitudes, affiliations, and opinions of Twitter users based on the data traces of their behavior on the platform (e.g. Barberá 2014; Conover et al. 2011; O'Connor et al. 2010; Tumasjan et al. 2010). The empirical results presented in this book suggest that these are two different endeavors for which data collected on Twitter might prove to be more or less well suited.

In Chap. 5, I showed that Twitter data allowed for the identification and analysis of events and topics of interest to politically vocal Twitter users during the campaign for the German federal election of 2009. This map of dynamics in the attention of politically vocal Twitter users did not provide us with an accurate picture of how the campaign evolved, be it to do with relevant events or topics discussed by political elites, the media, or the public. While some of these events or topics led users to post messages referring to them so that their shadows became discernible in Twitter data, most political events were ignored. Twitter data thus allows for the identification and analysis of events or topics of interest to its users, but this does not provide us with a true reflection of social or political reality. Instead, an image emerges that is mediated by the attention and interests of Twitter users.

In Chap. 7, I demonstrated that Twitter data allowed neither valid inferences on public opinion at large towards political parties nor an accurate prediction of their election results. While Twitter users mentioned parties in their tweets, these mentions proved to be indicative of attention but not of political support.

If we relate these two findings to Coleman's classical formulation of the problem in the analysis of macro-phenomena based on aggregates of data documenting micro-behavior (Coleman 1990), we begin to see a likely reason for these divergent results. Figure 8.1 shows a version of the by now familiar diagram illustrating the relationship between aggregates of Twitter data and social phenomena under examination. The diagram shows no direct link (4) between social phenomena or events (A) and data patterns in aggregates of Twitter messages (D). Instead, this relationship is mediated by at least two filters: first, by a filter based on attention and interests of Twitter users (1); and second, by a filter of affordances and channel-logics specific to the use of Twitter (2). These filters influence whether a Twitter user pays attention to an event or decides to react to a phenomena (B) and in which form this reaction manifests in a tweet (C). Only phenomena or events that make it through both filters can be identified in aggregates of Twitter messages (D), be it through the use of common cultural conventions, such as hashtags or common semantic patterns (3).

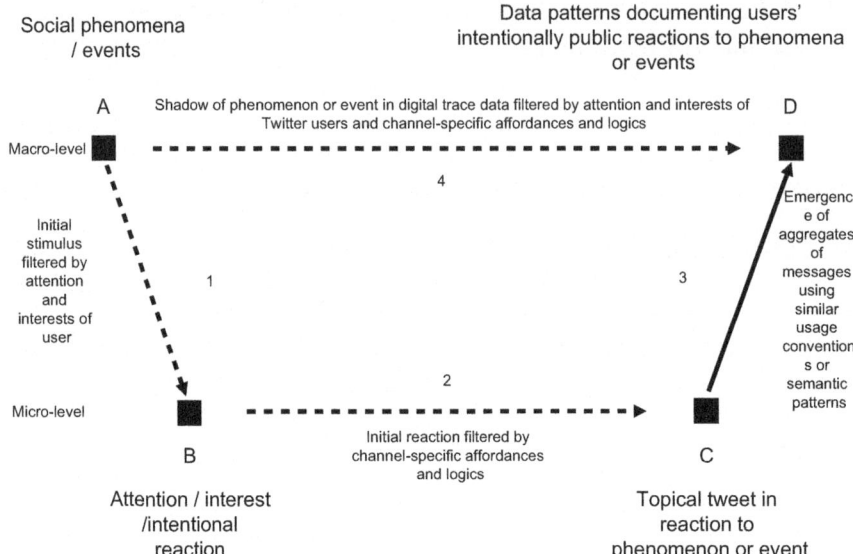

Fig. 8.1 Relationship between social phenomena and data patterns in aggregates of Twitter messages

Once we start thinking about the relationship between social phenomena and Twitter data in this way, it quickly becomes clear why specific social phenomena or events should leave discernible shadows in aggregates of Twitter messages and which phenomena or events should be less likely to leave traces. The analyses presented in Chap. 4 illustrated that messages referring to politics reacted strongly to outside stimuli, be it through links to content on the Web or by comments on live media coverage. While not every event or topic during the campaign created strong echoes in tweets those that did were clearly identifiable. Issues of collective attention by Twitter users can, therefore, be identified and public reactions to them analyzed. This is also illustrated by the formal representation of a mechanism explaining the publication of tweets that was introduced in Chap. 3:

$$Tweet_p = C + Tweets_{t-1} + S * I_{User} + \frac{\sum Tweets_{User}}{t_n} \qquad (8.1)$$

Here, the probability for a user to post a message $Tweet_p$ at $t1$ is understood as a function of channel-specific mediation processes—such as C, the social context of a tweet (e.g. day of the week, hour of the day); and $Tweets_{t-1}$, the state of the twittersphere in the time span directly preceding the publication of a tweet by identifying the number of Twitter messages that were posted at $t - 1$—external stimuli—such as S, the occurrence of an event of either personal or collective relevance—and individual factors—such as $\frac{\sum Tweets_{User}}{t_n}$, the overall propensity of a Twitter user to post messages; and $I_{User-to-Event}$, the interest a user has in a specific outside stimulus. Since, as illustrated in Chap. 3, many of these factors appear to follow regular patterns, the appearance of spikes in messages referring to the same topic or sharing semantic patterns can justifiably be taken as indicators that Twitter users reacted collectively to a common outside stimulus. The identification of these spikes and the analysis of messages contributing to them thus clearly allow us to make inferences about Twitter users' points of interest.

An analysis of users' political attitudes or their voting intentions, on the other hand, faces the challenge of connecting this type of social phenomenon to the posting or the content of a tweet. It might be that political attitudes are mediating factors in the decision to post tweets referring to politics or their content, but clearly this hypothetical influence is more indirect than the occurrence of an outside stimulus, such as the experience of an event or attention towards political media coverage. Traces of political attitudes should, therefore, be much harder to identify in aggregates of Twitter messages, if at all. This argument and the empirical evidence shown in the previous chapters show that it is sensible to expect that Twitter messages could hold information about objects of Twitter users' collective public attention but not about the political attitudes of Twitter users or of society at large.

To advance our understanding on the use of Twitter data in social research we have to focus on the mediation process of reality through user interactions with digital tools. In this, researchers could follow the example of communication research focusing on the mediation of reality in media coverage (Shoemaker and Reese 2014). A deeper understanding of the channel specific logics of various online tools is also important if we want to unlock the research potential of digital trace data.

8.4 Twitter: Political Communication Space and Mediator of Politics

All evidence presented in this book clearly indicates that Twitter constitutes a communication space that offers mediated reflections of politics. The microblogging service is a space where people publicly comment, interact, and link to political topics and stories. These public interactions offer a window into politically vocal Twitter users' interests, opinions, and objects of attention. Politicians, campaigners, and parties use Twitter to document their campaign activities, advertize their positions, counterframe media coverage, or statements by opponents, and mobilize their supporters. These interactions hold information on campaign agendas and the campaigning practices of political actors using Twitter actively. Naturally, data traces documenting these activities are of obvious interest for researchers of political communication and public opinion.

Still, the evidence presented in this book also indicates that data collected on Twitter does not provide a true image of political phenomena but instead an image of political reality mediated by the attention, attitudes, intentions, and interests of politically vocal Twitter users. This became most obvious in the identification of relevant events during the course of the campaign based on daily shifts in the dynamics of Twitter messages referring to politics and the attempt to infer public opinion towards political actors based on the volume of postings. Both analyses showed that relying on Twitter messages for the inference of political reality would have led to the emergence of a skewed image.

This skewness is not random but corresponds with attention, attitudes, intentions, and interests of users. Using Twitter to identify relevant political events leads to a nearly exclusive focus on highly advertized mediated events, indicating that only such political media coverage captures the attention of most politically vocal Twitter users. While some users regularly post messages referring to politics, most do so in reaction to an external stimulus catching their attention. Spikes in the volume of Twitter messages, therefore, do not necessarily mirror a political event but instead show that the collective attention of politically vocal Twitter users focused on one topic or event during a given time interval. Twitter thereby primarily becomes a sensor for shifts in attention to politics not politics itself.

Using Twitter to infer public opinion towards political actors would have produced equally skewed results. Taking relative mentions of political parties as an indicator of their support's strength would have led us to expect the Pirate Party to win the 2009 election. Obviously, they did not. Still, the relative strength of the Pirates on Twitter comes as no surprise. After all, their supporters comprised comparatively young, Internet savvy activists who used Twitter in their personal and professional lives. Naturally, parties with older and less Internet savvy supporters were underrepresented with regard to their mention counts. This shows that the unrepresentativeness of Twitter's user base might introduce biases in drawing inferences on political phenomena based on the activities of the highly self-selective behavior of politically vocal Twitter users. The evidence presented above also showed that there is no easy statistical approach to account for this bias as the share of mentions for political actors shifted daily. While the Pirates had a very high baseline of mentions, other parties and their candidates received sudden mention spikes as reaction to media coverage or controversies.

These patterns correspond with the view that Twitter offers a reflection of political reality mediated through the attention, interests, and intentions of politically vocal Twitter users and thereby will deviate from political reality generally. These mediating factors are a product of Twitter's data generating process. For a user to post a tweet referring to politics, she has to make a conscious decision in reacting to a stimulus she received by publicly posting a message. Analyzing patterns in aggregates of tweets, therefore, offers no window into the true opinions and attitudes of Twitter users; instead it offers insights into their reactions to stimuli which they consciously decided to make public. If we want to unlock Twitter's potential in the analysis of social and political phenomena, we have to take this data generating process seriously. This means systematically addressing and testing the impact of these mediating factors on the potential of Twitter data to speak with regard to the phenomenon in question.

It is highly likely that analyzing a series of social or political phenomena through Twitter data produces robust results against biases introduced by this mediation process; other results—as shown in this book—appear to be very fragile. It is crucial for researchers in proposing relationships between Twitter-based metrics and social or political phenomena to address the link, therefore, between Twitter's data generating process and the phenomenon under examination. In this discussion researchers should address and test how factors mediating the image of reality emerging from digital trace data collected on Twitter—such as Twitter's skewed user base or specific dynamics of Twitter as communication space—influence or otherwise are of no relevance to the validity of their findings.

This is a necessary development for the use of digital trace data in the social sciences irrespective of the service from which the data was collected. Each digital service has a specific data generating process dependent on its affordances, usage practices, accessibility, and technological design. Any analysis using digital trace data collected on digital services has, therefore, consciously to address the link between the specific underlying data generating process and the specific phenomenon under analysis. Without this step in the evolution of the field, the use of digital trace data in the social sciences will remain a novelty act, highly vulnerable to challenges on the methodological soundness of the approach and the validity of the reported findings.

References

Barberá P (2014) Birds of the same feather tweet together: Bayesian ideal point estimation using Twitter data. Polit Anal. doi:10.1093/pan/mpu011
Chadwick A (2013) The hybrid media system: politics and power. Oxford University Press, Oxford
Chaffee SH, Metzger MJ (2001) The end of mass communication? Mass Commun Soc 4(4):365–379. doi:10.1207/S15327825MCS0404_3
Chakrabarti D, Punera K (2011) Event summarization using tweets. In: Nicolov N, Shanahan JG, Adamic L, Baeza-Yates R, Counts S (eds) ICWSM 2011: proceedings of the 5th international AAAI conference on weblogs and social media, association for the advancement of artificial intelligence (AAAI), Menlo Park, pp 66–73
Coleman JS (1990) Foundations of social theory. Harvard University Press, Cambridge
Conover MD, Goncalves B, Ratkiewicz J, Flammini A, Menczer F (2011) Predicting the political alignment of Twitter users. In: SocialCom 2011: the 3rd IEEE international conference on social computing. IEEE, Washington, DC. http://cnets.indiana.edu/wp-content/uploads/conover_prediction_socialcom_pdfexpress_ok_version.pdf
Jungherr A (2014) Twitter in politics: a comprehensive literature review. Soc Sci Res Netw. http://papers.ssrn.com/sol3/papers.cfm?abstract_id=2402443
Jungherr A, Jürgens P (2014) Stuttgart's Black Thursday on Twitter: mapping political protests with social media data. In: Gibson R, Cantijoch M, Ward S (eds) Analyzing social media data and web networks. Palgrave Macmillan, New York, pp 154–196

Karpf D (2012) Social science research methods in internet time. Inf Commun Soc 15(5):639–661. 10.1080/1369118X.2012.665468

Margolis M, Resnick D (2000) Politics as usual: the cyberspace "revolution". SAGE Publications, Thousand Oaks

O'Connor B, Balasubramanyan R, Routledge BR, Smith NA (2010) From tweets to polls: linking text sentiment to public opinion time series. In: Hearst M, Cohen W, Gosling S (eds) ICWSM 2010: proceedings of the 4th international AAAI conference on weblogs and social media. Association for the Advancement of Artificial Intelligence (AAAI), Menlo Park, pp 122–129

Parks MR (2014) Big data in communication research: its contents and discontents. J Commun 64(2):355–360. doi:10.1111/jcom.12090

Sakaki T, Okazaki M, Matsuo Y (2010) Earthquake shakes Twitter users: real-time event detection by social sensors. In: Rappa M, Jones P, Freire J, Chakrabarti S (eds) WWW 2010: proceedings of the 19th international conference on the world wide web. ACM, New York, pp 851–860. doi:10.1145/1772690.1772777

Schweitzer EJ (2011) Normalization 2.0: a longitudinal analysis of German online campaigns in the national elections 2002–9. Eur J Commun 26(4):310–327. doi:10.1177/0267323111423378

Shamma DA, Kennedy L, Churchill EF (2011) Peaks and persistence: modeling the shape of microblog conversations. In: Hinds P, Tang JC, Wang J, Bardram J, Ducheneaut N (eds) CSCW 2011: proceedings of the ACM 2011 conference on computer supported cooperative work. ACM, New York, pp 355–358. doi:10.1145/1958824.1958878 10.1145/1958824.1958878

Shoemaker PJ, Reese SD (2014) Mediating the message in the 21st century, 3rd edn. Routledge, New York

Tumasjan A, Sprenger TO, Sandner PG, Welpe IM (2010) Predicting elections with Twitter: what 140 characters reveal about political sentiment. In: Hearst M, Cohen W, Gosling S (eds) ICWSM 2010: proceedings of the 4th international AAAI conference on weblogs and social media. Association for the Advancement of Artificial Intelligence (AAAI), Menlo Park, pp 178–185

The manufacturer's authorised representative in the EU is Springer Nature Customer Service Centre GmbH, Europaplatz 3, 69115 Heidelberg, Germany. If you have any concerns regarding our products, please contact ProductSafety@springernature.com

Printed and bound by CPI Group (UK) Ltd, Croydon, CR0 4YY
23/03/2026
02076667-0014